Pocket Rough Guide

NEW YORK CITY

written and researched by

STEPHEN KEELING AND
ANDREW ROSENBERG

Contents

<< VIEW OF EMPIRE STATE BUILDING
< MANHATTAN BRIDGE

INTRODUCTION TO
NEW YORK CITY

No superlative, no cliché does New York City justice. It may not serve as the official capital of the US or even of New York State, but it's the undisputed capital of the world in many regards. High finance, media, art, architecture, food, fashion, popular culture, urban style, street life... it's all here, in plenitude and peak form. Best of all for visitors (and residents), you don't have to look too hard for any of it. Often the sights, both big and small, are just staring you right in the face: the money fortresses of Wall Street; the raised torch of the Statue of Liberty; the iconic Empire State Building; the hype and hustle of Times Square; Fifth Avenue's foot traffic; the proud lions of the Public Library. For energy and dynamism, cultural impact and sheer diversity, New York cannot be beaten.

CENTRAL PARK

You could spend weeks here and still barely scratch the surface, but there are some key attractions and pleasures you won't want to miss. The city is packed with vibrant ethnic neighbourhoods, like Chinatown and Harlem, and boasts the artsy enclaves of Chelsea, Tribeca and Greenwich Village. Of course, you will find the celebrated modern architecture of corporate Manhattan in Midtown and the Financial District, complemented by row upon row of elegant brownstones in landmarked areas like Brooklyn Heights. Then there are the city's renowned museums, not just the Metropolitan Museum of Art or the Museum of Modern Art, but countless smaller collections – the Old Masters at the Frick, the prints and manuscripts of the Morgan Library – that afford days of happy wandering.

In between sights, you can (and should) eat just about anything, cooked in any style: silky Korean pork buns to pressed sea urchin sandwiches, Jewish deli to Jamaican food cart. You can drink in virtually any company at any time in any type of watering hole imaginable: unmarked cocktail dens that mix up the latest artisanal concoctions or joints where folks will look at you sideways if you order anything but a bottle of beer. You can see comedy or cabaret, hear jazz combos or jug bands, and attend obscure movies. The more established arts – dance, theatre, opera and classical music – are superbly catered for; and New York's clubs are varied and exciting.

Best places for bagels and lox

A bagel with cream cheese and lox is the city's classic bite, found all over at cafés, delis, bagelries and speciality food shops – though best sampled from a Jewish "appetizing" store (basically, a place that sells fish and dairy products) such as hundred-year-old, family-owned Russ & Daughters (p.65). Our other favourites include Absolute Bagels (p.150), Barney Greengrass (p.150) and Zabar's (p.150).

QUEENSBORO BRIDGE

For the avid consumer, the choice of shops is vast, almost numbingly exhaustive, in this heartland of the great capitalist dream. You can spend your dollars at big names like Bloomingdale's or contemporary designers like Marc Jacobs, and visit boutiques full of vintage garments or thrift stores with clothes priced by the pound.

New York City comprises the central island of Manhattan along with four outer boroughs – Brooklyn, Queens, the Bronx and Staten Island. To many, Manhattan is New York, and you're likely to spend a bulk of your time here – though Brooklyn and, increasingly, Queens demand plenty of visitor attention. The former has the ragged glory of Coney Island and the hip nightlife of Williamsburg and Greenpoint; the latter a number of cool art spaces, including the uplifting Noguchi Museum in Long Island City. Don't overlook the Bronx either, for baseball at Yankee Stadium and a stunning botanical garden a bit further north. These are just a few of the attractions that make worthy detours, and you'll find great neighbourhood restaurants and bars along the way. The subway and bus system can take you everywhere, but New York is great to explore on foot too.

When to visit

Pretty much any time is a good time to visit New York. Winter can be bitingly cold but the city can be delightful during the run-up to Christmas, when the trees are lit up, the windows decorated and shops open extra-late. It's coldest in January and February, coinciding with one of the few times to find bargains on flights and hotels, and in any case New York has some wonderful crisp and clear sunny days even then. Spring, early summer, and the fall are the most appealing times to visit, when temperatures can be comfortably warm. It's wise to avoid visiting between mid-July and August: the temperatures tend be sweltering and the humidity worse. On the other hand, locals tend to leave town then, so weekends are less crowded.

NEW YORK CITY AT A GLANCE

>> EATING

From street food to haute cuisine, it's here, it's excellent and it's in abundance. **Chinatown** is most accessible for ethnic eats. The **Lower East Side**, traditional home to Jewish food, now teems with fashionable restaurants, while the **East Village** is the locus for great late-night eats – bowls of ramen, slices of pizza and hot dogs. Continue up to **Midtown** for powerhouse names like *Aquavit* and *Oyster Bar*, one of the city's quintessential eateries. Further north, **Harlem** has fabulous soul food, barbecue and African restaurants. **Queens**' Astoria has great international spots, and **Brooklyn**'s Williamsburg and Carroll Gardens are packed with voguish options.

>> DRINKING

Bars are everywhere and come in every stripe: pubs, dives, beer gardens, hidden speakeasies, exclusive hotel lounges. Drinkers descend on the **Lower East Side** and **East Village**, especially streets like Ludlow and Avenue A, which can seem like a carnival – but are good destinations nonetheless. Rocker hangouts and swanky wine bars also hover around **Union Square**, and **Ninth Avenue**, starting in **Chelsea** and moving up to **Hell's Kitchen**. The most exciting and characterful places are in the outer boroughs, specifically **Long Island City** and **Williamsburg**. Most bars and pubs are typically open till the wee hours of morning.

>> NIGHTLIFE

Clubbing hotspots jump around: the lower western edge of **Soho** one year, 27th Street in the far west of **Chelsea** another. The **East and West Villages** always offer a few standbys, and the **Meatpacking District** can be good if you're looking for busy places to put on your dancing shoes. Keep your ears open, get current listings magazines and generally aim downtown. Music venues are more established: the **West Village** and **Harlem** have historic venues for jazz; **Lincoln Center** holds top spots for classical music, dance and opera, with **Carnegie Hall** just a few blocks away; and the coolest rock clubs are mostly in Williamsburg and the **Lower East Side**.

>> SHOPPING

For big-ticket retail, look no further than Midtown, specifically **Fifth Avenue**, where Saks, Bergdorf Goodman and many others congregate. **Madison Avenue** on the Upper East Side also has its share of famous brands. Somewhat edgier fashion can be found in **Soho** and **Nolita**: Prince and Spring streets are crammed with designer boutiques and hip jewellery and shoe shops. Those looking for vintage duds or the truly avant-garde might find the **Lower East Side** and **Williamsburg** more suitable. Antique hunters will have fun trolling around **Chelsea** and on weekends, the **Hell's Kitchen Flea Market**.

OUR RECOMMENDATIONS ON WHERE TO EAT, DRINK AND SHOP ARE LISTED AT THE END OF EACH PLACES CHAPTER.

Day One in New York City

1 Starting point: Battery Park
> p.38. Ferries set out from here to the Harbor Islands; leave early and plan on a full morning.

2 Statue of Liberty > p.40. One of the city's most potent symbols is just as exciting up close as from a distance, especially if you climb the steps to the crown.

3 Ellis Island > p.40. The sensitive and moving museum drives home New York's immigrant roots.

🍴 > p.43. Back on shore, stop for lunch at *Adrienne's Pizzabar* on pedestrianized Stone Street.

4 Stroll along **Wall Street** to see the buildings at the heart of world finance, then head up **Trinity Place** (Church Street) to the 1766 **St Paul's Chapel**, with its 9/11 exhibit. The **National September 11 Memorial** is across the street.

5 The High Line > p.92. If you've got the time on your way uptown, take a stroll along this elevated promenade on the West Side.

🍴 > For a pre-theatre meal, choose from traditional dining spots such as *Chez Napoleon* (p.128) and *Joe Allen* (p.129).

6 Taking in a Broadway play or musical is a must for theatre-lovers; any venue will suffice, as long as the show is up to standard.

🍷 > p.130. Atmospheric *Jimmy's Corner* is full of crusty barflies and boxing memorabilia; a drink at the bar provides a fitting end to a full day.

Day Two in New York City

1 Starting point: Zabar's > p.150.
Pick up some provisions at *Zabar's*
and enjoy them in the attached café or
head for a picnic in Central Park.

2 Central Park > p.132. Wander
across the park, starting at Strawberry
Fields in the west, then walking along
the Lake and across the Ramble or
Great Lawn, emerging on the east side.

3 Metropolitan Museum of Art
> p.138. Goya, Vermeer, the Hudson
River School and the Temple of Dendur
are among the highlights at this
colossal museum.

4 Grand Central > p.109.
Lunchtime tours (Wed and Fri) of
Grand Central Terminal help illuminate
the magnificent Main Concourse and
other features of this architectural
marvel.

Oyster Bar > p.120. Enjoy
a late lunch in the bowels of
Grand Central at this timeless Midtown
hangout.

5 Empire State Building > p.103.
The obligatory trip to the 320m-high
viewing platform provides just what
you'd expect: a great vantage point
of the city.

6 Soho shopping > p.48. Prada and
the Apple Store are destination shops,
but there's plenty more to browse
along Spring, Prince, Broadway and
the smaller side streets.

> p.44. **Soho** and **Tribeca**
are full of excellent high-end
restaurants; if you can foot the bill,
Aquagrill, *Bouley* or *Blue Ribbon Sushi*
will certainly fit the bill.

Budget New York

New York can be an expensive place to visit, but there are a surprising number of inspiring sights and activities that are cheap or completely free.

1 Staten Island Ferry > p.39. The free boat ride across New York harbour offers mesmerizing views of the city and the Statue of Liberty.

2 Governors Island > p.40. Explore the historic houses, parks and galleries of this tranquil island – bikes are free weekdays 10am–noon.

🍴 Pizza slices at Artichoke > p.76. The iconic NYC budget snack is done to perfection at this tiny, low-key East Village pizza joint.

3 Chelsea art galleries > p.96. Wander a neighbourhood packed with cutting-edge contemporary art galleries (all free).

4 Free Fridays MoMA (p.116), the Morgan Library (p.108), Neue Galerie (p.140), the Whitney Museum of American Art (p.92) and the Asia Society (p.143) are free or donation only on Friday evenings.

🍴 Dinner in Chinatown > p.60. Best-value meals in Manhattan – eat like an emperor for less than $20 at *Great N.Y. Noodletown*.

Kids' New York

Most sights are perfectly appropriate for kids, but beyond the expected – such as the Statue of Liberty – you can easily tailor a day or two to their interests.

Good Enough to Eat > p.152. Load up with pancakes, French toast or corned beef hash at this relaxed restaurant.

1 American Museum of Natural History > p.148. Go early to miss the crowds for the innovative special exhibits.

2 Carousel in Central Park > p.134. If the kids are too old for this, check out the skaters and performance artists at the nearby Mall or Sheep Meadow.

3 Flatiron and Chrysler buildings > p.102 & p.110. Their supporting roles in *Spiderman* and other action movies should compensate for any initial reticence about checking out architecture.

4 Madison Square Park > p.102. Besides places to run and play, Madison Square boasts the *Shake Shack*, perfect for lunch or a midday snack.

5 Books of Wonder > p.104. If it's a weekend, you might hear a reading at this kids' bookstore; regardless, there are plenty of volumes to browse.

6 The Museum of the Moving Image > p.165. Swing a trip to Queens for interactive film fun, movie memorabilia and quirky screenings.

Zenon Taverna > p.171. Astoria is filled with cheerful, family-friendly Greek restaurants along the lines of this affordable spot.

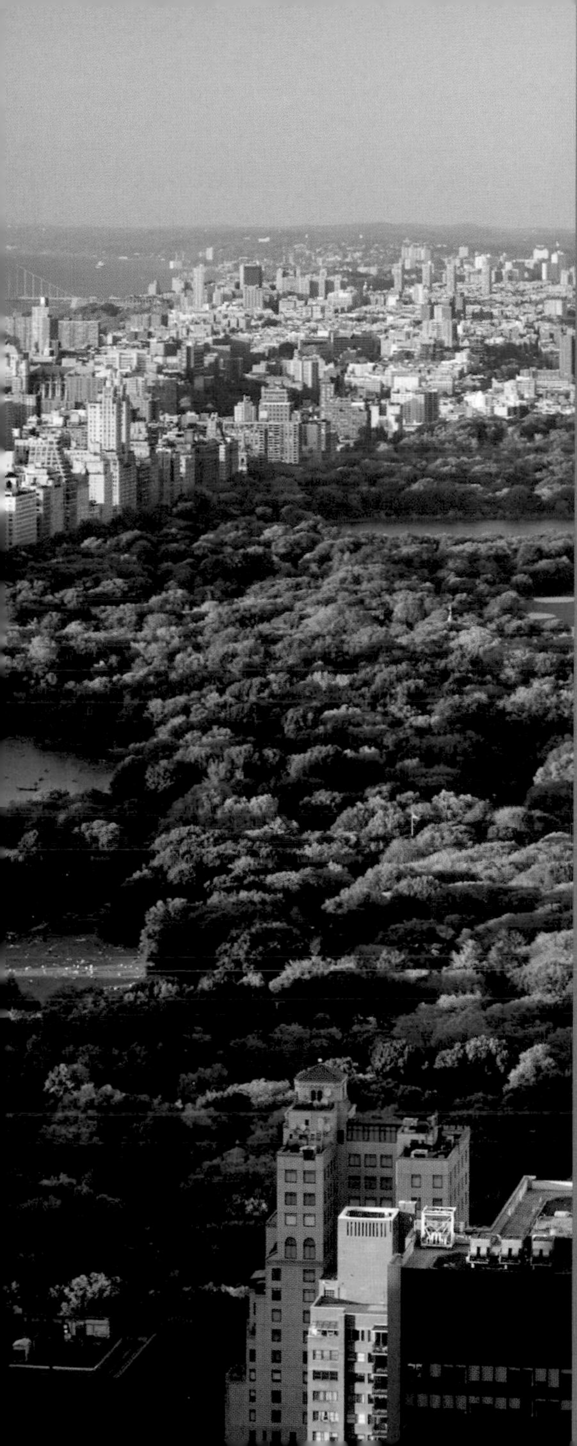

BEST OF NEW YORK CITY

Big sights

1 Brooklyn Bridge The elegant gateways, magnificent views and undeniable romance add up to a memorable walk whichever way you cross. > **p.42**

2 Central Park It's hard to imagine the city without this green and fantastically landscaped sanctuary. > **p.132**

3 Empire State Building The king of Midtown's skyline, the Empire State is the skyscraper fixed in the public's imagination. > **p.103**

4 Statue of Liberty The views of Lower Manhattan and the trip to the crown make this the ultimate New York experience. > **p.40**

5 The Met Spend a week exploring the museum's extensive holdings, or focus on a favourite section, such as the Vermeers or the Impressionist collection. > **p.138**

Brooklyn

1 Red Hook This waterfront neighbourhood, full of art galleries and restaurant gems, is well worth a wander. > **p.162**

2 Coney Island The city's summertime playground has thrill rides and a carnivalesque vibe. > **p.164**

3 Brooklyn Museum An art collection to rival most of the biggies across the river. > **p.162**

4 Hipster bars Bingo night at *Pete's Candy Store*? Shuffleboard at *Royal Palms*? Brooklyn's bar scene couldn't be more cool. > **p.172**

5 Smorgasburg The culinary-driven offshoot of the Brooklyn Flea has artisans vending every food concoction under the sun. > **p.168**

Museums and galleries

1 **Frick Collection** This Fifth Avenue mansion houses one of the city's most beautifully presented collections of fine art. ≥ **p.138**

2 Tenement Museum
A Lower East Side apartment dwelling turned museum, this local treasure brilliantly captures the lives of three generations of immigrants. > **p.63**

3 The American Museum of Natural History One of the world's best natural history collections, with a first-class planetarium and a must-see ensemble of dinosaur fossils. > **p.148**

4 Whitney Museum of American Art Its new Meatpacking District home shows off modern American art, with a healthy dose of terrace views. > **p.92**

5 MoMA Gallery of fabulous modern art and photography, from Monet and Cézanne to Picasso, Dalí, Rothko and Warhol. > **p.116**

Classic eats

1 Katz's Ask for a taste at the meat counter, then settle in with your delicious, overstuffed pastrami sandwich. > **p.66**

2 Peter Luger Steak House In the face of relentless, newfangled competition, 125-year-old Peter Luger remains at the top of the steakhouse heap. > **p.170**

3 Lombardi's America's oldest pizzeria still knocks out huge coal-oven pizzas like it's 1905. > **p.60**

4 Shopsin's Kenny Shopsin's tiny Essex Market diner is famed for its idiosyncratic owner as much as his huge menu of tasty breakfasts and sandwiches. > **p.67**

5 Momofuku Noodle Bar Around for over a decade, David Chang's first restaurant was a ramen, fried chicken and pork bun trendsetter. > **p.79**

Drinking

1 Outdoor The authentic Czech *Bohemian Hall and Beer Garden* is New York's favourite outdoor bar, well worth a foray into Queens. > **p.171**

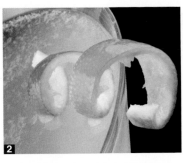

2 Cocktails Cocktail connoisseurs flock to *Pegu Club*, a colonial-style lounge bar, famed for its potent Gin-Gin Mule. **p.53**

3 Dives 1930s dive bar *Subway Inn* moved into new digs in 2015, but it's still perfect for a no-frills, late-afternoon beer. **p.145**

4 Rooftop *The Delancey* is a lounge and live music venue in the Lower East Side, with a popular, canopied roof deck. **p.68**

5 Historic *Ear Inn*, a cosy nineteenth-century seaman's pub, is a neighbourhood classic. **p.52**

Live music

1 Music Hall of Williamsburg An industrial vibe, mingled with lounge space, solid acoustics and killer bookings, makes for an enjoyable night out. > **p.173**

2 Arlene's Grocery Charmingly grungy spot for some indie punk or to take your own turn on the stage during Monday's rock'n'roll karaoke. > **p.69**

3 Village Vanguard Probably the city's signature venue for jazz, the *Vanguard* has been showcasing big names for 75 years. > **p.91**

4 Terra Blues New York's last authentic blues club offers live sets from all the greats, seven days a week. > **p.91**

5 Shrine This African themed Harlem joint hosts everything from World Music to jazz, especially on Sundays. > **p.159**

25

Shopping

1 Beacon's Closet Brooklyn's secondhand fashion paradise, specializing in high-quality modern labels as well as vintage attire. > **p.168**

3 Apple Store All the latest laptops and iPods on display, as well as tech support at the "Genius Bar" and all kinds of tutorials. **> p.118**

2 Brooklyn Flea This weekend-only market has morphed into event shopping, with local gourmets providing gustatory accompaniment. **> p.168**

4 Bloomingdale's Famous department store that stocks everything and somehow manages to remain the epitome of Upper East Side style. **> p.118**

5 Strand Bookstore This venerable bookstore with "18 miles of books" specializes in secondhand titles, recent review copies and new books at half price. **> p.75**

Sports

1 **Cycling the parks and riverbanks** The Hudson River Greenway is just one waterfront path you can trace on two wheels. **> p.46**

2 Ice skating in Bryant Park
Renting blades to zoom around
an ice rink with Midtown skyline
architecture all around trumps
most winter thrills. > **p.113**

3 US Open Tennis For two weeks
in late summer, you can get close
to Grand Slam action in Queens.
> **p.193**

4 Kayaking on the Hudson
The active alternative to a ferry
ride, kayak along the Hudson
for free (at weekends) from
Pier 40 in the West Village.
> **p.86**

5 Yankee Stadium Baseball's
Bronx Bombers are the most
famous team in the US – and
for the time being, the stadium
hosts soccer too. > **p.167**

LACES

Financial District and the Harbor Islands

New York was born on the southern tip of Manhattan in the 1620s. Today, the heart of the world's financial markets is also home to some of the city's most historic streets, sights and One World Trade Center, scene of the nation's biggest tragedy and now its most ambitious development. In recent years the neighbourhood has become increasingly residential, as former bank buildings are converted to luxury condos. To the north, City Hall Park remains the seat of New York's government, while the Brooklyn Bridge zooms eastward from here over the river. Take to the water to visit some of the city's offshore highlights and experience unbeatable views of Manhattan's celebrated skyline; just to the south of the Financial District, in New York Harbor, lies historic Ellis Island, the Statue of Liberty and the bucolic charms of Governors Island.

WALL STREET

Subway #4, #5, #2, #3 to Wall St.
MAP P.34–35, POCKET MAP 023

Wall Street was named after the wooden stockade built by the Dutch at the edge of New Amsterdam in 1653, to protect themselves from the British colonies further north. The street has been associated with money for hundreds of years, and remains the apex of the global financial system thanks to the Stock Exchange. Yet Wall Street has gained a new leisurely air since much of it has been closed to traffic, and fitness studios have opened up in empty office spaces. The old Bank of Manhattan Trust at no. 40 was briefly the world's tallest building in 1930 (927ft) – today it's known as the Trump Building after the flamboyant tycoon who bought it in 1995.

WALL STREET

TRINITY CHURCH

79 Broadway, at Wall St. Subway #4, #5 to Wall St ☎ 212 602 0800, 🌐 www .trinitywallstreet.org. Daily 8am–6pm. Free.
MAP P.34–35, POCKET MAP C23

Trinity Church held its first service at the western end of Wall Street in 1698, but this striking neo-Gothic version – the third model – only went up in 1846, and for fifty years was the city's tallest building. Trinity has the air of an English church (Richard Upjohn, its architect, was English), especially the sheltered graveyard, resting place of the first Secretary of the Treasury, Alexander Hamilton, and steamboat king Robert Fulton.

NEW YORK STOCK EXCHANGE

11 Wall St. Subway #4, #5, #2, #3 to Wall St Ⓦ www.nyse.com. Closed to the public. MAP P.34–35, POCKET MAP D23

Behind the imposing Neoclassical facade of the **New York Stock Exchange** (on Broad St and usually draped with a giant US flag), the purse strings of the capitalist world are pulled. First established in 1817, two to three billion shares are now traded and $50 billion changes hands on an average day. Owing to security concerns, the public can no longer view the frenzied trading floor.

FEDERAL HALL NATIONAL MEMORIAL

26 Wall St. Subway #4, #5, #2, #3 to Wall St ☏ 212 825 6888, Ⓦ www.nps.gov/feha. Mon–Fri 9am–5pm. Free. MAP P.34–35, POCKET MAP D23

One of New York's finest examples of Greek Revival architecture, **Federal Hall** was completed in 1842 on the site of the old city hall, and is best known for the monumental statue of George Washington on its steps. Exhibits inside cover the heady days of 1789 when Washington was sworn in as America's first president here, as well as the later incarnations of the hall as US Customs House and Treasury. Washington's inaugural Bible is displayed, and there are

special exhibits on Alexander Hamilton.

THE MUSEUM OF AMERICAN FINANCE

48 Wall St. Subway #4, #5, #2, #3 to Wall St ☏ 212 908 4110, Ⓦ www.moaf.org. Tues–Sat 10am–4pm. $8. MAP P.34–35, POCKET MAP D23

Housed in the opulent banking hall of the former headquarters of the Bank of New York, the **Museum of American Finance** is the best place to gain an understanding of what's going on in the streets outside. Stocks, bonds and futures trading are demystified through multimedia presentations and a stack of rare artefacts, including a bond signed by Washington, and a stretch of ticker tape from the opening moments of 1929's Great Crash. Despite the inclusion of a detailed timeline of the 2008–2009 financial crisis, the overall message is unequivocally positive; that financial markets are a crucial factor in the development of modern society.

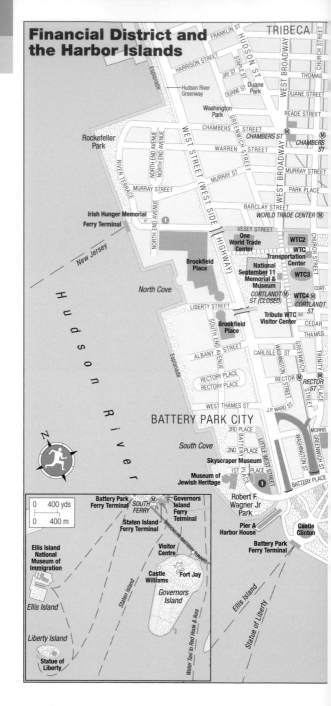

Financial District and the Harbor Islands

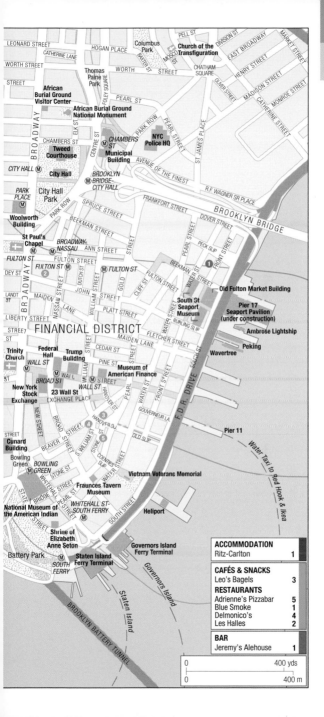

LEONARD STREET
CATHERINE LANE
HOGAN PLACE
Columbus Park
PELL ST
DIVISION ST
EAST BROADWAY
MARKET STREET
Church of the Transfiguration
WORTH STREET
BAXTER ST
MOTT ST
CHATHAM SQUARE
HENRY STREET
MADISON STREET
MONROE STREET
STREET
Thomas Paine Park
WORTH STREET
FOLEY SQ
OLIVER STREET
CATHERINE STREET
African Burial Ground Visitor Center
PEARL ST
PARK ROW
CHAMBERS ST
ELK ST
CENTRE ST
African Burial Ground National Monument
PEARL STREET
ST JAMES PLACE
BROADWAY
CHAMBERS ST Ⓜ
Tweed Courthouse
CHAMBERS ST
Municipal Building
CHAMBERS Ⓜ ST
NYC Police HQ
CITY HALL Ⓜ
City Hall
BROOKLYN BRIDGE-CITY HALL Ⓜ
AVENUE OF THE FINEST
R.F WAGNER SR PLACE
PARK PLACE Ⓜ
City Hall Park
PARK ROW
SPRUCE STREET
FRANKFORT STREET
BROOKLYN BRIDGE
Woolworth Building
BEEKMAN STREET
DOVER STREET
St Paul's Chapel
BROADWAY-NASSAU Ⓜ
ANN STREET
PEARL STREET
PECK SLIP
FRONT STREET
FULTON ST Ⓜ
FULTON STREET
FULTON ST Ⓜ
DUTCH ST
WATER STREET
❶
DEY ST
JOHN STREET
GOLD STREET
CLIFF STREET
FULTON STREET
BEEKMAN STREET
LANDT ST
MAIDEN
NASSAU STREET
WILLIAM STREET
PLATT STREET
Old Fulton Market Building
LIBERTY STREET
LANE
South St Seaport Museum
Pier 17 Seaport Pavilion (under construction)
STREET
FINANCIAL DISTRICT
MAIDEN LANE
FLETCHER STREET
BURLING SLIP
Ambrose Lightship
CEDAR STREET
Peking
Trinity Church
Federal Hall
Trump Building
PINE ST
Museum of American Finance
FRONT STREET
SOUTH ST
Wavertree
WALL ST Ⓜ
WALL Ⓜ ST
New York Stock Exchange
BROAD ST Ⓜ
23 Wall St
WALL STREET
WILLIAM STREET
PEARL STREET
WATER STREET
F.D.R. DRIVE
NEW STREET
EXCHANGE PLACE
HANOVER ST
GOUVERNEUR LA
Pier 11
Cunard Building
BROAD STREET
❸
BEAVER STREET
❹
STONE ST
WILLIAM ST S
HANOVER SQ
OLD SLIP
Water Taxi to Red Hook & Ikea
Bowling Green
BOWLING GREEN Ⓜ
STONE STREET
❺
COUNTIES SLIP
WATER STREET
STREET
STATE STREET
WHITEHALL STREET
BRIDGE ST
Fraunces Tavern Museum
PEARL ST
Vietnam Veterans Memorial
National Museum of the American Indian
WHITEHALL ST-SOUTH FERRY Ⓜ
SOUTH STREET
Heliport
STREET
Shrine of Elizabeth Anne Seton
Battery Park
SOUTH FERRY Ⓜ
Staten Island Ferry Terminal
Governors Island Ferry Terminal
Governors Island
BROOKLYN BATTERY TUNNEL
Staten Island

ACCOMMODATION	
Ritz-Carlton	1

CAFÉS & SNACKS	
Leo's Bagels	3
RESTAURANTS	
Adrienne's Pizzabar	5
Blue Smoke	1
Delmonico's	4
Les Halles	2

BAR	
Jeremy's Alehouse	1

0	400 yds
0	400 m

ST PAUL'S CHAPEL

209 Broadway, at Fulton St. Subway E to
World Trade Center; A, C, #4, #5 to Fulton St
☎ 212 233 4164, ⓦ www.saintpaulschapel
.org. Mon–Sat 10am–6pm, Sun 7am–6pm.
Free. MAP P.34–35, POCKET MAP C22

St Paul's Chapel dates from
1766, making it almost
prehistoric by New York
standards. The main attraction
inside is Unwavering Spirit, a
poignant exhibition on 9/11.
For eight months after the
September 11 attacks, the
chapel served as a sanctuary
for rescue workers, and the
exhibit chronicles this period,
with a moving ensemble of
photos, artefacts and
testimonies. Even George
Washington's pew, preserved
shrine-like from 1789, forms
part of the exhibition (it served
as a foot treatment chair for
firefighters).

NATIONAL SEPTEMBER 11 MEMORIAL & MUSEUM

180 Greenwich St, between Fulton and
Liberty sts. Subway: R to Cortland St; #1 to
Rector St, #4, #5 to Fulton St. ☎ 212 266
5211, ⓦ www.911memorial.org. Memorial daily
7.30am–9pm; museum Sun–Thurs 9am–8pm,
last entry 6pm, Fri & Sat 9am–9pm, last entry
7pm. Free (memorial); $24, children 7–17 $15
(museum). MAP P.34–35, POCKET MAP C22–23

The incredibly moving
**National September 11
Memorial & Museum** was
dedicated on 11 September
2011 to commemorate the
ten-year anniversary of the
9/11 attacks. The two
memorial pools, representing
the footprints of the original
towers, are each around one
acre in size, with 30ft
waterfalls tumbling down their
sides. The names of the 9/11
victims are inscribed on
bronze parapets surrounding
the pools, while the
contemplative eight-acre
Memorial Plaza is filled with

nearly four hundred oak trees.
The underground **9/11
Memorial Museum** (which
you have to pay to enter, and
go through airport-like
security) lies in between the
two memorial pools. Ramps
lead down to the **Foundation
Hall**, containing remnants of
the original Twin Towers, a
half-crushed FDNY fire truck
and the heavily inscribed "Last
Column", the last piece of steel
to be removed from Ground
Zero in 2002. The heart of the
museum is the **September 11,
2001 Historical Exhibition**, a
poignant blend of images,
recordings and videos
covering the 9/11 attacks
minute by minute.

ONE WORLD TRADE CENTER

285 Fulton St (enter on West St, at Vesey
St). Subway: A, C, #2, #3, #4, #5 to Fulton
St; E to World Trade Center; R to Cortland St;
#1 to Rector St. ☎ 844 696 1776, ⓦ www
.oneworldobservatory.com. Daily: early May–
early Sept 9am–10pm (last entry 9.15pm);
early Sept–early May 9am–8pm (last entry
7.15pm). $32, children 6–12 $26 (reserve
tickets online). MAP P.34–35, POCKET MAP C22–23

The tallest skyscraper in the
US (if the spire is included),
One World Trade Center
(1776ft) finally opened to the
public in 2015, with visits to
the **observatory** on floors 100,
101 and 102 (1250ft) – five
high-speed elevators called
Sky Pods will whisk you to the
top in just sixty seconds,
where sensational views of the
city await. There are also
dining options up here, but
you must have an Observatory
ticket to visit them.

TRIBUTE WTC VISITOR CENTER

120 Liberty St. Subway R to Cortland St; #1 to
Rector St; #4, #5 to Fulton St. ☎ 212 393 9160,
ⓦ www.tributewtc.org. Mon–Sat 10am–6pm,
Sun 10am–5pm. $15 (tours $25).
MAP P.34–35, POCKET MAP C23

Facing the World Trade Center site, the **Tribute WTC Visitor Center** commemorates the 9/11 attacks with a touching exhibit about the day itself, embellished with video and taped accounts of survivors. Items from the site make heart rending symbols of the tragedy.

IRISH HUNGER MEMORIAL

290 Vesey St, at North End Ave. Subway E to World Trade Center; #1, #2, #3 to Chambers St. Daily 8am–6.30pm. Free. MAP P.34–35, POCKET MAP B22

This sobering monument to the more than one million Irish people who starved to death during the Great Famine of 1845–52 was designed by artist Brian Tolle in 2002. He transported an authentic famine-era stone cottage from County Mayo, and set it on a 25ft embankment overlooking the Hudson River. The passageway underneath echoes with haunting Irish folk songs, and there is a meandering path through the grassy garden.

MUSEUM OF JEWISH HERITAGE

36 Battery Place. Subway R to Whitehall St; #4, #5 to Bowling Green ☎ 646 437 4200, ⓦ www.mjhnyc.org. Sun–Tues & Thurs 10am–5.45pm, Wed 10am–8pm, Fri 10am–5pm; Nov–Feb museum closes at 3pm on Fri. $12, free Wed 4–8pm. MAP P.34–35, POCKET MAP C24

This moving and informative museum begins with everyday Eastern European Jewish life, before moving on to the horrors of the Holocaust. It ends with the establishment of Israel and subsequent Jewish achievements, even covering the successes of entertainers and artists like Samuel Goldwyn and Allen Ginsberg. The Zen-like "Garden of Stones" is on the second-floor terrace.

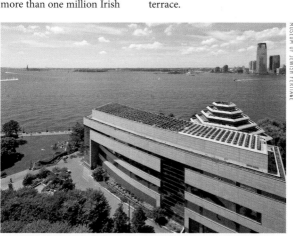

NATIONAL MUSEUM OF THE AMERICAN INDIAN

THE NATIONAL MUSEUM OF THE AMERICAN INDIAN

1 Bowling Green, the US Customs House. Subway R to Whitehall St; #4, #5 to Bowling Green ☎ 212 514 3700, Ⓦ www.nmai.si.edu. Daily 10am–5pm, Thurs 10am–8pm. Free. MAP P.34–35, POCKET MAP D24

Cass Gilbert's US Customs House is now home to the Smithsonian's **National Museum of the American Indian**, a thoughtful collection of artefacts from almost every tribe native to the Americas. The permanent collection includes intricate basketry and woodcarvings, quilled hides, feathered bonnets, and objects of ceremonial significance. Completed in 1907 and in use till 1973, the Beaux Arts **Customs House** is itself part of the attraction. The facade is adorned with elaborate statuary representing the major continents (carved by Daniel Chester French) and the world's great commercial centres, while the spectacular marble-clad Great Hall and Rotunda are beautifully decorated; the sixteen murals covering the 135ft dome were painted by Reginald Marsh in 1937.

THE FRAUNCES TAVERN MUSEUM

54 Pearl St, at Broad St. Subway #1 to South Ferry; #4, #5 to Bowling Green; R to Whitehall St ☎ 212 425 1778, Ⓦ www.frauncestavernmuseum.org. Mon–Fri noon–5pm, Sat & Sun 11am–5pm. $7. MAP P.34–35, POCKET MAP D24

Having survived extensive modification, several fires and nineteenth-century use as a hotel, the three-storey, ochre-and-red-brick **Fraunces Tavern** was almost totally reconstructed in 1907 to mimic its appearance on December 4, 1783, when, after hammering the Brits, a weeping George Washington took leave of his assembled officers, intent on returning to rural life in Virginia. The **Long Room** where his speech was made has been decked out in the style of the time, while the adjacent Federal-style **Clinton Room** is smothered in florid French wallpaper from 1838. The tavern's upper floors contain exhibits tracing the site's history, two hundred flags and a collection of Revolutionary War artefacts; look out for the lock of Washington's hair.

BATTERY PARK

Subway #1 to South Ferry; #4, #5 to Bowling Green; R to Whitehall St. MAP P.34–35, POCKET MAP C24

Lower Manhattan lets out its breath in **Battery Park**, a

Visiting the Harbor Islands

The only way to get to any of the Harbor Islands is by ferry. Take the #1 train to South Ferry or the #4 or #5 trains to Bowling Green, then walk to the boat pier in Battery Park. From the pier, Statue Cruises go to Liberty Island, then on to Ellis Island (daily, every 30–45min, 9.30am–3.30pm; last ferry departs Liberty Island at 5pm and Ellis Island at 5.15pm; round-trip $18, audio guide included). Note that you must be at security 30 minutes before departure. You can buy tickets at Castle Clinton (in the park), or buy them in advance (recommended) at ☏877 523 9849 or ⊛www.statuecruises.com. Queues can be extremely long at any time of year (45min or more), but they're especially bad in the summer; you must queue to buy tickets, and then join another queue to clear security before boarding the ferry. Start out early: keep in mind that if you take the last ferry of the day to Liberty Island, you won't be able to see Ellis. Ferries to Governors Island (May–Sept; hourly: Mon–Fri 10am–4pm; last ferry back 6pm; Sat & Sun every 30min 10am–5.30pm; last ferry back 7pm; $2; free Sat & Sun before noon) depart from the Battery Maritime Building just northeast of the Staten Island Ferry Terminal and Battery Park.

To simply get a closer view of the islands, catch the Staten Island Ferry (every 30min; free; ☏212 639 9675; ⊛www.siferry.com), which departs from the terminal north of Battery Park. The twenty-five-minute ride across to Staten Island provides a beautiful panorama of the harbour and downtown skyline.

bright and breezy landscaped area in which memorials and souvenir vendors lead up to a sweeping view of America's largest harbour. The squat 1811 **Castle Clinton** (daily 8am–5pm; free), on the west side of the park, is the place to buy tickets for and board ferries to the Statue of Liberty and Ellis Island, visible in the distance. Jutting into the harbour on the western side of Battery Park, **Pier A Harbor House** is a lavish nineteenth-century relic dating from 1886, originally the headquarters of the New York Harbor Police. A mammoth renovation has filled the old wooden structure with a mix of shops, oyster bar and restaurants, plus plenty of outdoor seating.

LOWER MANHATTAN

THE STATUE OF LIBERTY

Liberty Island ☎ 212 363 3200, ⓦ www.nps
.gov/stli. Daily 9am–5.15pm. Free (with ferry
ticket). MAP P.34–35, POCKET MAP A16

Standing tall and proud in the middle of New York Harbor, the **Statue of Liberty** has served as a symbol of the American Dream since its dedication in 1886. The monument was the creation of the French sculptor Frédéric Auguste Bartholdi, a gift from France in recognition of the fraternity between the French and American people. The 151ft statue (305ft with pedestal), which consists of thin copper sheets bolted together and supported by an iron framework designed by Gustave Eiffel (of Eiffel Tower fame), was built in Paris between 1874 and 1884.

The basic ferry ticket (see p.39) allows entry to Liberty Island grounds only. To access the interior of the statue, the museum inside and the pedestal observation deck (168 steps up), you must buy a special ticket in advance (no extra charge). To enjoy the spectacular views from the crown of the statue, you'll need to book a Crown Ticket ($21; includes ferry) and climb 354 steps. You must pass another security screening at the statue.

ELLIS ISLAND

☎ 212 363 3200, ⓦ www.nps.gov/elis or
ⓦ www.libertyellisfoundation.org. Museum
open daily 9am–5.15pm. Free. MAP P.34–35,
POCKET MAP A15

Just across the water from Liberty Island, **Ellis Island** became an immigration station in 1892. It was the first stop for more than twelve million immigrants, all steerage-class passengers, and today some one hundred million Americans can trace their roots here. Closed in 1954, it reopened in 1990 as a **Museum of Immigration**, an ambitious project that eloquently recaptures the spirit of the place with artefacts, photographs, maps, and personal testimonies of the immigrants who passed through. On the first floor, the excellent permanent exhibit, "Peopling of America", chronicles four centuries of immigration, while the huge, vaulted Registry Room upstairs has been left imposingly bare.

GOVERNORS ISLAND

Ferry from 10 South St, Slip 7 ☎ 212 825
3045, ⓦ www.nps.gov/gois or ⓦ www
.govisland.com. Late May to Sept Mon–Fri
10am–6pm, Sat & Sun 10am–7pm. Free. MAP
P.34–35, POCKET MAP B15–16

Until the mid-1990s, **Governors Island** was the largest and most expensively run Coast Guard installation in the world, but today it's being developed into a leafy historical park, the island's bucolic village greens and colonial architecture reminiscent of a New England college campus. Many of the buildings are being restored as art galleries and craft stores, and the **Historic Landmark District** at the northern end is managed by the National Park Service.

WALL OF HONOR, ELLIS ISLAND

Tasi-Teic

Ferries arrive at Soissons Dock, where you'll find the small visitors' centre. From here it's a short stroll up to the solid walls of Fort Jay, completed in 1794, and the nearby shady lanes of Nolan Park, home to some beautifully preserved Neoclassical and Federal-style mansions. Other highlights include Castle Williams, a circular fort completed in 1811, but there are also plenty of green spaces in which to lounge in the sun, an artificial beach in the summer, and a breezy promenade with stellar views of Manhattan.

SOUTH STREET SEAPORT

Fulton St, at Water St. Subway: A, C, J, Z, #2, #3, #4, #5 to Fulton St. ☎ 212 748 8600, ⓦ www.southstreetseaportmuseum.org. Museum Wed–Sun 11am 5pm. $12. MAP P.34–35, POCKET MAP E22

The cobbled streets and busy promenade of **South Street Seaport** were devastated by Hurricane Sandy in 2012, prompting a massive redevelopment of the site. Plans include a new marina, food market, the opening of iPic Theaters in the old Fulton Market Building and a controversial hotel/condo skyscraper, while the new **Pier 17** should be open in 2017. The **South Street Seaport Museum**, lodged in a series of painstakingly restored 1830s warehouses showing maritime art and trade exhibits, reopened in 2016, with access to moored ships like the *Peking* (1911), the *Ambrose Lightship* (1908) and the *Wavertree* (1855).

CITY HALL

Subway J, Z to Chambers St; R to City Hall; #2, #3 to Park Place; #4, #5, #6 to Brooklyn Bridge-City Hall. MAP P.34–35, POCKET MAP D22

At the north end of City Hall Park sits graceful **City Hall**, completed in 1812. It's the oldest city hall in the US to retain its original government function; inside is the mayor's office and city council. The sumptuous interior can be seen on free prearranged tours via the Art Commission (Thurs 10am; 1hr; ☎212 788 2656, ⓦwww.nyc.gov) or by just signing up for the public tours (Wed noon) at the tourist kiosk opposite the Woolworth Building. Tours include the sensational, white coffered Rotunda.

WOOLWORTH BUILDING

THE WOOLWORTH BUILDING

233 Broadway, between Barclay St and Park Place. Subway R to City Hall; #2, #3 to Park Place; #4, #5, #6 to Brooklyn Bridge-City Hall. ☎ 203 966 9663, ⓦ www .woolworthtours.com. 30min tours Thurs & Sat 1pm ($20); 1hr tours Thurs & Fri 2pm, Sat 11.30am, also Mon 2pm May–Sept only ($30); 1hr 30min tours Tues, Wed, Sat & Sun 2pm ($45). MAP P.34–35, POCKET MAP C22

The world's tallest skyscraper until 1930, the **Woolworth Building** (792ft) exudes money, ornament and prestige. The soaring, graceful lines of Cass Gilbert's 1913 "Cathedral of Commerce" are fringed with Gothic-style gargoyles and elaborate decorations. Guided tours must be booked online in advance.

AFRICAN BURIAL GROUND NATIONAL MONUMENT

Monument, at Duane St and Elk St; visitor centre at 290 Broadway. Subway J, Z to Chambers St; R to City Hall ☎ 212 637 2019, ⓦ www.nps.gov/afbg. Mon–Sat 10am–5pm, visitor centre Tues–Sat 10am–4pm. Free. MAP P.34–35, POCKET MAP D21

In 1991 construction workers uncovered the remains of 419 skeletons near Broadway, a tiny portion of an African burial ground that covered five blocks during the 1700s. After being examined, the skeletons were re-interred at this site in 2003, marked by seven grassy mounds and a highly polished black granite monument, a symbolic counterpoint to the infamous "gate of no return" on Gorée Island in Senegal. To learn more, walk around the corner to the visitor centre (look for the dedicated entrance). Videos, displays and replicas of the artefacts found here are used to recount the history of the site, and shed light on the brutal life of the city's oft forgotten enslaved population.

THE BROOKLYN BRIDGE

Subway (Manhattan) J, Z to Chambers St; #4, #5, #6 to Brooklyn Bridge-City Hall; (Brooklyn) A, C to High St. MAP P.34–35, POCKET MAP D22–F22

Completed in 1883, the **Brooklyn Bridge** was the first to connect what were the then two separate cities of New York and Brooklyn across the East River, and for twenty years after it was the world's longest suspension bridge. Indeed, the bridge's meeting of art and function, of romantic Gothic and daring practicality, became a sort of spiritual model for the next generation's skyscrapers. But the bridge didn't go up without difficulties: John Augustus Roebling, its architect and engineer, crushed his foot taking measurements and died of tetanus, and twenty workers perished during construction. The entrance to the boardwalk that carries walkers above the traffic is opposite City Hall Park. It's best not to look back till you're midway: the Financial District's giants cluster shoulder to shoulder through the spidery latticework of the cables, a mesmerizing glimpse of the twenty-first-century metropolis.

Cafés and snacks

LEO'S BAGELS

3 Hanover Sq, at Stone St. Subway #2, #3
to Wall St. Mon–Fri 6am–5pm, Sat & Sun
7am–5pm. MAP P.34–35, POCKET MAP D23

Get your bagel fix at this popular
local joint, with the hand-rolled,
chewy main event going for
$1.25 or $2.75–4.95 with huge
dollops of cream cheese and
various *schmears*.

Restaurants

ADRIENNE'S PIZZABAR

54 Stone St. Subway #2, #3 to Wall St ☎ 212
248 3838. Mon–Sat 11am–midnight, Sun
11am–10pm. MAP P.34–35, POCKET MAP D23

One of the better Italian
restaurants downtown, with
alfresco seating in the summer.
Serves nonna-style square
pizzas with a crispy crust; the
crumbled sausage topping is
especially tasty (from $23).

BLUE SMOKE

255 Vesey St, between West St and North
End Ave. Subway J, Z to Broad St, #2, #3 to
Wall St ☎ 212 889 2005. Mon–Thurs
11.30am–10pm, Fri 11.30am–11pm, Sat
11am–11pm, Sun 11am–10pm.
MAP P.34–35, POCKET MAP B22

Authentic Southern barbecue
comes to FiDi courtesy of
pitmaster Kenny Callaghan and
the Danny Meyer empire, with
a perfect brisket burnt-end
sandwich ($16) and classics
such as North Carolina pulled
pork, smoked over hickory and
apple wood ($30).

DELMONICO'S

56 Beaver St, at S William St. Subway #2, #3
to Wall St ☎ 212 509 1144. Mon–Fri
11.30am–10pm, Sat 5–10pm.
MAP P.34–35, POCKET MAP D23

Many a million-dollar deal has
been made at this 1837
landmark restaurant that
features pillars from Pompeii
and classics like lobster Newburg
($24) and succulent steaks (from
$49); next door *Delmonico's Grill*
is cheaper (dishes from $17).

LES HALLES

15 John St, between Broadway and Nassau
St. Subway A, C, J, Z, #2, #3, #4, #5 to Fulton
St ☎ 212 285 8585. Daily 8am–midnight.
MAP P.34–35, POCKET MAP D22

This heady French bistro was
the Rive Gauche fantasy of
celebratory chef Anthony
Bourdain, and still churns out
reasonably priced Gallic
classics, such as escargots in
garlic butter ($10), *moules*
($21) and steak frites ($24).

Bar

JEREMY'S ALEHOUSE

228 Front St, at Peck Slip. Subway A, C, J,
Z, #2, #3, #4, #5 to Fulton St. Mon–Fri
8am–midnight, Sat 10am–midnight,
Sun noon–midnight. MAP P.34–35,
POCKET MAP E22

This local bar, with bras and
ties hanging from the rafters
(donated by happy patrons),
serves pints of beer from $6 (in
plastic cups) and excellent
burgers ($6.50) – happy hour
Mon–Fri 4–6pm.

JEREMY'S ALEHOUSE

Soho and Tribeca

North of the Financial District, Tribeca, the "Triangle Below Canal Street", is a former wholesale garment district that has been transformed into a gentrified community that mixes commercial establishments with loft residences, galleries, celebrity hangouts and chic restaurants. To the northeast, the historic district between Houston and Canal known as Soho (short for "South of Houston") owes its distinction to the cast-iron architecture used by nineteenth-century manufacturers and wholesalers. Decades after toiling immigrant women had left the premises, artists reclaimed the abandoned lofty factory floors as living spaces and studios in the 1960s. Since then, Soho has come to signify fashion chic, urbane shopping and art, and its high-end chains attract celebrities and hordes of tourists; it's a grand place for brunch and browsing, and there are still a few good galleries to speak of.

DUANE PARK

Subway #1, #2, #3 to Chambers St.
MAP P.45, POCKET MAP C21

Duane Park, at the confluence of Duane, Hudson and Greenwich streets, was the first open space acquired by the city specifically to be a public park. Once part of a 62-acre farm, the city bought the park in 1797 for $5, scaled it down and watched it go through various stages of beauty and neglect. From the 1940s, trees and flowers were replaced with patches of concrete, until the park became a scar of what it once was. The most recent restoration was completed in 1999, harking back to its genteel days of 1887 and the design of Samuel Parsons, Jr and Calvert Vaux, famous for their work on Central Park. Wrought-iron fences are back, as are the World's Fair-style benches, historic-looking streetlights and cobblestones.

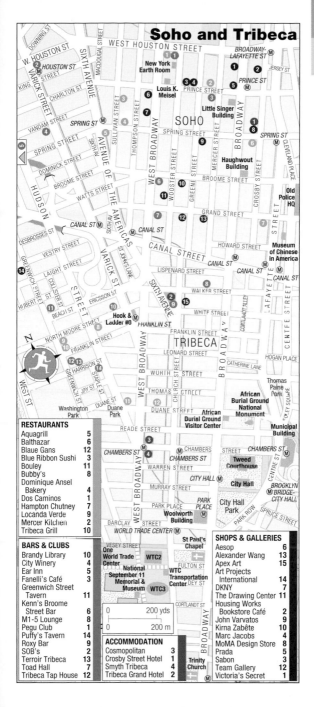

Soho and Tribeca

RESTAURANTS

Aquagrill	5
Balthazar	6
Blaue Gans	12
Blue Ribbon Sushi	3
Bouley	11
Bubby's	8
Dominique Ansel Bakery	4
Dos Caminos	1
Hampton Chutney	7
Locanda Verde	9
Mercer Kitchen	2
Tribeca Grill	10

BARS & CLUBS

Brandy Library	10
City Winery	4
Ear Inn	5
Fanelli's Café	3
Greenwich Street Tavern	11
Kenn's Broome Street Bar	6
M1-5 Lounge	8
Pegu Club	1
Puffy's Tavern	14
Roxy Bar	9
SOB's	2
Terroir Tribeca	13
Toad Hall	7
Tribeca Tap House	12

ACCOMMODATION

Cosmopolitan	3
Crosby Street Hotel	1
Smyth Tribeca	4
Tribeca Grand Hotel	2

SHOPS & GALLERIES

Aesop	6
Alexander Wang	13
Apex Art	15
Art Projects International	14
DKNY	7
The Drawing Center	11
Housing Works Bookstore Café	2
John Varvatos	9
Kirna Zabête	10
Marc Jacobs	4
MoMA Design Store	8
Prada	5
Sabon	3
Team Gallery	12
Victoria's Secret	1

ROCKEFELLER PARK AND HUDSON RIVER PARK

Subway #1, #2, #3 to Chambers St.
MAP P.45, POCKET MAP B21

At the far western end of Chambers Street is **Rockefeller Park**, a charming parcel of lawn and gardens jutting into the Hudson River with fabulous views of New Jersey. In the summer, expect to see the wide lawn filled with sunbathers and the large playground jumping with children. From here you can stroll along **Hudson River Park** north towards Chelsea and Midtown, and south along the shady Battery Park City Esplanade, or cycle the parallel **Hudson River Greenway** all the way to Harlem.

WEST BROADWAY

Subway #1, #2, #3 to Chambers St.
MAP P.45, POCKET MAP C21

West Broadway is one of Tribeca's main thoroughfares, with several of the neighbourhood's best boutiques and restaurants, old and new. Across **West Broadway**, at 14 North Moore at the intersection of Varick, stands the New York Fire Department's **Hook and**

Cast-iron architecture

Soho contains one of the largest collections of cast-iron buildings in the world, erected between 1869 and 1895. **Cast-iron architecture** was designed so that buildings could be assembled quickly and cheaply, with iron beams rather than heavy walls carrying the weight of the floors. The result was greater space for windows and remarkably decorative facades. Glorifying Soho's sweatshops, architects indulged themselves in Baroque balustrades, forests of Renaissance columns, and all the effusion of the French Second Empire. Many fine examples of cast-iron architecture can be glimpsed along **Broadway** and **Greene Street**.

Ladder Company #8, a nineteenth-century brick-and-stone firehouse that starred in the *Ghostbusters* movies (note the mural on the sidewalk outside), and played a crucial role in the rescue efforts of September 11. As it is a working firehouse, you can't do more than admire it externally.

HUDSON RIVER PARK

THE HAUGHWOUT BUILDING

488–492 Broadway. Subway R, N to Prince St; #6 to Spring St. MAP P.45, POCKET MAP D20

The magnificent 1857 **Haughwout Building** is perhaps the ultimate in the cast-iron architectural genre. Rhythmically repeated motifs of colonnaded arches are framed behind taller columns in this thin sliver of a Venetian-style palace – the first building ever to boast a steam-powered Otis elevator. The first two floors opened as a fashion store in 2010 (it's otherwise closed to the public).

SPRING STREET

Subway R, N to Prince St; #6 to Spring St. MAP P.45, POCKET MAP C19–D19

Cutting across the heart of Soho, **Spring Street** east of Sixth Avenue is lined with old buildings, plush restaurants and boutiques; mostly high-end brands such as Chanel and John Varvatos, as well as trendy labels like Ben Sherman, especially as you get closer to Broadway. You'll find a few French bistros and cafés towards Sixth Avenue, while there's a small craft market on the corner of Wooster Street.

THE LITTLE SINGER BUILDING

561 Broadway. Subway R, N to Prince St; #6 to Spring St. MAP P.45, POCKET MAP D19

In 1904, Ernest Flagg took the possibilities of cast iron to their conclusion in this office and warehouse for the sewing machine company, a twelve-storey terracotta design whose use of wide window frames pointed the way to the glass curtain wall of the 1950s. The first floor is a Mango fashion store, but you won't get much sense of the building inside (the rest is off limits).

HAUGHWOUT BUILDING

PRINCE STREET

Subway R, N to Prince St. MAP P.45, POCKET MAP C19–D19

The pulse beats here between Sixth Avenue and The Bowery, where the streets are always packed with shoppers looking to max out their credit cards at the Apple Store, Camper and Michael Kors. In between the shops are small cafés and art galleries, such as **Louis K. Meisel** (where *Sex and the City* character Charlotte worked). On clear days, artists peddle original artwork and handmade jewellery from the sidewalks, though the crowds can get stifling at the weekends. The Belgian-block pavements of nearby Mercer and Greene streets retain the neighbourhood's historical charm. Just north of Prince Street at 141 Wooster Street, the **New York Earth Room** (Wed–Sun noon–3pm and 3.30–6pm; free; Ⓦwww.diaart.org) is a permanent installation by land artist Walter de Maria; a second-floor loft completely covered in two feet of moist brown earth. The installation is closed from mid-June to mid-September.

Shops and galleries

AESOP

438 W Broadway, at Prince St. Subway C to Spring St, R, N to Prince St. Daily 11am–8pm. MAP P.45 POCKET MAP C19

The current darling of the skincare industry, Aussie-born Aesop crafts lush, all-natural products such as bergamot face wash and geranium leaf body scrub. The store is spare but inviting.

ALEXANDER WANG

103 Grand St, between Greene and Mercer sts. Subway N, Q, R to Canal St, #6 to Spring St. Mon–Sat 11am–7pm, Sun noon–6pm. MAP P.45, POCKET MAP C20

This avant-garde Taiwanese American designer is a bonafide international brand. Wang is the brains behind a number of very successful fashion collaborations with houses both high (Balenciaga) and fast (H&M).

APEX ART

291 Church St, between Walker and White sts. Subway N, Q, R to Canal St; #1 to Franklin St. Tues–Sat 11am–6pm. MAP P.45, POCKET MAP C20

Founded in 1994, the thematic multimedia exhibits here are known for their intellectual diversity. Seven group exhibitions are presented each year, with a focus on contextualizing contemporary world art and culture.

ART PROJECTS INTERNATIONAL

434 Greenwich St, at Vestry St. Subway #1 to Canal St. Tues–Sat 11am–6pm. MAP P.45, POCKET MAP B20

Highly respected for showing leading contemporary artists from Asia, this gallery's engaging exhibits are mostly in print and have featured artists like Zheng Xuewu, Gwenn Thomas and Richard Tsao. No sign – just walk in.

DKNY

420 West Broadway, between Prince and Spring sts. Subway N, R to Prince St. Mon–Sat 11am–8pm, Sun noon–7pm. MAP P.45, POCKET MAP C19

This landmark store is great to wander, with enticing coffee-table books and houseware in addition to the expensive clothes.

THE DRAWING CENTER

35 Wooster St, between Grand and Broome sts. Subway A, C, E, N, R, Q to Canal St. Wed, Fri–Sun noon–6pm, Thurs noon–8pm. MAP P.45, POCKET MAP C20

Masters like Marcel Duchamp and Richard Tuttle, as well as emerging and unknown artists, are shown together at this committed nonprofit organization.

HOUSING WORKS BOOKSTORE CAFÉ

126 Crosby St, between Houston and Prince sts. Subway B, D, F, M to Broadway-Lafayette, N, R to Prince St; #6 to Bleecker St. Mon–Fri 9am–9pm, Sat & Sun 10am–5pm. MAP P.45, POCKET MAP D19

Extra-cheap and secondhand books in a spacious and comfy

APEX ART

environment, with a café at the back. Proceeds benefit AIDS charities.

JOHN VARVATOS

122 Spring St, at Greene St. Subway N, R to Prince St, #6 to Spring St. Mon–Sat 11am–7pm, Sun noon–6pm. MAP P.45, POCKET MAP C19

Boxy though flattering casual wear and suits, plus the New York-based American designer's highly successful line of leather Converse trainers.

KIRNA ZABÊTE

477 Broome St, between Greene and Wooster sts. Subway N, R to Prince St. Mon–Sat 11am–7pm, Sun noon–6pm. MAP P.45, POCKET MAP C20

Fashion-forward store that stocks hand-picked highlights from hot designers such as Jason Wu, Rick Owens and Proenza Schouler.

MARC JACOBS

113 Prince St. Subway N, R to Prince St, Mon–Sat 11am–7pm, Sun noon–6pm. MAP P.45, POCKET MAP C19

Doyen of the New York fashion world, Jacobs sells his women's ready-to-wear lines, accessories, shoes and men's clothes at this minimalist store.

MOMA DESIGN STORE

81 Spring St, between Broadway and Crosby St. Subway N, R to Prince St, #6 to Spring St. Mon–Sat 10am–8pm, Sun 11am–7pm. MAP P.45, POCKET MAP D19

A trove of creatively designed goods that range from cheap to astronomical.

PRADA

575 Broadway, at Prince St. Subway N, R to Prince St. Mon–Sat 11am–7pm, Sun 11am–6pm. MAP P.45, POCKET MAP D19

This jaw-dropping flagship store designed by Rem Koolhaas is as much of a sight as the famous clothes inside.

SABON

SABON

123 Prince St, at Wooster St. Subway R, N to Prince St, #6 to Spring St. Jan–April Mon–Sat 10am–9pm & Sun 11am–8pm; May–Dec Mon–Sat 10am–10pm & Sun 11am–8.30pm. MAP P.45, POCKET MAP C19

Luxury body and bath fragrances, soaps and aromatic oils from Israel; friendly assistants help you try the products at the old-fashioned sink in the middle of the store.

TEAM GALLERY

83 Grand St, at Greene St. Subway N, Q, R to Canal St. Tues–Sat 10am–6pm, Sun noon–6pm. MAP P.45, POCKET MAP C20

Beautiful, voyeuristic and cutting-edge work by artists such as Tracey Emin and Genesis P-Orridge, and web artist Cory Arcangel, is shown here.

VICTORIA'S SECRET

565 Broadway, at Houston St. Subway N, R to Prince St. Mon–Sat 10am–9pm, Sun 11am–8pm. MAP P.45, POCKET MAP D19

The enduring appeal of the "world's most glamorous lingerie" is about quality, comfort and design, as much as their celebrity models.

Restaurants

AQUAGRILL

210 Spring St, at Sixth Ave. Subway C, E to Spring St ☎ 212 274 0505. Mon–Thurs noon–3pm & 6–11pm, Fri noon–3pm & 6pm–midnight, Sat noon–4pm & 6pm–midnight, Sun noon–4pm & 6–10.30pm.
MAP P.45, POCKET MAP C19

At this enticing Soho spot, you'll find seafood so fresh it's still flapping. Russian Osetra Caviar chimes in at $165 per ounce, or try the grilled yellowfin tuna for $30. The excellent raw bar and Sunday brunch dishes are not prohibitively expensive, between $15.50 and $26.50. Reservations recommended.

BALTHAZAR

80 Spring St, between Crosby St and Broadway. Subway #6 to Spring St ☎ 212 965 1414. Mon–Thurs 7.30am–12.30am, Fri 7.30am–1.30am, Sat 8am–1.30am, Sun 8am–12.30am. MAP P.45, POCKET MAP D19

Still one of the hottest reservations in town, *Balthazar's* tastefully ornate Parisian decor and stylish clientele keep your eyes busy until the food arrives. Then you can savour highlights such as the fresh oysters ($24/dozen) or exquisite pastries. Entrées $21–47.

BALTHAZAR

BLAUE GANS

139 Duane St, between Church St and W Broadway. Subway A, C, #1, #2, #3 to Chambers St ☎ 212 571 8880. Sun–Wed 11am–11pm, Thurs–Sat 11am–midnight.
MAP P.45, POCKET MAP C21

Poster-filled walls and a long bar made of zinc add personality to this bright Austro-German restaurant, with tasty *schnitzels*, goulash and fresh fish (entrées $19–28) the highlights of chef Kurt Gutenbruner's menu. The beer selection includes some unusual German draughts.

BLUE RIBBON SUSHI

119 Sullivan St, between Prince and Spring sts. Subway C, E to Spring St ☎ 212 343 0404. Daily noon–2am. MAP P.45, POCKET MAP C19

Widely considered one of the best and freshest sushi restaurants in New York, with fish flown in daily from Japan. Have some cold sake and dine at the sushi bar or in the cosy back room. Special rolls from $7, platters from $18.

BOULEY

163 Duane St, at Hudson St. Subway #1, #2, #3 to Chambers St ☎ 212 964 2525. Mon–Sat 11.30am–2.45pm & 5.30–11pm. MAP P.45, POCKET MAP C21

Modern French food made from the freshest ingredients by one of the city's most renowned chefs, David Bouley. Prices are fairly steep (entrées $38–50); soften costs by opting for one of the prix-fixe lunch options (from $55). Jackets required.

BUBBY'S

120 Hudson St, between Franklin and N Moore sts. Subway #1 to Franklin St ☎ 212 219 0666. Sun–Thurs 8am–10pm, Fri & Sat 8am–11pm. MAP P.45, POCKET MAP C21

A relaxed place serving comfort food like matzo-ball soup ($10) and barbecued meats ($24). The pies really pull in the crowds though – try the key lime ($8).

DOMINIQUE ANSEL BAKERY

189 Spring St, between Thompson and Sullivan sts. Subway C, E to Spring St. ☎ 212 219 2773. Mon–Sat 8am–7pm, Sun 9am–7pm. MAP P.45, POCKET MAP C19

The bakery responsible for the "Cronut" craze that swept NYC in 2013; fans still line up an hour before opening to get their hands on the fried, flaky (and trademarked) delight that's a cross between a donut and a croissant ($5.50).

DOS CAMINOS

475 W Broadway, at Houston St. Subway #1 to Houston St ☎ 212 277 4300. Mon–Wed 11.30am–10pm, Thurs 11.30am–10.30pm, Fri 11.30am–11.30pm, Sat 11am–11.30pm, Sun 11am–10pm. MAP P.45, POCKET MAP C19

Thoughtful, real-deal Mexican served with style – try the table-side guacamole. Brunch should set you back $20–25 per person, while dinner entrées range between $19 and $28.

HAMPTON CHUTNEY

143 Grand St, between Lafayette and Crosby sts. Subway J, N, Q, R, Z, #6 to Canal St ☎ 212 226 9996. Mon–Sat 11am–8.30pm, Sun 11am–6pm. MAP P.45, POCKET MAP D20

This place is all about dosas ($8.95), uttapas and naan breads, traditional south Indian fare, albeit with plenty of American ingredients. Orders are spiced up with a choice of fresh, home-made chutneys: cilantro, curry, mango, tomato or peanut.

LOCANDA VERDE

377 Greenwich St, at N Moore St. Subway #1 to Franklin St ☎ 212 925 3797. Mon–Thurs 7am–3pm & 5.30–11pm; Fri 7am–3pm & 5.30–11.30pm, Sat 8am–3pm & 5.30–11.30pm, Sun 8am–3pm & 5.30–11pm. MAP P.45, POCKET MAP C21

This casual Italian taverna is a showcase for star chef Andrew Carmellini's exceptional creations; try the *porchetta*

DOS CAMINOS

sandwich ($21), roasted skate ($32) or his fabulous pastas ($25–28).

MERCER KITCHEN

99 Prince St, at Mercer St in Mercer Hotel. Subway R, N to Prince St ☎ 212 966 5454. Mon–Thurs 7am–midnight, Fri & Sat 7am–1am, Sun 7am–11pm. MAP P.45, POCKET MAP C19

This hip basement hangout and restaurant for hotel guests and scenesters entices with the casual culinary creations of star chef Jean Georges Vongerichten, who makes ample use of his raw bar and wood-burning oven. Brunch items between $15 and $22 and dinner plates from $24.

TRIBECA GRILL

375 Greenwich St, at Franklin St. Subway #1 to Franklin St ☎ 212 941 3900. Mon–Thurs 11.30am–10.30pm, Fri 11.30am–11.30pm, Sat 5.30–11.30pm, Sun 11am–10pm. MAP P.45, POCKET MAP C21

The Grill is part-owned by Robert De Niro, but it's really the food – fine American cooking with Asian and Italian accents – that takes centre stage. The setting is attractive, too: an airy, brick-walled eating area in a 1905 warehouse, around a central Tiffany bar. Main dishes range $23 to $39 (for the steak).

Bars and clubs

BRANDY LIBRARY

26 N Moore St, at Varick St. Subway #1 to Franklin St. Sun–Wed 5pm–1am, Thurs 4pm–2am, Fri & Sat 4pm–4am. MAP P.45, POCKET MAP C20

Stylish lounge bar, with rows of bottles lining the "bookshelves" and a menu of over 100 cocktails, rare single malt whiskeys and the signature cognacs.

CITY WINERY

155 Varick St, at Vandam St. Subway #1 to Houston St, C, E to Spring St. Mon–Thurs & Sun 11.30am–3.30pm & 5pm–midnight, Fri 11.30am–3.30pm & 5pm–2am, Sat 5pm–2am. MAP P.45, POCKET MAP B19

City Winery puts on a fine roster of rock, folk and roots music performers on its stage; it has full dinner service (food is OK, nothing special) and wine is actually made on the premises. Tickets $15–50.

EAR INN

326 Spring St, between Washington and Greenwich sts. Subway C, E to Spring St, #1 to Houston St. Daily noon–4am. MAP P.45, POCKET MAP B20

"Ear" as in "Bar" with half the neon "B" chipped off. This historic pub near the Hudson opened in 1890 (the building dates from 1817). Its creaky interior is as cosy as a Cornish inn, with a good mix of beers on tap and basic, reasonably priced American food.

FANELLI'S CAFÉ

94 Prince St at Mercer St. Sun–Thurs 9.30am–12.30am, Fri & Sat 9.30am–1.30am. MAP P.45, POCKET MAP D19

Established in 1922 (the building dates from 1853), *Fanelli's* is one of the city's oldest pubs, relaxed and informal and a favourite of the not-too-hip after-work crowd.

FANELLI'S CAFÉ

GREENWICH STREET TAVERN

399 Greenwich St, at Beach St. Subway #1 to Franklin St. Sun & Mon 11am–10pm, Tues & Wed 11am–11pm, Thurs–Sat 11am–1am. MAP P.45, POCKET MAP B20

Friendly neighbourhood bar, refreshingly unpretentious for this part of town, with a solid menu of snack food, easy-going (generally male) clientele and beers for $3 in happy hour (Mon–Fri 5–8pm).

KENN'S BROOME STREET BAR

363 W Broadway, at Broome St. Subway #1 to Franklin St. Sun–Thurs 11am–1.30am, Fri & Sat 11am–2.30am. MAP P.45, POCKET MAP C20

Open since 1972 but set in an ageing 1825 Federal-style house, this comfortable bar offers 15 beers (eight draughts), from Brooklyn Lager to Dogfish IPA (they also have Stella on tap), and serves food, including decent burgers from $9.75.

M1-5 LOUNGE

52 Walker St, between Church St and Broadway. Subway N, Q, R to Canal St. Mon–Fri 4pm–4am, Sat 8pm–4am. MAP P.45, POCKET MAP C20

Ultra-hip lounge bar, with a decent range of beers, wines and cocktails to accompany the sleek design and good food. Live music and DJs set the scene.

PEGU CLUB

77 W Houston St, at West Broadway. Subway B, D, F, M to Broadway-Lafayette St, N, R to Prince St. Sun–Wed 5pm–2am, Thurs–Sat 5pm–4am. MAP P.45, POCKET MAP C19

One of NYC's most celebrated cocktail lounges, an elegant pioneer that perfected the Gin-Gin Mule (ginger beer with Tanqueray gin, fresh mint and lime juice).

PUFFY'S TAVERN

81 Hudson St, between Harrison and Jay sts. Subway #1 to Franklin St. Mon–Fri 11.30am–4am, Sat & Sun noon–4am. MAP P.45, POCKET MAP C21

Far from being P. Diddy's hangout, this small dive bar serves up cheap booze without an ounce of attitude, rare in this area. Italian sandwiches are served and its cool jukebox specializes in old 45s.

ROXY BAR

Roxy Hotel, 2 Sixth Ave, at White St. Subway A, C, E to Canal St, #1 to Franklin St ☏ 212 965 3565. Daily 7am–2am. MAP P.45, POCKET MAP C20

Fabulous hotel bar, set at the bottom of the *Roxy*'s spacious atrium – being surrounded by twinkling lights and beautiful people (it's much more atmospheric at night) eases the pain when it's time to pay.

SOB'S (SOUNDS OF BRAZIL)

204 Varick St, at W Houston St. Subway #1 to Houston St. Mon–Thurs hours vary, Fri 5pm–4am, Sat 6.30pm–4am, Sun noon–4pm. MAP P.45, POCKET MAP B19

Premier place to hear hip-hop, Brazilian, West Indian, Caribbean and World Music acts in Manhattan. Vibrant and danceable, with quality music.

TERROIR TRIBECA

24 Harrison St, at Greenwich St. Subway 1 to Franklin St. Mon & Tues 4pm–midnight, Wed–Sat 4pm–1am, Sun 4–11pm. MAP P.45, POCKET MAP C21

Tribeca outpost of the beloved wine bar, with more than 150 carefully curated bottles on the menu, plus eight beers on tap and select grape juices for non-drinkers. There's also a big choice of cheese, sandwiches and assorted finger foods.

TOAD HALL

57 Grand St, between W Broadway and Wooster St. Subway A, C, E to Canal St. Daily noon–4am. MAP P.45, POCKET MAP C20

With a pool table, good service and excellent bar snacks, this stylish alehouse is a little less hip and a little more of a local hangout than some of its neighbours.

TRIBECA TAP HOUSE

363 Greenwich St, between Harrison and Franklin sts. Subway #1 to Franklin St. Mon–Thurs 11am–1am, Fri–Sun 10am–1am. MAP P.45, POCKET MAP C21

Tribeca Tap House features twenty beers on tap, with plenty of microbrews on offer, as well as wine, cocktails, bar food, snacks and US sports events shown daily on big screens.

ROXY BAR

Chinatown, Little Italy and Nolita

Chinese immigrants have been coming to New York since the 1850s, making this Chinatown one of the oldest and biggest in the western hemisphere. Indeed, with over 100,000 residents, Chinatown is Manhattan's most densely populated ethnic neighbourhood. Since the 1980s it has pushed across its traditional border on Canal Street into the smaller enclave of Little Italy, and has begun to sprawl east across Division Street and East Broadway into the Lower East Side. Little Italy itself, now squeezed into a narrow strip along Mulberry Street, is far more dependent on tourists than Chinatown, but both neighbourhoods are fun places to eat, with cheap noodles, roast duck, gelato and huge plates of pasta on offer. On the northern fringes of Little Italy, the hip quarter known as Nolita ("North of Little Italy") is home to a number of chic restaurants, bars and boutiques.

CANAL STREET

Subway A, C, E, J, N, Q, R, Z, #1, #6 to Canal St. MAP P.55, POCKET MAP D20-E20

Canal Street is Chinatown's main all-hours artery crammed with jewellery shops and kiosks hawking sunglasses, T-shirts and fake Rolexes. At the eastern end of the thoroughfare, the majestic Byzantine dome of the former Citizen's Savings Bank (now HSBC) and the 1909 Manhattan Bridge's grand Beaux Arts entrance seem out of place amid the neon signs and market stalls.

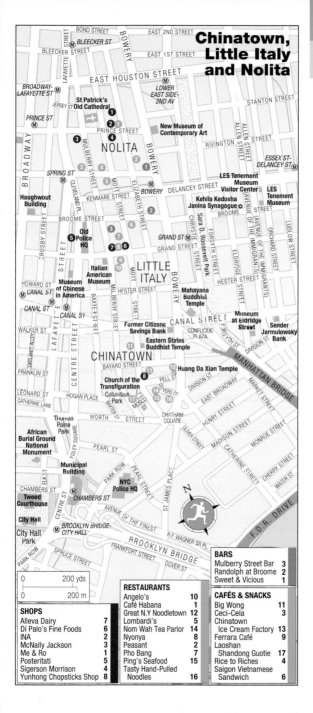

Chinatown, Little Italy and Nolita

BARS
Mulberry Street Bar	3
Randolph at Broome	2
Sweet & Vicious	1

RESTAURANTS
Angelo's	10
Café Habana	1
Great N.Y Noodletown	12
Lombardi's	5
Nom Wah Tea Parlor	14
Nyonya	8
Peasant	2
Pho Bang	7
Ping's Seafood	15
Tasty Hand-Pulled Noodles	16

CAFÉS & SNACKS
Big Wong	11
Ceci-Cela	3
Chinatown Ice Cream Factory	13
Ferrara Café	9
Laoshan Shandong Guotie	17
Rice to Riches	4
Saigon Vietnamese Sandwich	6

SHOPS
Alleva Dairy	7
Di Palo's Fine Foods	6
INA	2
McNally Jackson	3
Me & Ro	1
Posteritati	5
Sigerson Morrison	4
Yunhong Chopsticks Shop	8

CHURCH OF THE TRANSFIGURATION

29 Mott St. Subway J, N, Q, R, Z, #6 to Canal St ☎ 212 962 5157, ⓦ www
.transfigurationnyc.org. Sat 2–5pm, otherwise services only. Free. MAP P.55, POCKET MAP E21

This elegant green-domed Georgian edifice is known as the "church of immigrants" for good reason. Since opening in 1801 as a Lutheran parish, it has also served Irish and Italian church-goers. Today, Mass is said daily in Cantonese, English and Mandarin.

MOTT STREET

Subway J, N, Q, R, Z, #6 to Canal St. MAP P.55, POCKET MAP E20-21

Mott Street is Chinatown's most touristy restaurant row, although the streets around – Canal, Pell, Bayard, Doyers and Bowery – host a glut of authentic canteens, tea and rice shops. Cantonese cuisine predominates, but many restaurants also specialize in spicier Sichuan and Hunan dishes. Most restaurants start closing around 10pm.

GRAND STREET

Subway B, D to Grand St. MAP P.55, POCKET MAP E20-F20

Grand Street was the city's Main Street in the mid-1800s, and nowadays you will find outdoor fruit, vegetable and

GRAND STREET

live seafood stands lining the curbs, offering bean curd, fungi and dried sea cucumbers. Ribs, whole chickens and roast ducks glisten in the storefront windows, alongside those of Chinese herbalists.

MUSEUM OF CHINESE IN AMERICA

215 Centre St between Howard and Grand sts. Subway J, N, Q, R, Z, #6 to Canal St ☎ 212 619 4785, ⓦ www.mocanyc.org. Tues–Sun 11am–6pm, Thurs 11am–9pm. $10, free Thurs. MAP P.55, POCKET MAP D20

This fascinating museum was designed by Maya Lin in 2009, its core exhibition providing an historical overview of the Chinese in the US through evocative multimedia displays, artefacts and filmed interviews. Galleries are

Chinatown temples

Chinatown is a good place to observe traditional Chinese temple rituals, though the architecture is usually modern – most temples occupy converted shopfronts. **The Eastern States Buddhist Temple**, 64 Mott St (daily 8am–6pm), was established in 1962 as a social club for elderly Chinese men. The main deity here is Sakyamuni Buddha, but there's also a glass-encased gold statue of the "four-faced Buddha", a replica of the revered image in Bangkok's Erawan Shrine. Chinese influence is more obvious at the gilded and peaceful **Mahayana Buddhist Temple**, 133 Canal St (daily 8am–6pm). Candlelight and blue neon glow around the giant gold Buddha on the main altar. At the corner of Pell St and the Bowery is one of Chinatown's few Taoist temples: **Huang Daxian Temple** (daily 9am–6pm).

arranged around a sun-lit courtyard reminiscent of a traditional Chinese house.

ITALIAN AMERICAN MUSEUM AND MULBERRY STREET

155 Mulberry St. Subway J, N, Q, R, #6 to Canal St ☎ 212 965 9000, Ⓦ www .italianamericanmuseum.org. Fri–Sun noon–6pm. Donation $5. MAP P.55, POCKET MAP D20

Little Italy's main strip, **Mulberry Street**, is home to many of the area's cafés and restaurants – and filled with tourists. The former site of *Umberto's Clam House*, on the corner of Mulberry and Hester streets, was once notorious as the scene of the vicious gangland murder of Joe "Crazy Joey" Gallo in 1972. On the corner of Grand Street, the **Italian American Museum**, housed in the former 1885 Banca Stabile building, holds small exhibits on the old neighbourhood.

ST PATRICK'S OLD CATHEDRAL

263 Mulberry St, at Prince St. Subway R, N to Prince St ☎ 212 226 8075, Ⓦ www .oldcathedral.org. Daily 8am–6pm. Free. MAP P.55, POCKET MAP D19

The first Catholic cathedral in the city, **St Patrick's Old Cathedral** began by serving the Irish immigrant community in 1809 and is the parent church to its much more famous offspring on Fifth Avenue and 50th Street.

NEW MUSEUM OF CONTEMPORARY ART AND THE BOWERY

235 Bowery, at Prince St. Subway R, N to Prince St, #6 to Spring St ☎ 212 219 1222, Ⓦ www.newmuseum.org. Wed & Fri–Sun 11am–6pm, Thurs 11am–9pm. $16, "pay what you wish" (suggested $2 minimum) Thurs 7–9pm. MAP P.55, POCKET MAP E19

Powerful symbol of the Bowery's rebirth, this avant-garde art gallery is housed in a stack of seven shimmering aluminium boxes. The warehouse-like galleries are spacious, but still small enough to digest without overdosing on the diverse range of temporary exhibits inside. The **Bowery** itself was until relatively recently a byword for poverty and destitution, America's original skid row. At its peak, in 1949, around 14,000 homeless people could be found here, most dossing down in hostels known as flophouses. Today only a few flophouses remain, and the street is increasingly lined with smart, contemporary buildings, stores and bars.

Shops

ALLEVA DAIRY

188 Grand St, at Mulberry St. Subway J, Z, #6 to Canal St. Daily 9am–7pm. MAP P.55, POCKET MAP D20

The oldest Italian *formaggiaio* (cheesemonger) and grocery in America (1892). Makes its own smoked mozzarella, provolone and ricotta.

DI PALO'S FINE FOODS

200 Grand St, at Mott St. Subway B, D to Grand St. Mon–Sat 9am–6.30pm, Sun 9am–4pm. MAP P.55, POCKET MAP D20

Charming and authoritative family-run business, open since 1925, that sells some of the city's best ricotta, along with a fine selection of aged balsamic vinegars, oils and home-made pastas.

INA

21 Prince St, between Elizabeth and Mott sts. Subway R, N to Prince St. Mon–Sat noon–8pm, Sun noon–7pm. MAP P.55, POCKET MAP D19

Favourite consignment shop selling recent season cast-offs. Full of bargains; there's a men's branch at 19 Prince St (next door; same hours).

DI PALO'S

MCNALLY JACKSON

52 Prince St, between Mulberry and Lafayette sts. Subway N, R to Prince St. Mon–Sat 10am–10pm, Sun 10am–9pm. MAP P.55, POCKET MAP D19

This independent local bookstore has a great café and excellent literary events.

ME & RO

241 Elizabeth St, between Houston and Prince sts. Subway B, D, F, M to Broadway-Lafayette, R, N to Prince St. Mon–Sat noon–6pm. MAP P.55, POCKET MAP D19

The hottest, most distinctive jewellery designer in Manhattan, with tasteful Modernist designs inspired by the traditions of China, India and Tibet.

POSTERITATI

239 Centre St, between Broome and Grand sts. Subway #6 to Spring St. Tues–Sat 11am–7pm. MAP P.55, POCKET MAP D20

Vast selection of over nine thousand movie posters, from classics such as *20,000 Leagues Under the Sea* and *Goldfinger* to modern blockbusters like *Avatar*.

SIGERSON MORRISON

28 Prince St, at Mott St. Subway R, N to Prince St. Mon–Sat 11am–7pm, Sun noon–6pm. MAP P.55, POCKET MAP D19

Timeless, elegant shoes for women by Kari Sigerson and Miranda Morrison, a real pilgrimage for any shoe lover.

YUNHONG CHOPSTICKS SHOP

50 Mott St, between Bayard and Pell sts. Subway A, C, E, J, N, Q, R, Z, #1, #6 to Canal St. Daily 10.30am–8.30pm. MAP P.55, POCKET MAP D21

The only US branch of this Beijing chopstick maker, with more than 200 different styles made from mahogany, ebony and silver, and hand-painted. Some feature famous quotes from Chairman Mao.

Cafés and snacks

BIG WONG

67 Mott St, between Bayard and Canal sts. Subway J, N, Q, R, Z, #6 to Canal St. Daily 8.30am–11pm. MAP P.55, POCKET MAP D20

This cafeteria-style Cantonese BBQ joint serves some of Chinatown's tastiest duck and congee (savoury rice stew), all for $6–12.

CECI-CELA

55 Spring St, between Mulberry and Lafayette sts. Subway #6 to Spring St. Mon–Thurs 6.30am–8pm, Fri 6.30am–9pm, Sat 7am–9pm & Sun 7am–8pm. MAP P.55, POCKET MAP D19

Tiny French patisserie with tables in the back, selling delectable baked goods. Divine almond croissants and palmiers (elephant-ear-shaped, sugar-coated pastries).

CHINATOWN ICE CREAM FACTORY

65 Bayard St, between Mott and Elizabeth sts. Subway J, N, Q, R, Z, #6 to Canal St. Daily 11am–10pm. MAP P.55, POCKET MAP D21

An essential stop after dinner at one of the restaurants nearby. Specialties include green tea, ginger and almond cookie ice cream.

FERRARA CAFÉ

195 Grand St, between Mott and Mulberry sts. Subway J, N, Q, R, Z, #6 to Canal St B, D to Grand St. Sun–Fri 8am–midnight, Sat 8am–1am. MAP P.55, POCKET MAP D20

The best-known and most traditional of Little Italy's coffeehouses, this neighbourhood landmark has been around since 1892. Try the New York cheesecake or, in summer, *granite* (Italian ices). Outdoor seating is available in warmer weather.

FERRARA CAFÉ

LAOSHAN SHANDONG GUOTIE

106 Mosco St. Subway J, Z, #6 to Canal St. Daily 8am–9pm. MAP P.55, POCKET MAP D21

Identified simply by a "Fried Dumpling" sign in English, this bargain hole-in-the-wall specializes in pan-fried dumplings characteristic of northern China ($1 for 5).

RICE TO RICHES

37 Spring St, between Mott and Mulberry sts. Subway #6 to Spring St. Sun–Thurs 11am–11pm, Fri & Sat 11am–1am. MAP P.55, POCKET MAP D19

Utterly irresistible rice pudding, served up in this fashionable space in a variety of sweet flavours, from peanut butter and choc chip to mango and cinnamon. Bowls start at $8.

SAIGON VIETNAMESE SANDWICH

369 Broome St, at Mott St. Subway #6 to Spring St. Daily 9am–7pm. MAP P.55, POCKET MAP D20

One of the best makers of Vietnamese sandwiches (known as *bánh mì*) in the city. The classic is a large chunk of French bread stuffed with pork, sausage and pickled vegetables – all for $5.50 (cash only).

Restaurants

ANGELO'S

146 Mulberry St, between Hester and Grand sts. Subway N, R, #6 to Canal St. Tues–Thurs & Sun noon–11.30pm, Fri noon–12.30am, Sat noon–1am. MAP P.55, POCKET MAP D20

Little Italy's red-sauce restaurants cater firmly to tourists these days, but this 1902 classic is the best place to get a sense of the area's original style and flavours.

CAFÉ HABANA

17 Prince St, at Elizabeth St. Subway R to Prince St ☎ 212 625 2001. Daily 9am–midnight. MAP P.55, POCKET MAP D19

Small and always crowded, this Cuban–South American option features some of the best skirt steak and fried plantains this side of Cuba. A takeout window next door serves great *café con leche* (daily 11am–11pm).

GREAT N.Y. NOODLETOWN

28 Bowery, at Bayard St. Subway B, D to Grand St, J, Z, #6 to Canal St ☎ 212 349 0923. Daily 9am–4am. MAP P.55, POCKET MAP E21

Despite the name, noodles aren't the real draw at this down-to-earth restaurant – the soft-shell crabs (in season) are crisp, salty and delicious. Good roast meats (try the baby pig) and soups too.

LOMBARDI'S

32 Spring St, at Mott St. Subway #6 to Spring St ☎ 212 941 7994. Sun–Thurs 11.30am–11pm, Fri & Sat 11.30am–midnight. MAP P.55, POCKET MAP D19

The oldest pizzeria in the US (since 1905) serves some of the best pies in town, including an amazing clam pizza; no slices, though. Ask for roasted garlic on the side.

NOM WAH TEA PARLOR

13 Doyers St. Subway J, N, Q, R, Z, #6 to Canal St. ☎ 212 962 6047. Sun–Thurs 10.30am–9pm, Fri & Sat 10.30am–10pm. MAP P.55, POCKET MAP E21

Dating back to 1920 but spruced up in 2010, this elegant and old-fashioned dim sum place offers a select menu of tasty snacks, from taro and shrimp dumplings to salt and pepper shrimp and their original egg roll.

NYONYA

199 Grand St, between Mott and Mulberry sts. Subway B, D to Grand St, J, Z, #6 to Canal St ☎ 212 334 3669. Sun–Thurs 11am–11.30pm, Fri & Sat 11am–midnight. MAP P.55, POCKET MAP D20

Superb Malaysian grub at wallet-friendly prices. Try the chicken curry, spicy squid or clay-pot noodles. Cash only.

PEASANT

194 Elizabeth St, between Prince and Spring sts. Subway R, N to Prince St; J, Z to Bowery, #6 to Spring St ☎ 212 965 9511. Tues–Sun 6pm–2am. MAP P.55, POCKET MAP D19

A bit of a hangout after hours for city chefs, here you'll pay around $24–26 for Frank De Carlo's beautifully crafted Italian food such as *porchetta*

PING'S SEAFOOD

LOMBARDI'S

Freshly cooked and delicious hand-pulled noodles made to order – choose from seven different types, then opt for pan-fried or boiled noodles with pork, fish, beef, chicken, shrimp and several other combos.

Bars

MULBERRY STREET BAR

176-1/2 Mulberry St, between Broome and Grand sts. Subway J, Z to Bowery, #6 to Canal St. Mon–Sat 11am–4am, Sun noon–4am. MAP P.55, POCKET MAP D20

Donnie Brasco and *The Sopranos* had scenes shot in this favourite local dive bar, located in the heart of Little Italy. Formerly known as *Mare Chiaro*, the wooden bar, subway tile floor and pressed tin roof have barely changed since it opened in 1908.

RANDOLPH AT BROOME

349 Broome St, between Elizabeth St and the Bowery. Subway J, Z to Bowery, B, D to Grand St. Mon–Fri 5pm–4am; Sat & Sun noon–4am. MAP P.55, POCKET MAP D20

Friendly European café that serves artisanal cocktails and gourmet coffee from the Brooklyn Roasting Company (till 5pm). Happy hour is Mon–Fri 5–8pm, and there's a cosy outdoor patio at the front.

SWEET & VICIOUS

5 Spring St, between Bowery and Elizabeth St. Subway J, Z to Bowery. Daily 2pm–4am. MAP P.55, POCKET MAP D19

This bar is a neighbourhood favourite and the epitome of rustic chic, with exposed brick and wood and antique chandeliers. The tempting cocktail list features berry Cosmopolitans and lemondrop Martinis. A back garden and a cosy atmosphere add to its charm.

arrosto (roasted suckling pig) or $16 for brick-oven-fired pizzas.

PHO BANG

157 Mott St, between Grand and Broome sts. Subway B, D to Grand St, J, Z, #6 to Canal St ☎ 212 966 3797. Daily 10am–10pm. MAP P.55, POCKET MAP D20

One of the most popular Vietnamese restaurants in the city, often packed at weekends. The main event is *pho*, Vietnamese beef noodle soup, which comes in several varieties, but the crispy spring rolls and chicken curry are also excellent.

PING'S SEAFOOD

22 Mott St, between Chatham Square and Pell St. Subway R, N, J, Z, #6 to Canal St ☎ 212 602 9988. Mon–Fri 10.30am–11pm, Sat & Sun 9am–11pm. MAP P.55, POCKET MAP F21

While this Hong Kong seafood restaurant is good anytime, it's most enjoyable at weekends for dim sum, when carts of tasty, bite-size delicacies whirl by for the taking every thirty seconds. This place offers superb bang for your buck.

TASTY HAND-PULLED NOODLES

1 Doyers St, at the Bowery. Subway J, N, Q, R, Z, #6 to Canal St ☎ 212 791 1817. Daily 10.30am–10.30pm. MAP P.55, POCKET MAP F21

The Lower East Side

Historically the epitome of the American ethnic melting pot, the Lower East Side has been a revolving door for immigrants since the 1830s, when Irish and German populations moved in. The second wave came from Southern Italian and Eastern European Jewish communities arriving in the 1880s. By 1915, Jews had the largest representation in the Lower East Side, numbering more than 320,000. While a fair proportion of inhabitants today are working-class Latino or Asian, you are just as likely to find students, moneyed artsy types and other refugees from the overly-gentrified areas of Soho and the nearby East Village, a blend that makes this one of the city's most enthralling neighbourhoods and one of its hippest areas for shopping, drinking, dancing and – what else? – food.

ORCHARD STREET

Subway F, J, M, Z to Delancey St/Essex St, B, D to Grand St. MAP P.63, POCKET MAP E19

The centre of the Lower East Side's so-called Bargain District, Orchard is best visited at weekends, when filled with stalls and storefronts hawking discounted designer clothes and bags, though note that many Jewish-owned stores are closed on Saturdays. The rooms above the stores used to house sweatshops, so named because whatever the weather, a stove had to be kept warm for pressing the clothes made there. Much of the garment industry moved uptown ages ago, and the rooms are a bit more salubrious now – often home to pricey apartments.

TENEMENT MUSEUM

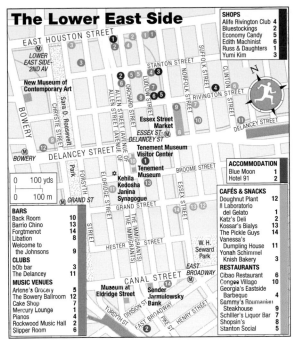

The Lower East Side

SHOPS

Alife Rivington Club	4
Bluestockings	2
Economy Candy	5
Edith Machinist	6
Russ & Daughters	1
Yumi Kim	3

ACCOMMODATION

Blue Moon	1
Hotel 91	2

CAFÉS & SNACKS

Doughnut Plant	12
Il Laboratorio del Gelato	1
Katz's Deli	2
Kossar's Bialys	13
The Pickle Guys	14
Vanessa's Dumpling House	11
Yonah Schimmel Knish Bakery	3

RESTAURANTS

Cibao Restaurant	6
Congee Village	10
Georgia's Eastside Barbeque	4
Sammy's Roumanian Steakhouse	9
Schiller's Liquor Bar	7
Shopsin's	8
Stanton Social	5

BARS

Back Room	10
Barrio Chino	13
Forgtmenot	14
Libation	8
Welcome to the Johnsons	9

CLUBS

bOb bar	3
The Delancey	11

MUSIC VENUES

Arlene's Grocery	5
The Bowery Ballroom	12
Cake Shop	7
Mercury Lounge	1
Pianos	4
Rockwood Music Hall	2
Slipper Room	6

TENEMENT MUSEUM

97 Orchard St, between Broome and Delancey sts. Subway D, D to Grand St, F, J, M, Z to Delancey St/Essex St ☎ 212 982 8420, ⌨ www.tenement.org. $25; for tickets go to the visitor centre at 103 Orchard St (Fri–Wed 10am–6.30pm, Thurs 10am–8.30pm).

MAP P.63, POCKET MAP E20

This illuminating museum offers a glimpse into the crumbling and claustrophobic interior of an 1863 tenement, with its deceptively elegant entry hall and two communal toilets for every four families. Museum guides expertly bring to life the building's past and present, aided by documents, photographs and artefacts found on-site, and concentrating on the area's multiple ethnic heritages.

Various apartments inside have been renovated with period furnishings to reflect the lives of tenants, from the mid-nineteenth century to the mid-twentieth century – when many families ran cottage industries from home.

The tenement is accessible only by themed **guided tours** (1hr, every 15–30min; daily 10.30am–5pm). These include "Hard Times", which focuses on a German-Jewish family and Italian family during the economic depressions of 1863 and 1935; "Irish Outsiders", which examines the grim life of the Irish Moore family from 1868–69; and "Sweatshop Workers", a visit to the Levine family's garment workshop and the Rogarshevskys' Sabbath table at the turn of the twentieth century. "Foods of the Lower East Side" ($45) is a two-hour tour of the neighbourhood (Fri & Sat only) that complements the tenement tours.

ESSEX STREET MARKET

120 Essex St, at Delancey St. Subway F, J, M,
Z to Delancey St/Essex St ☎ 212 388 0449,
Ⓦ www.essexstreetmarket.com. Mon–Sat
8am–7pm & Sun 10am–6pm. MAP P.63,
POCKET MAP E19

On the north side of Delancey
Street sprawls the **Essex Street
Market**, erected under the
aegis of Mayor LaGuardia in
the 1930s. Here you'll find all
sorts of fresh fruit, fish and
vegetables, along with artisan
chocolates, cheese and *Shopsin's*
restaurant (p.67).

MUSEUM AT ELDRIDGE STREET

12 Eldridge St, between Canal and Division
sts. Subway B, D to Grand St, F to East
Broadway ☎ 212 219 0302, Ⓦ www
.eldridgestreet.org. Mon–Thurs & Sun
10am–5pm, Fri 10am–3pm by tour only, every
30min (1hr); $14. MAP P.63, POCKET MAP E20

Built in 1887, this wonderfully
restored synagogue is one of the
neighbourhood jewels: a brick
and terracotta hybrid of Moorish
and Gothic influences, with rich
woodwork and stained-glass
windows, including the
spectacular west-wing rose
window. The synagogue is still in
use, but tours visit the main
sanctuary upstairs, while
exhibits introduce the history of
the building and the area.

Exploring the Jewish Lower East Side

Though its Jewish population has dwindled, the Lower East Side retains
a rich legacy of Jewish food, stores and, especially, Jewish buildings.
Several synagogues are well maintained and most accept visitors
Sun–Thurs. Perhaps the best preserved is the Museum at Eldridge St (see
above), but you can also visit the 1927 **Kehila Kedosha Janina
Synagogue and Museum** (☎ 212 431 1619, Ⓦ www.kkjsm.org. Sun
11am–4pm; free; Map p.63, Pocket map E20) at 280 Broome Street (at Allen
St), home of the Romaniote Jews from Greece, an obscure branch of
Judaism with roots in the Roman era. Enthusiastic volunteers introduce
Jewish art and various exhibits. Further south at 54–58 Canal St is the
ornate facade of the **Sender Jarmulowsky Bank** (now being developed as
office space). Founded in 1873 by a Russian peddler who made his fortune
reselling ship tickets, the bank catered to the financial needs of the area's
non-English-speaking immigrants (the building dates from 1912). In 1914,
the bank collapsed; on its closure, thousands lost what little savings they
had accumulated. At 7 Willett St, near the junction of Grand St and East
Broadway, **Bialystoker Synagogue** (☎ 212 475 0165, Ⓦ www.bialystoker
.org; Mon–Thurs 7–10am, to visit you must call in advance; free; Pocket
map F19), is a trove of stained glass, gold leaf and exuberant murals of
zodiac signs, all beautifully restored. For more in-depth tours, contact the
Lower East Side Jewish Conservancy (☎ 212 374 4100, Ⓦ www.esjc.org).

Shops

ALIFE RIVINGTON CLUB

158 Rivington St, at Clinton St. Subway J, M, Z to Essex St, F to Delancey St. Mon–Sat noon–7pm, Sun noon–6pm. MAP P.63, POCKET MAP F19

A shrine to designer sneakers, with special-edition Nikes going for as much as $900, as well as $150 sunglasses and other accessories for sale. The hip T-shirts are "just" $32.

BLUESTOCKINGS

172 Allen St, between Rivington and Stanton sts. Subway F to Lower East Side-Second Ave. Daily 11am–11pm. MAP P.63, POCKET MAP E19

Bluestockings sells new and used books on gay and gender studies, feminism, police and prisons, democracy studies and black liberation.

ECONOMY CANDY

108 Rivington St, between Essex and Ludlow sts. Subway J, M, Z to Essex St, F to Delancey St. Mon 10am–6pm, Tues–Fri & Sun 9am–6pm, Sat 10am–6pm. MAP P.63, POCKET MAP E19

Old-fashioned sweet store that sells hundreds of kinds of chocolates, candies, nuts, dried fruits and halvah.

EDITH MACHINIST

104 Rivington St, at Ludlow St. Subway J, M, Z to Essex St, F to Delancey St. Sun, Mon & Fri noon–6pm; Tues–Thurs & Sat noon–7pm. MAP P.63, POCKET MAP E19

This trendy used clothes store holds some exceptional finds (particularly shoes and top designers) but at a fraction of their Fifth Avenue price tags.

RUSS & DAUGHTERS

179 E Houston St, between Allen and Orchard sts. Subway F to Lower East Side-Second Ave. Mon–Fri 8am–8pm, Sat 8am–7pm, Sun 8am–5.30pm. MAP P.63, POCKET MAP E19

The original Manhattan gourmet shop, it was set up in 1914 to sate the appetites of homesick immigrant Jews with smoked fish, pickled vegetables, cheese and amazing bagels with smoky lox ($10).

YUMI KIM

105 Stanton St, at Ludlow St. Subway F to Delancey St, J, M, Z to Essex St. Mon–Sat noon–8pm. MAP P.63, POCKET MAP E19

Downtown chic clothing by New York-based Kim Phan, whose silk printed dresses, vintage bodies and flirty prints have been a big hit since launching in 2004.

Cafés and snacks

DOUGHNUT PLANT

379 Grand St, between Essex and Norfolk sts. Subway J, M, Z to Essex St, F to Delancey St. Sun–Thurs 6.30am–8pm, Fri & Sat 6.30am–9pm. MAP P.63, POCKET MAP F20

Serious (and seriously delicious) doughnuts; make sure you sample the seasonal flavours and glazes, including pumpkin and passion fruit.

IL LABORATORIO DEL GELATO

188 Ludlow St, at Houston St. Subway J, Z to Essex St, F to Delancey St. Mon–Thurs 7.30am–10pm, Fri 7.30am–midnight, Sat 10am–midnight, Sun 10am–10pm. MAP P.63, POCKET MAP E19

This shrine to cream and sugar serves up over 230 flavours (48 weekly; from $4.50), from honey lavender and toasted sesame to tarragon pink pepper.

KATZ'S DELI

205 E Houston St, at Ludlow St. Subway F to Lower East Side-Second Ave. Mon–Wed 8am–10.45pm, Thurs 8am–2.45am, Fri 8am–Sun 10.45pm (24hr). MAP P.63, POCKET MAP E19

Venerable Lower East Side Jewish deli since 1888, serving archetypal overstuffed pastrami and corned-beef sandwiches ($18.90), bagels, hot dogs and Ruebens ($20.25). Famous for the faux-gasm scene from *When Harry Met Sally*.

KOSSAR'S BIALYS

367 Grand St, between Essex and Norfolk sts. Subway J, M, Z to Essex St, F to Delancey St. Daily 6am–8pm. MAP P.63, POCKET MAP F20

A generations-old kosher treasure serves, bar none, the city's best bagels and bialys ($1), a flattened savoury dough traditionally topped with onion or garlic. Kossar's moved to this location in 1960.

THE PICKLE GUYS

49 Essex St, at Grand St. Subway R, N, J, Z, #6 to Canal St. Sun–Thurs 9am–6pm, Fri 9am–4pm. MAP P.63, POCKET MAP F20

Come here for fresh home-made pickles, olives and other yummy picnic staples from huge barrels of garlicky brine.

VANESSA'S DUMPLING HOUSE

118A Eldridge St, between Grand and Broome sts. Subway B, D to Grand St. Mon–Sat 10.30am–10.30pm, Sun 10.30am–10pm. MAP P.63, POCKET MAP E20

This always busy Chinese restaurant knocks out various combinations of steamed or fried pork, shrimp and vegetable dumplings at the bargain price of $1.50 for 4.

YONAH SCHIMMEL KNISH BAKERY

137 E Houston St, between First and Second aves. Subway F to Lower East Side-Second Ave. Daily 9.30am–7pm. MAP P.63, POCKET MAP E19

This place has been making and selling some of New York's best knishes ($3.50–4) since 1910: rounds of vegetable- or meat-stuffed dough, baked fresh on the premises, as are the wonderful bagels.

Restaurants

CIBAO RESTAURANT

72 Clinton St, at Rivington St. Subway J, M, Z to Essex St, F to Delancey St ☎ 212 228 0703. Daily 7am–2am. MAP P.63, POCKET MAP F19

El Cibao is the best Dominican restaurant on the Lower East Side. Hearty portions of roast chicken ($10) and huge sandwiches, particularly the Cubano ($6), are bargains.

CONGEE VILLAGE

100 Allen St, at Delancey St. Subway J, M, Z to Essex St, F to Delancey St ☎ 212 941 1818. Daily 10.30am–2am. MAP P.63, POCKET MAP E19

This Cantonese restaurant is a shrine to the eponymous fragrant, soupy rice dish and a wide range of other Hong Kong favourites for less than $20.

GEORGIA'S EASTSIDE BARBEQUE

192 Orchard St, at Houston St. Subway F to Lower East Side-Second Ave ☎ 212 253 6280. Sun & Mon noon–10pm, Tues–Sat noon–11pm. MAP P.63, POCKET MAP E19

Not smoked but equally mouth-watering oven-roasted, slow-cooked ribs ($19), tender pulled pork ($15), crunchy fried chicken ($15) and fried catfish sandwich ($10). Cash only.

SAMMY'S ROUMANIAN STEAKHOUSE

157 Chrystie St, at Delancey St. Subway B, D to Grand St, J, Z to Bowery, F to Lower East Side-Second Ave ☎ 212 673 0330. Sun–Thurs 4–10pm, Fri & Sat 4–11pm. MAP P.63, POCKET MAP E19

This basement Jewish steakhouse gives diners more than they bargained for: schmaltzy songs, delicious food (topped off by home-made *rugalach* and egg creams for dessert) and chilled vodka.

SCHILLER'S LIQUOR BAR

131 Rivington St, at Norfolk St. Subway F to Delancey St, J, M, Z to Essex St ☎ 212 260 4555. Mon–Thurs 11am–1am, Fri 11am–3am, Sat 10am–3am, Sun 10am–midnight. MAP P.63, POCKET MAP F19

Trendy bistro with beautiful clientele. The menu features salads and steak frites and chicken pot pie (entrées $15–30).

SHOPSIN'S

Stall 16, Essex St Market, 120 Essex St. Subway F to Delancey St, J, M, Z to Essex St (no phone). Wed–Sat 9am–2pm, Sun 10am–2pm. MAP P.63, POCKET MAP F19

A New York institution, Kenny Shopsin ran his idiosyncratic diner in the West Village for years, but was forced out by high rents. His creations – like peanut-butter-filled pancakes – have a loyal following.

STANTON SOCIAL

99 Stanton St, between Ludlow and Orchard sts. Subway F to Lower East Side-Second Ave ☎ 212 995 0099. Mon–Thurs 5pm–midnight, Fri 5pm–1am, Sat 11.30am–1am, Sun 11.30am–11pm. MAP P.63, POCKET MAP E19

Chandeliers, lizard-skin banquettes and retro booths draw a young, hip crowd to this restaurant-cum-lounge bar. Food, such as zesty snapper tacos with mango salsa, is designed for sharing.

Bars

BACK ROOM

102 Norfolk St, between Delancey and Rivington sts. Subway F to Delancey St, J, M, Z to Essex St. Sun–Thurs 7pm–3am, Fri & Sat 7.30pm–4am. MAP P.63, POCKET MAP F19

With a hidden, back-alley entrance, this former speakeasy was reputedly once a haunt of gangster Meyer Lansky. Booze is served in teacups as a nod to its Prohibition days.

BARRIO CHINO

253 Broome St, at Orchard St. Subway B, D to Grand St. Daily 11.30am–4.30pm & 5.30pm–1am. MAP P.63, POCKET MAP E20

Don't be confused by the Chinese lanterns or drink umbrellas – the speciality here is tequila, and there are over fifty to choose from. Shots are even served with the traditional sangria chaser.

FORGTMENOT

138 Division St, between Ludlow and Orchard sts. Subway F to East Broadway. Daily noon–11pm. MAP P.63, POCKET MAP E20

This quirky bar and restaurant is smothered with bumper stickers, graffiti and 1980s memorabilia, a favourite local hangout that also serves tasty pub food. Try the watermelon spicy margarita.

LIBATION

137 Ludlow St, between Stanton and Rivington sts. Subway F to Delancey St, J, M, Z to Essex St. Wed 5pm–midnight, Thurs 5pm–1am, Fri 5pm–4am, Sat noon–4am, Sun noon–midnight. MAP P.63, POCKET MAP E19

A sexy lounge spanning two floors. It's a bit eclectic, with $12 cocktails, a boozy weekend brunch ($45; bottomless mimosas and bloody Marys), American-style tapas menu, and DJs spinning '80s, hip-hop and everything in between.

WELCOME TO THE JOHNSONS

123 Rivington St, between Essex and Norfolk sts. Subway F to Delancey St, J, M, Z to Essex St. Mon–Fri 3pm–4am, Sat & Sun noon–4pm. MAP P.63, POCKET MAP E19

This 1970s throwback dive bar is all about rockin' out and chillin' out, and you can do both without any friction. Good beers, great bartenders.

Clubs

BOB BAR

235 Eldridge St, between Houston and Stanton sts. Subway F to Lower East Side-Second Ave. Tues & Wed 6pm–1am, Thurs–Sun 6pm–4am. MAP P.63, POCKET MAP E19

This cosy bar turns into one of the best dance parties in town after midnight, with DJs spinning a mix of hip-hop, reggae and R&B. Cover from $5.

THE DELANCEY

168 Delancey St, at Clinton St. Subway F to Delancey St, J, M, Z to Essex St ✆www .thedelancey.com. Daily 5pm–4am. MAP P.63, POCKET MAP F19

Williamsburg hipsters meet Lower East Side chic at this rooftop lounge and nightclub. Things can get frisky in the basement, which pulsates with loud music and live acts.

CAKE SHOP

Music venues

ARLENE'S GROCERY

95 Stanton St, between Ludlow and Orchard sts. Subway F to Lower East Side-Second Ave ☎ 212 358 1633, ⓦ www.arlenesgrocery .net. Daily 5pm–2am. MAP P.63, POCKET MAP E19

This intimate venue hosts free gigs by local indie talent every night. Monday (free) is "Rock and Roll Karaoke" night, when you can wail along (with a live band) to your favourite songs. Tues–Sun cover $8–10.

THE BOWERY BALLROOM

6 Delancey St, at the Bowery. Subway J, Z to Bowery, B, D to Grand St ☎ 212 533 2111, ⓦ www.boweryballroom.com. Daily from 7pm. MAP P.63, POCKET MAP E19

Great acoustics make this a favourite local venue to see well-known indie rock bands. Shows cost $15–55. Pay in cash at the *Mercury Lounge* box office (see opposite), at the door or through Ticketweb.

CAKE SHOP

152 Ludlow St, between Rivington and Stanton sts. Subway F to Delancey St, J, M, Z to Essex St ☎ 212 253 0036 ⓦ www .cake-shop.com. Sun–Thurs 9am–2am, Fri & Sat 9am–4am. MAP P.63, POCKET MAP E19

This unassuming coffee shop and record store becomes a cutting-edge venue for indie rock most evenings – cover ranges from $7–10.

MERCURY LOUNGE

217 E Houston St, between Ludlow and Essex sts. Subway F to Lower East Side-Second Ave ☎ 212 260 4700, ⓦ www .mercuryloungenyc.com. Daily shows from 7pm. MAP P.63, POCKET MAP E19

The dark, medium-sized space showcases local, national and international pop and rock acts. Events cost around $10–25. Pay in cash at the box office, at the door or via Ticketweb.

MERCURY LOUNGE

PIANOS

158 Ludlow St, at Rivington St. Subway F to Delancey St, J, M, Z to Essex St ☎ 212 505 3733, ⓦ www.pianosnyc.com. Daily 3pm–4am. MAP P.63, POCKET MAP E19

This converted piano factory hosts an endless roster of mostly rock bands (expect four choices nightly) in the back room ($8–10) and excellent DJs from 10pm.

ROCKWOOD MUSIC HALL

196 Allen St, between Houston and Stanton sts. Subway F to Lower East Side-Second Ave ☎ 212 614 2494, ⓦ rockwoodmusichall.com. Mon–Fri 6pm–4am, Sat & Sun 3pm–4am. MAP P.63, POCKET MAP E19

Come early: though there are no bad seats in the house, seven nights of live music draw locals to this three-stage venue.

SLIPPER ROOM

167 Orchard St, at Stanton St. Subway F to Second Ave. Daily 7pm–2am. MAP P.63, POCKET MAP E19

Gilded ceilings and elaborate decor provide the backdrop for entertainment that ranges from neo-burlesque and cabaret to comedy and live music, including Seth Herzog's variety show, "Sweet" (Tues $5–7; cover other nights ranges $10–20).

The East Village

Once a solidly working-class refuge of immigrants, the East Village, ranging east of Broadway to Avenue D between Houston and 14th streets, became home to New York's nonconformist intelligentsia in the early part of the twentieth century; in the 1950s, it was one of the main haunts of the Beat poets – Kerouac, Burroughs, Ginsberg. By the 1980s it was home to radical artists, including Keith Haring, Jeff Koons and Jean-Michel Basquiat, while Chinese artist Ai Weiwei lived on East 7th and East 3rd streets between 1983 and 1993. During the Nineties, escalating rents forced many people out, and the East Village is no longer the hotbed of dissidence and artistry that it once was. Nevertheless, it remains one of Downtown Manhattan's most vibrant neighbourhoods, with boutiques, thrift stores, record shops, bars and restaurants, populated by old-world Ukrainians, students and Japanese hairdressers.

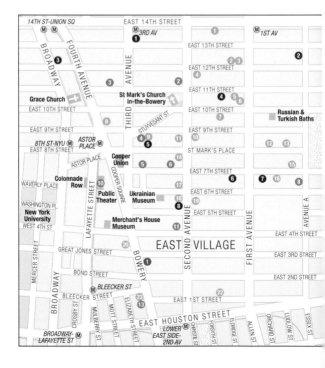

ASTOR PLACE

Subway N, R to 8th St, #6 to Astor Place.
MAP P.70–71, POCKET MAP D18

Astor Place marks the western fringe of the East Village, named after real-estate tycoon John Jacob Astor. Infamous for his greed, Astor was the wealthiest person in the US at the time of his death in 1848 (worth $115bn in modern terms). Beneath the replicated old-fashioned kiosk of the Astor Place subway station, the platform walls sport reliefs of beavers, recalling Astor's first big killings – in the fur trade. The teen hangout here is the balancing black steel cube *Alamo* (1967) by Tony Rosenthal, which dominates the centre of the intersection. In the 1830s, **Lafayette St**, which runs south from Astor Place, was home to the

city's wealthiest residents; **Colonnade Row**, a strip of four 1833 Greek Revival houses with Corinthian columns, is all that remains.

The stocky brownstone-and-brick building across Lafayette was once the **Astor Library**. Built with a bequest from Astor between 1853 and 1881, it was the first public library in New York. It became the Public Theater in 1967. **Astor Place Opera House** was erected on the corner of Astor Place and East 8th Street in 1847, infamous as the site of the Astor Place Riot two years later. Supporters of local stage-star Edwin Forrest tried to stop the performance of English Shakespearean actor William Macready, and in the resulting clashes 22 people died. The theatre closed in 1850.

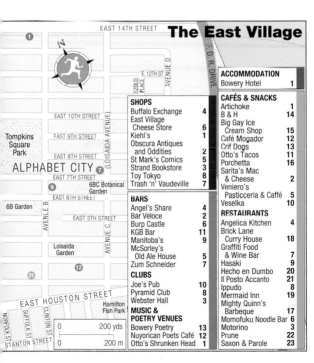

The East Village map

SHOPS	
Buffalo Exchange	4
East Village Cheese Store	6
Kiehl's	1
Obscura Antiques and Oddities	2
St Mark's Comics	5
Strand Bookstore	3
Toy Tokyo	8
Trash 'n' Vaudeville	7

BARS	
Angel's Share	4
Bar Veloce	2
Burp Castle	6
KGB Bar	11
Manitoba's	9
McSorley's Old Ale House	5
Zum Schneider	7

CLUBS	
Joe's Pub	10
Pyramid Club	8
Webster Hall	3

MUSIC & POETRY VENUES	
Bowery Poetry	13
Nuyorican Poets Café	12
Otto's Shrunken Head	1

ACCOMMODATION	
Bowery Hotel	1

CAFÉS & SNACKS	
Artichoke	1
B & H	14
Big Gay Ice Cream Shop	15
Café Mogador	12
Crif Dogs	13
Otto's Tacos	11
Porchetta	16
Sarita's Mac & Cheese	2
Veniero's Pasticceria & Caffé	5
Veselka	10

RESTAURANTS	
Angelica Kitchen	4
Brick Lane Curry House	18
Graffiti Food & Wine Bar	7
Hasaki	9
Hecho en Dumbo	20
Il Posto Accanto	21
Ippudo	8
Mermaid Inn	19
Mighty Quinn's Barbeque	17
Momofuku Noodle Bar	6
Motorino	3
Prune	22
Saxon & Parole	23

GRACE CHURCH

802 Broadway, at E 10th St. Subway N, R to 8th St ☎ 212 254 2000, ⓦ www .gracechurchnyc.org. Daily noon–5pm. Free. MAP P.70–71, POCKET MAP D17

The lacy marble of **Grace Church** was designed and built in 1846 by James Renwick (of St Patrick's Cathedral fame) in a delicate neo-Gothic style. Dark and aisled, with a flattened, web-vaulted ceiling, it was something of a society church in its day. Nowadays it is one of the city's most secretive escapes, and frequently offers shelter to the less fortunate.

MERCHANT'S HOUSE MUSEUM

29 E 4th St, between Lafayette St and the Bowery. Subway B, D, F, M to Broadway-Lafayette, N, R to 8th St, #6 to Astor Place ☎ 212 777 1089, ⓦ www.merchantshouse.com. Thurs noon–8pm, Fri–Mon noon–5pm. $13. MAP P.70–71, POCKET MAP D18

Constructed in 1832, this elegant Federal-style row house offers a rare and intimate glimpse of domestic life in New York during the 1850s. The house was purchased by Seabury Tredwell in 1835, a successful metal merchant, when the area was an up-and-coming suburb for the

middle class. Remarkably, much of the mid-nineteenth-century interior remains in pristine condition, largely thanks to Seabury's daughter Gertrude, who lived here until 1933 – it was preserved as a museum three years later. Highlights include furniture fashioned by New York's best cabinetmakers, the mahogany four-poster beds, and the tiny brass bells in the basement, used to summon the servants.

COOPER UNION – FOUNDATION BUILDING

7 E 7th St, Cooper Square, between Third and Fourth aves. Subway N, R to 8th St, #6 to Astor Place ☎ 212 353 4100, ⓦ www .cooper.edu. MAP P.70–71, POCKET MAP D18

Erected in 1859 by wealthy industrialist Peter Cooper (1791–1883) as a college for the poor, the **Foundation Building of Cooper Union** is best known as the place where, in 1860, Abraham Lincoln wowed an audience of top New Yorkers with his so-called "right makes might" speech, in which he boldly criticized the pro-slavery policies of the Southern states – an event that helped propel him to the White House later that year. In 1909 it was also the site of the first open meeting of the NAACP (National Association for the Advancement of Colored People), chaired by W.E.B. Du Bois. Today, Cooper Union is a prestigious art, engineering and architecture school, whose nineteenth-century glory is evoked with a statue of the benevolent Cooper by Augustus Saint-Gaudens just in front of the hall. From the entrance hall the guards normally allow you to walk downstairs to the Great Hall, where historical exhibits are displayed in the gallery outside.

ST MARK'S PLACE

Subway N, R to 8th St, #6 to Astor Place.
MAP P.70–71, POCKET MAP D18–E18

The East Village's main drag gets a name, not a number (it could have been called East 8th Street). **St Mark's Place** stretches east from Cooper Union to Tompkins Square Park. Between Third Avenue and Avenue A it's lined with souvenir stalls, punk and hippie-chic clothing shops and newly installed chain restaurants, signalling the end of the gritty atmosphere that had dominated this thoroughfare for years.

ST MARK'S CHURCH IN-THE-BOWERY

131 E 10th St, at Second Ave. Subway N, R to 8th St, #6 to Astor Place ☎ 212 674 6377, ⓦ www.stmarksbowery.org.
MAP P.70–71, POCKET MAP D17

In 1660, New Amsterdam Director-General Peter Stuyvesant built a small chapel here close to his farm, and was buried inside in 1672 (his tombstone is now set into the outer walls). The box-like Episcopalian house of worship that currently occupies this space was completed in 1799 over his tomb, and sports a Neoclassical portico that was added fifty years later. The church is still used for services and is normally locked – walk up to the office on the second floor (side door) and someone will let you in to see the vivid stained-glass windows. The church was home to Beat poetry readings in the 1950s, and in the 1960s the **St Mark's Poetry Project** (ⓦ www.poetryproject.com) was founded here to ignite artistic and social change. It remains an important cultural rendezvous, with poetry readings Monday, Wednesday and Friday evenings at 8pm, dance performances by the Danspace Project (ⓦ www.danspaceproject.org) and from New York Theatre Ballet (ⓦ www.nytb.org).

RUSSIAN & TURKISH BATHS

UKRAINIAN MUSEUM

222 E 6th St, between Second and Third aves. Subway N, R to 8th St, #6 to Astor Place ☎ 212 228 0110, ⓦ www.ukrainianmuseum.org. Wed–Sun 11.30am–5pm. $8. MAP P.70–71, POCKET MAP D18

Dedicated to chronicling the history of the Ukrainian immigrant community. The varied collection contains ethnic items such as Ukrainian costumes and examples of the country's famous painted eggs; lectures are also held here.

RUSSIAN & TURKISH BATHS

268 E 10th St, between First Ave and Ave A. Subway L to First Ave ☎ 212 674 9250, ⓦ www.russianturkishbaths.com. Mon, Tues, Thurs, Fri noon–10pm, Wed 10am–10pm, Sat 9am–10pm, Sun 8am–10pm. $40. MAP P.70–71, POCKET MAP E17

A neighbourhood landmark that's still going strong, with an ice-cold pool, Russian sauna (filled with 20,000lbs of red-hot rocks), a modern cherry-wood sauna and a Turkish steam room, as well as massage rooms and a restaurant. Free soap, towel, robe and slippers. Check the website for details of mixed and single-sex sessions.

TOMPKINS SQUARE PARK

Subway L to First Ave, N, R to 8th St, #6 to Astor Place. MAP P70–71, POCKET MAP F17–F18

Fringed by avenues A and B and East 7th and East 10th streets, **Tompkins Square Park** was one of the city's great centres for political protest and homes of radical thought. In the 1960s, regular demonstrations were organized here, and during the 1980s, the park was more or less a shantytown until the homeless were kicked out in 1991. Today it has a playground, dog run and a summer jazz festival. The famous saxophonist and composer Charlie "Bird" Parker lived at 151 Avenue B, a simple whitewashed 1849 house with a Gothic doorway (closed to the public). Bird lived here from 1950 until 1954, when he died of a pneumonia-related haemorrhage.

ALPHABET CITY

Subway L to First Ave, N, R to 8th St, #6 to Astor Place. MAP P70–71, POCKET MAP F18

Named after the avenues known as A–D, where the island bulges east beyond the city's grid structure, **Alphabet City** was not long ago a notoriously unsafe patch, with burnt-out buildings that were well-known dens for the brisk heroin trade. Now it's one of the most dramatically revitalized areas of Manhattan: crime is down, many of the vacant lots have been made into community gardens, and the streets have become the haunt of moneyed twenty-somethings and students. These avenues have some of the coolest bars, cafés and stores in the city.

COMMUNITY GARDENS

Subway L to First Ave, N, R to 8th St, #6 to Astor Place. MAP P70–71, POCKET MAP F18

In the 1970s, pockets of the East Village burned to the ground after cuts in the city's fire-fighting budget closed many of the local firehouses. Green Thumb, founded in 1978, helped locals transform vacant lots into vibrant green spaces, turning the rubble-filled messes into some of the prettiest and most verdant spaces in lower Manhattan. Of particular note is the **East 6th Street and Avenue B** affair, overgrown with wildflowers, vegetables, trees and roses. Other gardens include the very serene **6 B/C Botanical Garden** on East 6th Street between B and C, and **Loisaida Garden** on East 4th Street between B and C.

TOMPKINS SQUARE PARK

Shops

BUFFALO EXCHANGE

332 E 11th St, at Second Ave. Subway L to First Ave. Mon–Sat 11am–8pm, Sun noon–7pm. MAP P.70–71, POCKET MAP E17

US clothes exchange that started in Arizona in the 1970s; bring in your former threads for a trade-in or cash on the spot.

EAST VILLAGE CHEESE STORE

80 E 7th St, between First and Second aves. Subway R to 8th St, #6 to Astor Place. Daily 8.30am–6.30pm. MAP P.70–71, POCKET MAP E18

The city's most affordable source for cheese; its front-of-the-store bins sell pungent blocks and wedges starting at just a few dollars (cash only).

KIEHL'S

109 Third Ave, at E 13th St. Subway L to Third Ave. Mon–Sat 10am–9pm, Sun 11am–7pm. MAP P.70–71, POCKET MAP D17

An exclusive 160-year-old pharmacy that sells its own range of natural ingredient-based classic creams, soaps and oils.

OBSCURA ANTIQUES AND ODDITIES

207 Ave A, between E 12th and E 13th sts. Subway L to First Ave. Mon–Sat noon–8pm, Sun noon–7pm. MAP P.70–71, POCKET MAP E17

This spooky East Village classic specializes in antiques, rare taxidermy and strange, freaky artefacts – owners Mike Zohn and Evan Michelson even have a show on the Discovery Channel (*Oddities*).

ST MARK'S COMICS

11 St Mark's Place, between Second and Third aves. Subway #6 to Astor Place. Mon & Tues 10am–11pm, Wed 9am–1am, Thurs–Sat 10am–1am, Sun 11am–11pm. MAP P.70–71, POCKET MAP D18

Pilgrimage site for comic,

STRAND BOOKSTORE

manga and graphic novel fans from all over the world, with plenty of rare memorabilia.

STRAND BOOKSTORE

828 Broadway, at E 12th St. Subway N, R, Q, L, #4, #5, #6 to Union Square. Mon–Sat 9.30am–10.30pm, Sun 11am–10.30pm MAP P.70–71, POCKET MAP D17

With about eighteen miles of books and a stock of more than 2.5 million, this is the largest book operation in the city.

TOY TOKYO

91 Second Ave, between E 5th and E 6th sts. Subway #6 to Astor Place. Sun–Thurs 1–9pm, Fri & Sat 12.30–9.30pm. MAP P.70–71, POCKET MAP E18

Dizzying ensemble of Asian toys and cult memorabilia, mostly from Japan and Hong Kong: action figures, vintage robots, roto-plastic figures and wind-ups.

TRASH 'N' VAUDEVILLE

96 E 7th St, between First Ave and Ave A. Subway #6 to Astor Place. Mon–Thurs noon–8pm, Fri 11.30am–8.30pm, Sat 11.30am–9pm, Sun 1–7.30pm. MAP P.70–71, POCKET MAP E18

Formerly located on St Mark's Place, this has been a Goth and punk mecca since the 1970s. Great clothes, new and "antique", in the true East Village spirit.

Cafés and snacks

ARTICHOKE

328 E 14th St, between First and Second aves. Subway L to First Ave. Daily 10am–5am. MAP P.70–71, POCKET MAP E17

Fabulous late-night pizza slices to take away in the early hours, with just a few choices: sumptuous cheese-laden Sicilian ($4.75), Margherita ($4.75), crab ($5) or the trademark artichoke-spinach pie, topped with a super-creamy sauce ($5).

B & H

127 Second Ave, between E 7th St and St Mark's Place. Subway #6 to Astor Place. Mon–Fri 7am–11.30pm, Sat & Sun 7am–midnight. MAP P.70–71, POCKET MAP E18

Good veggie choice, this tiny luncheonette serves home-made soup, *challah* and *latkes*. You can also create your own juice combination to stay or go.

BIG GAY ICE CREAM SHOP

125 E 7th St, between First Ave and Ave A. Subway L to First Ave. Winter: Sun–Thurs 1–10pm, Fri & Sat 1–11pm; summer Sun–Thurs noon–10pm, Fri & Sat noon–midnight. MAP P.70–71, POCKET MAP E18

The utterly addictive ice cream here has cheekily named flavours including the "salty pimp" (vanilla, dulce de leche, sea salt and chocolate dip) and the "gobbler" (pumpkin butter, maple syrup and pie pieces).

CAFÉ MOGADOR

101 St Mark's Place, between First Ave and Ave A. Subway #6 to Astor Place. Sun–Thurs 9am–midnight, Fri & Sat 9am–1am. MAP P.70–71, POCKET MAP E18

Young hipster-types frequent this romantic, Moroccan-themed mainstay. Expect crowds and stalled service, but the food is more than worth the wait. Try the *charmoulla* with either chicken or lamb. The brunch (Sat–Sun 9am–4pm) is especially good, with a choice of delicate mains such as Moroccan Benedict (eggs in a spicy tomato sauce) served with orange juice, coffee or tea for just $17.

CRIF DOGS

113 St Mark's Place, between First Ave and Ave A. Subway #6 to Astor Place. Sun–Thurs noon–2am, Fri & Sat noon–4am. MAP P.70–71, POCKET MAP E18

Hot-dog aficionados swear by these deep-fried, shiny wieners bursting with flavour (from $3.50), enjoyed Philly-steak style, smothered in cheese, or topped with avocado and bacon.

OTTO'S TACOS

141 Second Ave, between E 9th St and St Mark's Place. Subway #6 to Astor Place. Sun–Thurs 11am–11pm, Fri & Sat 11am–midnight. MAP P.70–71, POCKET MAP E17

No frills, rustic space for delicious corn tacos stuffed with carne asada (beef; $3.25), carnitas (pork; $3) and chicken ($3), all perfectly seasoned and accompanied by chips and guacamole ($3.75).

VENIERO'S

PORCHETTA

110 E 7th St, between First Ave and Ave A. Subway #6 to Astor Place. Sun–Thurs 11.30am–10pm, Fri & Sat 11.30am–11pm. MAP P.70–71, POCKET MAP E18

This tiny takeaout shop (with a few stools and counter inside) has developed a loyal following for its luscious Tuscan *porchetta* sandwiches ($12), thick slabs of roasted and seasoned pork in a ciabatta roll.

SARITA'S MAC & CHEESE

345 E 12th St, between Second and First aves. Subway L to First Ave. Sun–Thurs 11am–11pm, Fri & Sat 11am–midnight. MAP P.70–71, POCKET MAP E17

Indulge your macaroni and cheese cravings at this homey joint, with ten creative varieties on offer, blending cheddar, gruyère, brie and goat's cheese with herbs and meats. Pick your portion sizes: nosh, major munch or mongo ($5.75–19.75).

VENIERO'S PASTICCERIA & CAFFÉ

342 E 11th St, between First and Second aves. Subway L to First Ave; #6 to Astor Place. Sun–Thurs 8am–midnight, Fri & Sat 8am–1am. MAP P.70–71, POCKET MAP E17

A beloved East Village institution, tempting the neighbourhood with heavenly cheesecake ($4.50), tiramisu ($5.25) and Italian pastries since 1894 – the almond torte ($4.75) is their most famous snack. Sit inside the old-world marble-floor café, or takeout.

VESELKA

144 Second Ave, corner of E 9th St. Subway #6 to Astor Place. Daily 24hr. MAP P.70–71, POCKET MAP E17

This popular Ukrainian diner has been an East Village institution since the 1950s, offering fine home-made borscht from $4.95, *kielbasa* sausage ($17.50), *pierogi* ($6.95) and great burgers.

VESELKA

Restaurants

ANGELICA KITCHEN

300 E 12th St, between First and Second aves. Subway L to First Ave ☎ 212 228 2909. Daily 11.30am–10.30pm MAP P.70–71, POCKET MAP E17

Great veggie organic restaurant with various daily specials and a colourful downtown crowd. Main dishes $11–16.50. No reservations.

BRICK LANE CURRY HOUSE

99 Second Ave, at E 6th St. Subway #6 to Astor Place ☎ 212 979 8787. Sun–Thurs noon–11pm, Fri & Sat noon–1am. MAP P.70–71, POCKET MAP E18

Hands-down the best Indian in the East Village thanks to its expanded selection of traditional favourites ($16–28).

GRAFFITI FOOD & WINE BAR

244 E 10th St, between First and Second aves. Subway L to First Ave, #6 to Astor Place ☎ 212 677 0695. Tues & Sun 5.30–10.30pm, Wed–Sat 5.30–11.45pm. MAP P.70–71, POCKET MAP E17

Pastry chef Jehangir Mehta cooks up a fusion of Chinese, American and Indian flavours in this artsy space, with four tables and courses costing $9–17, including chilli pork dumplings and foie gras raspberry crostini.

HASAKI

210 E 9th St, at Stuyvesant St. Subway #6 to
Astor Place ☎ 212 473 3327. Mon & Tues
5.30–11pm, Wed–Fri noon–3pm & 5.30–11pm,
Sat & Sun 1–4pm & 5.30–11.30pm.
MAP P.70–71, POCKET MAP D17

Some of the best sushi in the
city is served at this popular
but mellow downstairs
cubbyhole. Sit at the bar and
the chefs will try to tempt you
with a variety of improvised
dishes (five pieces from $24).

HECHO EN DUMBO

354 Bowery, between Great Jones and E
4th sts. Subway #6 to Astor Place
☎212 937 4245. Mon–Thurs 5.30–11.30pm,
Fri 5.30pm–midnight, Sat 11.30am–4pm &
5.30pm–midnight, Sun 11.30am–4pm &
5.30–11pm. MAP P.70–71, POCKET MAP D18

This authentic Mexican diner
migrated across the East River
in 2010, but it still knocks out
wonderful small plates ($11–17)
and Mexico City contemporary
cuisine such as house-cured
beef, lamb shank confit and an
innovative selection of tacos and
burritos ($14–16).

IL POSTO ACCANTO

190 E 2nd Street, between aves A and B.
Subway F to Lower East Side–Second Ave
☎ 212 228 3562. Mon–Fri noon–3am, Sat &
Sun noon–3.30pm & 5.30pm–midnight.
MAP P.70–71, POCKET MAP F18

Nab a spot at a high wooden
table at this small, intimate wine
bar and restaurant serving a vast
array of Italian reds by the glass.
You can easily make a meal
from the excellent small plates
of pasta ($14–16), panini
($8.50–10) and the like. Can get
crowded, like its popular parent
restaurant next door (*Il
Bagatto*).

IPPUDO

65 Fourth Ave, between E 9th and E 10th
sts. Subway #6 to Astor Place ☎212 388
0088. Mon–Fri 11am–3.30pm & 5–11.30pm,
Sat 11am–3.30pm & 5pm–12.30am, Sun
11am–10.30pm.
MAP P.70–71, POCKET MAP D17

The first overseas outpost of
Fukuoka-based "ramen king"
Shigemi Kawahara, this
popular Japanese ramen shop
offers steaming bowls of classic
tonkotsu-style noodles for $15,
as well as tasty pork buns.

MERMAID INN

96 Second Ave, between E 5th and 6th sts.
Subway #6 to Astor Place ☎212 674 5870.
Sun & Mon 5–10pm, Tues–Sat 5–10.30pm.
MAP P.70–71, POCKET MAP E18

Serious seafood restaurant
serving simple and fresh dishes
in a Maine boathouse
atmosphere. There's an
excellent raw bar, and specials
change daily depending on the
catch; highlights include the
littleneck clams ($10) and
lobster sandwich ($29).

MIGHTY QUINN'S BARBEQUE

103 Second Ave, at E 6th St.
Subway L to Third Ave ☎ 212 677 3733.
Sun–Thurs 11.30am–11pm, Fri & Sat
11.30am–midnight. MAP P.70–71, POCKET MAP E18

Texas and Carolinas-inspired
slow-smoked barbecue, with a
no-nonsense menu of
lip-smacking burnt ends
($9.40), pulled pork ($8.80)
and ribs ($9.15), accompanied

MERMAID INN

IL POSTO ACCANTO

by burnt-end baked beans (from $3.25).

MOMOFUKU NOODLE BAR

171 First Ave, between E 10th and E 11th sts. Subway L to First Ave, #6 to Astor Place ☎212 777 7773. Mon–Thurs noon–4.30pm & 5.30–11pm, Fri noon–4.30pm & 5.30pm–1am. Sat noon–4pm & 5.30pm–1am, Sun noon–4pm & 5.30–11pm. MAP P.70-71, POCKET MAP E17

Celebrated chef David Chang's first restaurant, where his simplest creations are still the best: silky steamed pork buns with hoisin sauce and pickled cucumbers ($13), or steaming bowls of chicken and pork ramen noodles ($16). If you're in the neighbourhood, it's worth checking out Chang's other ventures: the *Milk Bar* (251 E 13th St, at Second Ave; daily 9am–midnight) serves sweet treats.

MOTORINO

349 E 12th St, near First Ave. Subway L to First Ave ☎212 777 2644. Mon–Thurs & Sun 11am–midnight, Fri & Sat 11am–1am. MAP P.70-71, POCKET MAP E17

Some of the best pizza in the city, with a tongue-tingling Stracciatella (basil, olive oil and sea salt) and a cherry stone clam masterpiece.

PRUNE

54 E 1st St, between First and Second aves. Subway F to Lower East Side-Second Ave ☎212 677 6221. Mon–Fri 5.30–11pm, Sat & Sun 10am–3.30pm & 5.30 11pm. MAP P.70 71, POCKET MAP E19

Cramped, yet adventurous and full of surprises, this modern American bistro delivers one of the city's most exciting dining experiences, serving dishes such as sweetbreads wrapped in bacon, seared sea bass with Berber spices, and buttermilk ice cream with pistachio puff pastry. A choice of over ten Bloody Marys gives weekend brunch a bit of a kick.

SAXON & PAROLE

316 Bowery, at Bleecker St. Subway #6 to Bleecker St. ☎212 254 0350. Mon–Fri noon–3am, Sat & Sun noon–3.30pm & 5.30pm–midnight. MAP P.70-71, POCKET MAP D19

Modern American grill with amazing food; tea-smoked mussels, horseradish-whipped potatoes and whisky jelly with steaks, washed down with a celery gimlet and rounded off with the warm chocolate pudding with marshmallow and whiskey barrel smoke.

Bars

ANGEL'S SHARE

8 Stuyvesant St, between E 9th St and Third Ave. Subway #6 to Astor Place. Sun–Wed, 6pm–1.30am, Thurs 7pm–2.30am, Fri & Sat 6pm–1.30am. MAP P.70–71, POCKET MAP D17

This serene, Japanese-style haven is a great date spot and the cocktails are some of the best in the city. It can be hard to find, though: walk through the *Yokocho* restaurant, up the stairs.

BAR VELOCE

175 Second Ave, between E 11th and E 12th sts. Subway L to Third Ave. Mon–Thurs 5pm–2am, Fri & Sat 3pm–3am, Sun 3pm–2am. MAP P.70–71, POCKET MAP E17

Stylish Italian wine bar fit for the Mod Squad, with excellent hors d'oeuvres and a fine wine list (by the glass from $10).

BURP CASTLE

41 E 7th St, between Second and Third aves. Subway #6 to Astor Place. Mon–Fri 5pm–4am, Sat & Sun 4pm–4am. MAP P.70–71, POCKET MAP D18

Though bartenders no longer wear monks' habits and choral music is rarely piped in, you are encouraged to speak in tones below a whisper. Oh,

KGB BAR

85 E 4th St, at Second Ave. Subway F to Lower East Side-Second Ave, #6 to Astor Place. Daily 6.30pm–4am. MAP P.70–71, POCKET MAP E18

A dark bar on the second floor, which was the Ukrainian Labor Home social club in the 1950s, but is better known now for its marquee literary readings.

MANITOBA'S

99 Ave B, between E 6th and 7th sts. Subway L to First Ave, #6 to Astor Place. Daily 2pm–4am. MAP P.70–71, POCKET MAP F18

Run by Dick Manitoba, lead singer of the punk group The Dictators, the kickin' jukebox and rough-and-tumble vibe at this spot make it a drinkers' favourite.

MCSORLEY'S OLD ALE HOUSE

15 E 7th St, between Second and Third aves. Subway #6 to Astor Place. Mon–Sat 11am–1am, Sun 1pm–1am. MAP P.70–71, POCKET MAP D18

Yes, it's often full of tourists and NYU students, but you'll be drinking in history at this landmark bar that opened in 1854 – it's the oldest pub in the city. Today, it only pours its own ale – light or dark.

ZUM SCHNEIDER

107 Ave C, at E 7th St. Subway L to 1st Ave, #6 to Astor Place. Mon–Thurs 5pm–2am, Fri 4pm–4am, Sat 1pm–4am, Sun 1pm–midnight. MAP P.70–71, POCKET MAP F18

A Bavarian beer hall (and indoor garden) with a mega-list of brews from the Fatherland, and wursts too. Cash only.

Clubs

JOE'S PUB

425 Lafayette St, between Astor Place and E 4th St. Subway #6 to Astor Place 212 539 8770. MAP P.70–71, POCKET MAP D18

and there are still over 550 different types of beer.

ANGEL'S SHARE

The word "pub" is a misnomer for this swanky nightspot that features a vast array of musical, cabaret and dramatic performances. Shows nightly at 7.30pm, 9.30pm and 11pm (tickets $20–30).

PYRAMID CLUB

101 Ave A, between E 6th and 7th sts. Subway L to First Ave, #6 to Astor Place ☏ 212 228 4888. Thurs–Sat 8pm–4am. MAP P.70–71, POCKET MAP E18

This small club has been an East Village standby for years, but it's the insanely popular 1980s Dance Parties on Thursday to Saturday that are not to be missed ($6).

WEBSTER HALL

125 E 11th St, between Third and Fourth aves. Subway N, Q, R, L, #4, #5, #6 to Union Square ☏ 212 353 1600, ⓦ www.websterhall.com. Club nights Thurs–Sat 10pm–4am. Cover $15–35. MAP P.70–71, POCKET MAP D17

Four floors, a hip, young crowd and a big electro mash-up on Fridays and Saturdays make this a solid bet for a good night out.

Music and poetry venues

BOWERY POETRY

308 Bowery, at Bleecker St. Subway N, Q, R, L, #4, #5, #6 to Union Square. Poetry Sun 12.30–11pm, Mon 6.30–11pm. ☏ 212 353 1600, ⓦ www.bowerypoetry.com. MAP P.70–71, POCKET MAP D19

The old Bowery Poetry Club reopened in 2013 as a joint venue with Duane Park (burlesque shows on Sat), with the poetry programme presented by Bowery Arts + Science on Sundays ($6–10) and Mondays ($10–15).

ZUM SCHNEIDER

NUYORICAN POETS CAFÉ

236 E 3rd St, between aves B and C. Subway F to Lower East Side-Second Ave ☏ 212 505 8183, ⓦ www.nuyorican.org. Daily noon–2am. MAP P.70–71, POCKET MAP F18

The godfather of all slam venues often features stars of the poetry world who pop in unannounced. SlamOpen on Wednesdays 9pm (except the first Wednesday of every month) and the Friday Night Slam (10pm) cost $10 and $15 respectively. The café was founded in 1973 by Puerto Rican poet Miguel Algarín and playwright Miguel Piñero, moving to this location in 1980.

OTTO'S SHRUNKEN HEAD

538 E 14th St, between aves A and B. Subway L to First Ave ☏ 212 228 2240, ⓦ www.ottosshrunkenhead.com. Mon–Fri noon–4am, Sat & Sun 4pm–4am. MAP P.70–71, POCKET MAP F17

This East Village joint is hard to pigeonhole; a Tiki bar that hosts live indie and punk rock bands, as well as some of the most popular club nights on the island. Weekends also see a host of rock/punk parties. Usually no cover.

The West Village

For many visitors, the West Village, Greenwich Village – or simply "the Village" – is the most-loved neighbourhood in New York. It sports refined Federal and Greek Revival townhouses and a busy late-night streetlife, while cosy restaurants, bars and cafés clutter every corner – many of the attractions that first brought bohemians here around the start of World War I. The area proved fertile ground for struggling artists and intellectuals, and the neighbourhood's clubs and off-Broadway theatres came to define Village life, laying the path for rebellious, countercultural groups and musicians in the 1960s; John Coltrane, Bob Dylan and Jimmy Hendrix all built their early careers here. Today, the central part of the Village is dominated by the sprawling New York University campus, adding a youthful edge to this fashionable, historic and increasingly expensive corner of Manhattan.

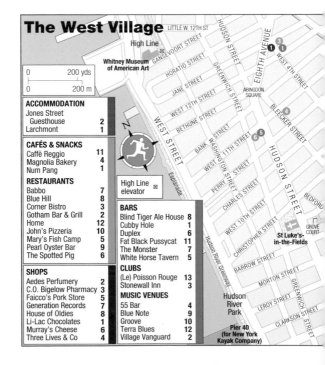

The West Village

| 0 | 200 yds |
| 0 | 200 m |

ACCOMMODATION

| Jones Street Guesthouse | 2 |
| Larchmont | 1 |

CAFÉS & SNACKS

Caffè Reggio	11
Magnolia Bakery	4
Num Pang	1

RESTAURANTS

Babbo	7
Blue Hill	8
Corner Bistro	3
Gotham Bar & Grill	2
Home	12
John's Pizzeria	10
Mary's Fish Camp	5
Pearl Oyster Bar	9
The Spotted Pig	6

SHOPS

Aedes Perfumery	2
C.O. Bigelow Pharmacy	3
Faicco's Pork Store	5
Generation Records	7
House of Oldies	8
Li-Lac Chocolates	1
Murray's Cheese	6
Three Lives & Co	4

BARS

Blind Tiger Ale House	8
Cubby Hole	1
Duplex	6
Fat Black Pussycat	11
The Monster	7
White Horse Tavern	5

CLUBS

| (Le) Poisson Rouge | 13 |
| Stonewall Inn | 3 |

MUSIC VENUES

55 Bar	4
Blue Note	9
Groove	10
Terra Blues	12
Village Vanguard	2

WASHINGTON SQUARE PARK

Subway A, B, C, D, E, F to West 4th St, N, R to 8th St. MAP P.82–63, POCKET MAP C18

The natural centre of the Village is **Washington Square Park**. Memorialized in Henry James's 1880 novel *Washington Square*, the city completed an extensive renovation of the park in 2012, though only the row of elegant Greek Revival mansions on its northern edge – the "solid, honourable dwellings" that James described – remind visitors of the area's more illustrious past.

Today, all these buildings belong to New York University (NYU). The most imposing monument in the park is Stanford White's **Washington Arch**, built in 1892 to commemorate the centenary of George Washington's

PLAYING CHESS IN WASHINGTON SQUARE PARK

presidential inauguration.

During the spring and summer months, the square becomes a combination of a running track, performance venue, giant chess tournament and social club; boiling over with life as skateboards flip, dogs run and guitar notes crash through the urgent cries of performers calling for the crowd's attention.

CHURCH OF THE ASCENSION

Fifth Ave and W 10th St. Subway N, Q, R, L, #4, #5, #6 to Union Square, F, L at 14th St 📞 212 254 8620, 🌐 www.ascensionnyc.org. Mon–Sat noon–1pm, Sun services only at 9am, 11am, 7pm. Free. MAP P.82–83. POCKET MAP C17

A small, restored structure originally built in 1841 by Richard Upjohn (architect of Trinity Church), the **Church of the Ascension** was later redecorated by Stanford White. Duck inside to see the gracefully toned La Farge altar painting and some fine stained glass on view.

FIRST PRESBYTERIAN CHURCH

12 W 12th St, at Fifth Ave. Subway N, Q, R, L, #4, #5, #6 to Union Square, F, L at 14th St 📞 212 675 6150, 🌐 www.fpcnyc.org. Mon, Wed & Fri noon–12.30pm, Sun 11am service only. Free. MAP P.82–83, POCKET MAP C17

Continuing the Gothic theme, Joseph Wells's bulky, chocolate-brown **First Presbyterian Church**, just across 11th Street from the Church of the Ascension, was completed in 1845 with a crenellated tower modelled on the one at Magdalen College in Oxford, England. Inside, you'll find carved black-walnut pews, a soaring altarpiece and fabulous Tiffany stained-glass windows, installed between 1893 and 1916.

JEFFERSON MARKET COURTHOUSE AND PATCHIN PLACE

425 Sixth Ave, at W 10th St. Subway A, B, C, D, E, F, M to West 4th St, #1 to Christopher St–Sheridan Sq 📞 212 243 4334. Library open Mon–Thurs 10am–8pm, Fri & Sat 10am–5pm, Sun 1–5pm. MAP P.82–83, POCKET MAP B17

Known for its fanciful clock tower, the nineteenth-century **Jefferson Market Courthouse** is an imposing High Victorian-style edifice, complete with gargoyles, which first served as an indoor market but went on to be a firehouse, jail, and finally a women's detention centre before enjoying its current incarnation as a public library. Adjacent to it and opening onto West 10th Street, **Patchin Place** (closed to the public) is a tiny mews constructed in 1848, whose neat row houses were home to the reclusive Djuna Barnes for more than forty years. Patchin Place has also been home to e.e. cummings, Marlon Brando, Ezra Pound and Eugene O'Neill.

BLEECKER STREET

Subway A, B, C, D, E, F to West 4th St, #1 to Christopher St–Sheridan Sq. MAP P.82–83, POCKET MAP B18

Cutting across from the Bowery to Hudson Street, **Bleecker Street**, with its

BLEECKER STREET

touristy concentration of shops, bars and restaurants, is to some extent the Main Street of the Village. It has all the best reasons you come to this part of town: all-day cafés, late-night bars, cheap record stores, traditional bakeries and food shops, and the occasional good restaurant or pizzeria.

At Sixth Avenue, the Italian-Renaissance-style **Our Lady of Pompeii Church**, built in 1929, hints at the area's Italian past; *Faicco's* butchers and *Rocco's* (best known for its crunchy nut *cannoli*) are still here, as well as celebrated deli *Murray's Cheese* (see p.87). Bob Dylan lived for a time at 161 West 4th St, and the cover of his iconic 1963 *Freewheelin'* album was shot a few paces away on Jones Street, just off Bleecker.

SHERIDAN SQUARE AND CHRISTOPHER PARK

Subway #1 to Christopher St-Sheridan Sq.
MAP P.82–83, POCKET MAP B18

Confusingly, **Christopher Park** holds a pompous-looking statue of Civil War cavalry commander General Sheridan, though **Sheridan Square** is actually the next space down, where West 4th Street meets Washington Place. Historically, the area is better

known, however, as the scene of one of the worst and bloodiest of New York's Draft Riots, when a marauding mob assembled here in 1863 and attacked members of the black community. Violence also erupted here in 1969 during the Stonewall Riots. The event is commemorated by George Segal's **Gay Liberation Monument**, unveiled in 1992. Further north, 66 Perry St, between Bleecker and West 4th Street, was used as the exterior of Carrie's apartment in *Sex and the City*, while there's almost always a queue of people waiting outside lauded *Magnolia Bakery* at Bleecker and West 11th St (see p.88). The historic *White Horse Tavern*, over at West 11th St and Hudson, is where legend claims Dylan Thomas had his last drink (see p.90).

CHRISTOPHER STREET

Subway #1 to Christopher St-Sheridan Sq.
MAP P.82–83, POCKET MAP B18

The Village's main gay artery runs from Sixth Avenue to West Street, passing by many a gay bar, sex toy shop and café. The lively street's weekend cruise scene is still strong, although the domain is by no means as exclusively gay as it once was.

BEDFORD STREET

BEDFORD STREET

Subway #1 to Christopher St-Sheridan Sq.
MAP P.82-83, POCKET MAP B18

Bedford Street runs west off Seventh Avenue to become one of the quietest and most desirable Village addresses. Edna St Vincent Millay, the young poet and playwright, lived at no. 75 1/2. At only 9ft wide, it is one of the narrowest houses in the city. The brick and clapboard structure next door at no. 77 is the **Isaacs-Hendricks House**, built in 1799 and the oldest house in the Village. The building at no. 90, right on the corner of Grove Street (above the *Little Owl*), served as the exterior for Monica's apartment in *Friends*, though the TV series was shot entirely in L.A. studios. Opposite is 17 Grove St, built in 1822 and one of the most complete wood-frame houses in the city.

GROVE STREET

Subway #1 to Christopher St-Sheridan Sq.
MAP P.82-83, POCKET MAP B18

Turn left down **Grove Street** from the *Little Owl* and you'll find Grove Court just off the street, one of the neighbourhood's most attractive and exclusive little mews. Heading back to Seventh Avenue on Grove Street, keep an eye out for *Marie's Crisis Café* at no. 59. Now a piano bar, this was the site of the rented rooms where English revolutionary writer and philosopher Thomas Paine died in 1809. Paine, who was reviled in England for his support of both the American and French revolutions, was the author of the eighteenth century's three bestselling pamphlets; *Common Sense*, published in 1776, is generally credited with turning public opinion in favour of US independence. The current building dates from 1839, the café named in part after Paine's masterful essay *The American Crisis*.

ST LUKE'S PLACE

Subway #1 to Christopher St-Sheridan Sq.
MAP P.82-83, POCKET MAP B18

One block south of Bedford Street is a section of Leroy Street known as **St. Luke's Place**; no. 10 was used as the exterior of the Cosby house (from the beloved 1980s TV show), while no. 6 is the former residence of Jimmy Walker, an extravagant mayor of New York in the 1920s.

NEW YORK KAYAK COMPANY

Pier 40, end of Houston St ☎ 212 924 1327,
ⓦ www.nykayak.com. Tues-Fri 10am–6pm,
Sat 10am–5pm. MAP P.82-83, POCKET MAP A19

This professional outfit offers kayaking classes and tours on the **Hudson River**, at the edge of the West Village. Classes start at $50/hr, and tours depend on ability, but the sensational views and the chance to work off all those cupcakes make this a fabulous deal (no children under 15; ages 15–18 must be accompanied by an adult).

Shops

AEDES PERFUMERY

7 Greenwich Ave, at Christopher St. Subway A, B, C, D, E, F, M to W 4th St, #1 to Christopher St. Mon–Sat noon–8pm, Sun 1–7pm. MAP P.82–83, POCKET MAP B17

Enchanting fragrance purveyor, with plenty of international offerings and perfume rarities; best of all, they'll wrap your purchase in fresh blooms.

C.O. BIGELOW PHARMACY

414 Sixth Ave, between W 8th and 9th sts. Subway A, B, C, D, E, F, M to W 4th St; #1 to Christopher St. Mon–Fri 7.30am–9pm, Sat 8.30am–7pm, Sun 8.30am–5.30pm. MAP P.82–83, POCKET MAP C17

Established in 1882, this is the oldest apothecary in the country – the Victorian shop-fittings are still in place. Specializes in homeopathic remedies.

FAICCO'S PORK STORE

260 Bleecker St, between Morton and Leroy sts. Subway A, B, C, D, E, F, M to W 4th St. Tues–Fri 8.30am–6pm, Sat 8am–6pm, Sun 9am–2pm. MAP P.82–83, POCKET MAP B18

This old-school Italian butcher serves some of the best-value meats, Italian products and sandwiches in the city.

GENERATION RECORDS

210 Thompson St, between Bleecker and W 3rd sts. Subway A, B, C, D, E, F, M to W 4th St. Sun–Thurs 11am–10pm, Fri & Sat 11am–11pm. MAP P.82–83, POCKET MAP C18

The focus here is on hardcore, metal and punk, with some indie rock thrown in. New CDs, vinyl and records on offer.

HOUSE OF OLDIES

35 Carmine St, between Bleecker St and Bedford St. Subway A, B, C, D, E, F, M to W 4th St; #1 to Houston St. Tues–Sat 9am–5pm. MAP P.82–83, POCKET MAP B18

This shop specializes in rare and out-of-print vinyl records from the 1950s, 1960s and 1970s.

LI-LAC CHOCOLATES

40 Eighth Ave, at Jane St. Subway A, C, E, L, #1, #2, #3 to 14th St. Mon–Thurs 11am–8pm, Fri & Sat 11am–9pm, Sun 11am–7pm. MAP P.82–83, POCKET MAP B17

Delicious chocolates handmade on the premises since 1923, including fresh fudge and hand-moulded Liberties and Empire States.

MURRAY'S CHEESE

254 Bleecker St, at Cornelia St. Subway A, B, C, D, E, F, M to W 4th St, #1 to Christopher St. Mon–Sat 8am–9pm, Sun 9am–8pm. MAP P.82–83, POCKET MAP B18

The exuberant and entertaining staff make any visit to this cheese-lovers' mecca a treat.

THREE LIVES & CO

154 W 10th St, at Waverly Place. Subway A, B, C, D, E, F, M to W 4th St, #1 to Christopher St. Sun noon–7pm, Mon & Tues noon–8pm, Wed–Sat 11am–8.30pm. MAP P.82–83, POCKET MAP B18

Excellent literary bookstore that has an especially good selection of books by and for women, as well as general titles.

MURRAY'S CHEESE

Cafés and snacks

CAFFÈ REGGIO

119 MacDougal St, between Bleecker and W 3rd sts. Subway A, B, C, D, E, F to W 4th St. Mon–Thurs 8am–3am, Fri & Sat 8am–4.30am, Sun 9am–3am. MAP P.82–83, POCKET MAP C18

Oldest coffee shop in the Village, dating back to 1927, and embellished with all sorts of Italian antiques, paintings and sculpture.

MAGNOLIA BAKERY

401 Bleecker St, at W 11th St. Subway #1 to Christopher St. Mon–Thurs & Sun 9am–11.30pm, Fri & Sat 9am–12.30am. MAP P.82–83, POCKET MAP B18

There are lots of baked goods on offer at this very popular bakery, but everyone comes for the good but slightly overrated cupcakes (celebrated in *Sex and the City*), $3.50 each.

NUM PANG

28 E 12th St, between University Place and Fifth Ave. Subway L, N, Q, R, #4, #5, #6 to Union Square ☎ 646 791 0439. Mon–Sat 11am–10pm, Sun noon–9pm. MAP P.82–83, POCKET MAP C17

Superb Cambodian-style sandwiches served on freshly toasted semolina flour baguettes with chilli mayo and home-made pickles; try the pulled duroc pork ($8.95).

Restaurants

BABBO

110 Waverly Place, between MacDougal St and Sixth Ave. Subway A, B, C, D, E, F, M to W 4th St, #1 to Christopher St ☎ 212 777 0303. Mon 5–11.15pm, Tues–Sat 11.30am–2pm & 5–11.15pm, Sun 4.30–10.45pm. MAP P.82–83, POCKET MAP C18

Some of the best pasta in the city; this Mario Batali mecca for Italian food-lovers is a must. Try the mint love letters or goose liver ravioli – they're worth the pinch on your wallet.

BLUE HILL

75 Washington Place, between Sixth Ave and Washington Square Park. Subway A, B, C, D, E, F to W 4th St, #1 to Christopher St ☎ 212 539 1776. Mon–Sat 5–11pm, Sun 5–10pm. MAP P.82–83, POCKET MAP C18

Rustic American and New England fare, including parsnip soup and braised cod, made with seasonal upstate ingredients. Don't miss the rich chocolate bread pudding.

CORNER BISTRO

331 W 4th St, at Jane St. Subway A, C, E, L to 14th St ☎ 212 242 9502. Mon–Sat 11.30am–4am, Sun noon–4am. MAP P.82–83, POCKET MAP B17

Popular no-frills tavern serving cheap beer and some of the best burgers ($8.95) in town. An excellent place to unwind and refuel in a friendly atmosphere. Cash only.

GOTHAM BAR & GRILL

12 E 12th St, between Fifth Ave and University Place. Subway L, N, Q, R, #4, #5, #6 to Union Sq ☎ 212 620 4020. Mon–Thurs noon–2.15pm & 5.30–10pm, Fri noon–2.15pm & 5.30–11pm, Sat 5–11pm, Sun 5–10pm. MAP P.82–83, POCKET MAP C17

One of the city's best restaurants, the *Gotham* features marvellous American food; at

the very least, it's worth a drink at the bar to people-watch.

HOME

20 Cornelia St, between Bleecker and W 4th sts. Subway A, B, C, D, E, F, M to W 4th St, #1 to Christopher St ☏ 212 243 9579. Mon–Fri 11am–11pm, Sat 10.30am–11pm, Sun 10.30am–10pm. MAP P.82–83, POCKET MAP B18

One of those rare places that manages to pull off cosy with flair. The creative and reasonably priced American food is always fresh and tasty, though it may be a better deal for lunch ($11–16) than dinner ($21–30).

JOHN'S PIZZERIA

278 Bleecker St, between Sixth and Seventh aves. Subway A, B, C, D, E, F, M to W 4th St, #1 to Christopher St ☏ 212 243 1680. Sun–Thurs 11.30am–11.30pm, Fri & Sat 11.30am–midnight. MAP P.82–83, POCKET MAP B18

This full-service restaurant serves some of the city's most popular pizzas, thin with a coal-charred crust ($17). Be prepared to queue for a table. They don't do slices.

MARY'S FISH CAMP

64 Charles St, at W 4th St. Subway #1 to Christopher St ☏ 646 486 2185. Mon–Sat noon–3pm & 6–11pm, Sun noon–4pm. MAP P.82–83, POCKET MAP B18

Lobster rolls, *bouillabaisse* and seasonal veggies adorn the menu at this intimate spot, where you can almost smell the salt air. Go early, as the queue lasts into the night (no reservations).

PEARL OYSTER BAR

18 Cornelia St, between Bleecker and W 4th sts. Subway A, B, C, D, E, F, M to W 4th St, #1 to Christopher St ☏ 212 691 8211. Mon–Fri noon–2.30pm & 6–11pm, Sat 6–11pm. MAP P.82–83, POCKET MAP B18

Upmarket version of a New England fish shack, best known for its lemony-fresh lobster roll. You may have to fight for a table here, but the thoughtfully executed dishes are worth it.

PEARL OYSTER BAR

THE SPOTTED PIG

314 W 11th St, at Greenwich St. Subway #1 to Christopher St ☏ 212 620 0393. Mon–Fri noon–2am, Sat & Sun 11am–2am. MAP P.82–83, POCKET MAP A18

New York's first gastro-pub, courtesy of chef April Bloomfield. The menu is several steps above ordinary bar food – featuring smoked-haddock chowder and sheep's ricotta *gnudi* – and the wine list is excellent. Entrées $25–36, with lunch plates under $20.

THE SPOTTED PIG

Bars

BLIND TIGER ALE HOUSE

281 Bleecker St, at Jones St. Subway A, B, C, D, E, F, M to W 4th St; #1 to Christopher St. Daily 11.30am–4am. MAP P.82–83, POCKET MAP B18

This wood-panelled pub is the home of serious ale connoisseurs, with 28 rotating draughts (primarily US microbrews such as Sixpoint and Smuttynose for around $7–8), a couple of casks and loads of bottled beers – they also serve cheese plates from Murray's. The prime location means it tends to get packed.

CUBBY HOLE

281 W 12th St, at W 4th St. Subway A, C, E, L to 14th St. Mon–Fri 4pm–4am, Sat & Sun 2pm–4am. MAP P.82–83, POCKET MAP B17

This pocket-sized lesbian bar is warm and welcoming, with a busy festive atmosphere and unpretentious clientele.

DUPLEX

61 Christopher St, at Seventh Ave S. Subway A, B, C, D, E, F, M to W 4th St, #1 to Christopher St. Daily 4pm–4am. MAP P.82–83, POCKET MAP B18

A village institution, this entertaining piano bar/cabaret elevates gay bar culture to a new level. A fun place for anyone, gay or straight, to stop for a tipple.

FAT BLACK PUSSYCAT

130 W 3rd St, between Sixth Ave and MacDougal St. Subway A, B, C, D, E, F, M to W 4th St. Daily 1pm–4am. MAP P.82–83, POCKET MAP C18

This pub is an NYU favourite, with popular happy hours (Sun–Fri 4–8pm), cosy wooden booths, darts and billiards. The pub's original location on MacDougal St is where Bob Dylan allegedly wrote *Blowin' in the Wind*.

THE MONSTER

80 Grove St, between Waverly Place and W 4th St. Subway A, B, C, D, E, F, M to W 4th St, #1 to Christopher St ☎ 212 924 3558, ⓦ www.monsterbarnyc.com. Mon–Fri 4pm–4am, Sat & Sun 2pm–4am. MAP P.82–83, POCKET MAP B18

Large, campy gay bar with drag cabaret, piano and downstairs dancefloor. Very popular, especially with tourists, yet has a strong neighbourhood feel. Cover $6–10 (Fri–Mon).

WHITE HORSE TAVERN

567 Hudson St, at W 11th St. Subway #1 to Christopher St. Daily 11am–3am. MAP P.82–83, POCKET MAP A18

Village institution, opening in 1880: Dylan Thomas supped his last here before being carted off to hospital with alcohol poisoning. The cheap beer and food are palatable, and there's outside seating in summer.

Clubs

(LE) POISSON ROUGE

158 Bleecker St, at Thompson St. Subway A, B, C, D, E, F, M to W 4th St ☎ 212 505 3474, ⓦ www.lpr.com. Daily 5pm–2am, Fri & Sat till 4am. MAP P.82–83, POCKET MAP C18

Club and live venue (from classical to live rock, folk, pop

and electronica), with dance nights most Fridays and Saturdays ("Back to the Eighties" from 11pm; $22). Cover usually ranges $15–20.

STONEWALL INN

53 Christopher St, between Seventh Ave and Waverly Place. Subway A, B, C, D, E, F, M to W 4th St, #1 to Christopher St ☎ 212 488 2705, Ⓦ www.thestonewallinnnyc.com. Daily 2pm–4am. MAP P.82–83, POCKET MAP B18

The gay civil-rights movement began outside this bar/club in the late 1960s and despite a few revamps hasn't changed much since. The crowd is mostly tourists and men, but everyone is made welcome.

Music venues

55 BAR

55 Christopher St, at Seventh Ave. Subway #1 to Christopher St. Ⓦ www.55bar.com. Daily 4.30pm–4am. MAP P.82–83, POCKET MAP B18

A gem of an underground jazz bar that's been around since the days of Prohibition, with a great jukebox, congenial clientele, and live jazz every night.

BLUE NOTE

131 W 3rd St, between Sixth Ave and MacDougal St. Subway A, B, C, D, E, F, M to W 4th St, #1 to Christopher St ☎ 212 475 8592, Ⓦ www.bluenote.net. Sun–Thurs 6pm–1am, Fri & Sat 6pm–3am. MAP P.82–83, POCKET MAP C18

Open since 1981 (and unrelated to the record label), this jazz institution regularly hosts top international performers, the likes of B.B King and Roberta Flack ($10–45).

GROOVE

125 MacDougal St, at W 3rd St. Subway A, B, C, D, E, F, M to W 4th St ☎ 212 254 9393, Ⓦ www.clubgroovenyc.com. Daily 4pm–4am. MAP P.82–83, POCKET MAP C18

This lively joint features live rhythm & blues and soul music

VILLAGE VANGUARD

every night; it's one of the city's best bargains. Sets at 7pm and 9.30pm. No cover Sun–Thurs.

TERRA BLUES

149 Bleecker St, between Thompson St and LaGuardia Place. Subway A, B, C, D, E, F, M to W 4th St ☎ 212 777 7776, Ⓦ www.terrablues.com. Mon–Thurs & Sun 7pm–3am, Fri 7pm–4am, Sat 6pm–4am. MAP P.82–83, POCKET MAP C18

The last remaining exclusive blues club in the city offers acoustic blues from 7.30pm and electric blues after 10pm, for $10–20 cover; all the big national names play here, and there's an excellent house band.

VILLAGE VANGUARD

178 Seventh Ave S, between W 11th and Perry sts. Subway #1, #2, #3 to 14th St. ☎ 212 255 4037, Ⓦ www.villagevanguard .com. Daily 7.30pm–1am. MAP P.82–83, POCKET MAP B17

A NYC jazz landmark, the *Village Vanguard* celebrated its seventieth anniversary in 2005. Sonny Rollins made a legendary recording here in 1957, John Coltrane followed in 1961 and there's still a regular diet of big names. Cover is $30, including a one-drink minimum ($5–16).

Chelsea and the Meatpacking District

A grid of tenements, row houses and warehouses west of Sixth Avenue between West 14th and 30th streets, Chelsea came to life with the gay community's arrival, beginning in the late 1970s. New York's art scene further transformed the neighbourhood in the 1990s with an explosion of galleries between Tenth and Twelfth avenues. These days the High Line park and the relocated Whitney Museum are responsible for the area's energy. The triangular wedge of land created by Fourteenth, Gansevoort and West streets, aka the Meatpacking District, is a trendy place for shopping and clubbing.

THE WHITNEY MUSEUM OF AMERICAN ART

99 Gansevoort St, between Tenth and Eleventh aves. Subway A, C, E, to 14th St, L to Eighth Ave ☎ 212 570 3600, ❖ www .whitney.org. Mon, Wed & Sun 10.30am–6pm, Thurs–Sat 10.30am–10pm. $22, under 18 free, after 7pm Fri free. Free tours daily roughly on the hour from noon. MAP P.93, POCKET MAP C11

Transplanted from its Upper East Side home (and closer to where it began back in the 1930s, in Greenwich Village), the **Whitney Museum of American Art** debuted its

Renzo Piano-designed building at the foot of the High Line in May 2015. The architecture – its industrial look, external stairs and roomy terraces – attracts nearly as much attention as the art. As for what's on display, a good chunk of the museum's permanent collection now has room to shine. Look for favourites like Alexander Calder's *Circus* and Edward Hopper's *Early Sunday Morning*; though temporary exhibitions frequently take top billing. The Whitney is, after all, most famous for its Biennial, which gives a provocative overview of contemporary American art.

THE HIGH LINE

Gansevoort St to W 30th St, roughly along Tenth Ave; entrances at Gansevoort, 14th, 16th, 18th, 20th, 23rd, 26th, 28th, 30th and 34th sts. Subway A, C, E to 14th St, C, E to 23rd St ❖ www.thehighline.org. Daily: April, May, Oct & Nov 7am–10pm; June–Sept 7am–11pm; Dec–March 7am–7pm. MAP P.93, POCKET MAP B10

An ambitious urban renewal project that spans the Meatpacking District and West Chelsea, the **High Line** opened

THE HIGH LINE

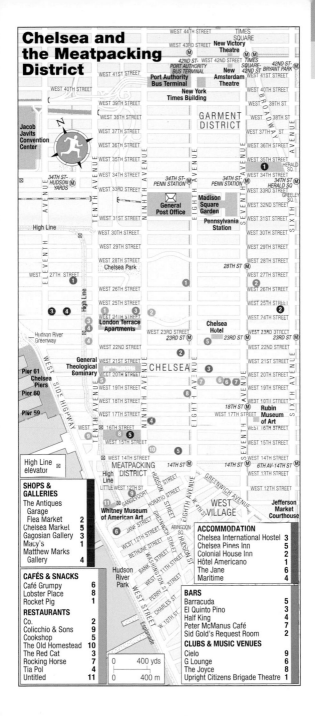

Chelsea and the Meatpacking District

SHOPS & GALLERIES

The Antiques Garage Flea Market	2
Chelsea Market	5
Gagosian Gallery	3
Macy's	1
Matthew Marks Gallery	4

CAFÉS & SNACKS

Café Grumpy	6
Lobster Place	8
Rocket Pig	1

RESTAURANTS

Co.	2
Colicchio & Sons	9
Cookshop	5
The Old Homestead	10
The Red Cat	3
Rocking Horse	7
Tia Pol	4
Untitled	11

ACCOMMODATION

Chelsea International Hostel	3
Chelsea Pines Inn	5
Colonial House Inn	2
Hôtel Americano	1
The Jane	6
Maritime	4

BARS

Barracuda	5
El Quinto Pino	3
Half King	4
Peter McManus Café	7
Sid Gold's Request Room	2

CLUBS & MUSIC VENUES

Cielo	9
G Lounge	6
The Joyce	8
Upright Citizens Brigade Theatre	1

93

in 2009. It's a stunning transformation of a disused railway that once moved goods and produce around lower Manhattan, then spent years threatened with demolition.

Basically an elevated promenade-cum-public park, it pays proper homage to its history – steel rails peek out from the ground; smooth pavement and wood echo the lines of train tracks; and wild growth patches have been left intact. The first stretch, from Gansevoort to 20th Street, has a subtle water feature between 14th and 15th streets and an amphitheatre a few blocks north. Between 20th and 30th streets the walkway feels narrower; at one point it is elevated on a metal catwalk right in the trees. The last part, the High Line at the Rail Yards, curves around the rail terminus and finishes along 34th Street, where a massive redevelopment is taking place.

RUBIN MUSEUM OF ART

150 W 17th St, between Sixth and Seventh aves. Subway #1 to 18th St, F, M to 14th St ☎ 212 620 5000, ⓦ www.rubinmuseum.org. Mon & Thurs 11am–5pm, Wed 11am–9pm, Fri 11am–10pm, Sat & Sun 11am–6pm, closed Tues. $15, free on Fri 6–10pm. MAP P.93, POCKET MAP D10

The serene **Rubin Museum** is one of the city's lesser-visited gems, a collection of a few thousand paintings, sculptures and textiles from the Himalayas and surrounding regions. The permanent exhibits on the second and third floors are organized and labelled with great care and thought, essential for a subject that will be familiar to few. While a few pieces manage to stand out, the thrust is less about individual artists and objects and more about understanding how and why art is created. The ground-floor café becomes the *K2 Lounge* on Friday nights, with DJs and cocktails.

THE CHELSEA HOTEL

222 W 23rd St, between Seventh and Eighth aves. Subway C, E to 23rd St ⓦ www .hotelchelsea.com. MAP P.93, POCKET MAP C10

Built as a luxury cooperative apartment in 1884 and converted to a hotel in 1903, the **Chelsea Hotel** has served as undisputed home to the city's harder-up literati and its musical vagabonds. Eugene O'Neill, Arthur Miller and Tennessee Williams lived here, and

HISTORIC CHELSEA ROWHOUSES

Brendan Behan and Dylan Thomas staggered in and out during their New York visits. Legend has it that Jack Kerouac typed *On the Road* nonstop onto a 120ft roll of paper while here, though most agree that took place at 454 W 20th Street, over a six-week period (and from existing journals, not just the top of his head). Bob Dylan wrote songs in and about the hotel, and Sid Vicious stabbed Nancy Spungen to death in 1978 in their suite, a few months before his own life ended with an overdose of heroin.

After years of closure and numerous rumours, the place is finally due to reopen in 2017 as a boutique hotel.

GENERAL THEOLOGICAL SEMINARY

440 W 21st St, between Ninth and Tenth aves. Subway C, E to 23rd St ☎ 212 243-5150, ⊕ www.gts.edu. Mon–Sat 10am–3pm; later in summer, but always call ahead. MAP P.93, POCKET MAP C10

Founded in 1817, this is a Chelsea secret, a harmonious assemblage of Gothic structures that feel like part of a college campus. Though the buildings still house a working Episcopalian seminary – the oldest in the US – it's possible to explore the grounds and small chapel. You'll need to get a special pass to check out their collection of Latin Bibles, one of the largest in the world.

CHELSEA PIERS

W 17th to W 23rd St, along Hudson River. Subway C, E to 23rd St ☎ 212 336 6666, ⊕ www.chelseapiers.com. Hours vary according to activity. MAP P.93, POCKET MAP B11

First opened in 1910, this was where the great transatlantic liners would disembark their passengers (it was en route to the **Chelsea Piers** in 1912 that the *Titanic* sank). By the 1960s,

THE GENERAL POST OFFICE

however, the piers had fallen into neglect. Reopened in 1995, the new Chelsea Piers stretches between piers 59 to 62 as a sports complex, with ice rinks and open-air roller rinks, as well as a bowling alley and a golf range. There's a nice waterfront walkway and skate park at the end of **Pier 62**.

THE GENERAL POST OFFICE

421 Eighth Ave, at W 33rd St. Subway A, C, E to 34th St ☎ 212 330 3296. Mon–Fri 7am–10pm, Sat 9am–9pm, Sun 11am–7pm. MAP P.93, POCKET MAP C9

The 1913 **General Post Office**, officially the James A Farley Station (named after a well-regarded postmaster general), is a relic from when municipal pride was all about making statements. Twenty huge columns stand beneath the sonorous inscription: "Neither snow nor rain nor heat nor gloom of night stays these couriers from the swift completion of their appointed rounds." The McKim, Mead, and White building is being refitted to serve as an entrance to Amtrak and LIRR trains at Penn Station; it is currently used for fashion events and other happenings.

Shops and galleries

THE ANTIQUES GARAGE FLEA MARKET

112 W 25th St, between Sixth and Seventh aves. Subway F, M, #1 to 23rd St. Sat & Sun 9am–5pm. MAP P.93, POCKET MAP D10

Packed into a bi-level garage, vendors come to peddle all sorts of old knick-knacks, antique jewellery, framed items, toys, cigarette lighters and more.

CHELSEA MARKET

75 Ninth Ave, between W 15th and 16th sts. Subway A, C, E to 14th St. Mon–Sat 7am–10pm, Sun 8am–9pm. MAP P.93, POCKET MAP A17

Food shops and restaurants line this former Nabisco factory warehouse's ground floor; go for *pad thai*, panini, tacos, sinful brownies or kitchenware. Tours are available too.

GAGOSIAN GALLERY

555 W 24th St, between Tenth and Eleventh aves, other locations at 522 W 21st St and 980 Madison Ave. Subway C, E to 23rd St ☎212 741 1111, ⊕www.gagosian.com. Tues–Sat 10am–6pm. MAP P.93, POCKET MAP B10

This art world powerbroker shows heavyweights such as Richard Serra and Damien Hirst.

CHELSEA MARKET

MACY'S

MACY'S

151 Broadway, at W 34th St at Herald Square. Subway B, D, F, M, N, Q, R to 34th St. Mon–Fri 9am–9.30pm, Sat 9am–11pm, Sun 11am–8.30pm. MAP P.93, POCKET MAP O9

One of the world's largest department stores, Macy's stocks fairly mediocre brands (except for the excellent Cellar houseware department). If you're from abroad, head to the Visitor Center (Balcony Level) to receive a ten percent discount; bring your passport.

MATTHEW MARKS GALLERY

522 W 22nd St, between Tenth and Eleventh aves, with three other branches in Chelsea. Subway C, E to 23rd St ☎212 243 0200, ⊕www.matthewmarks.com. Tues–Sat 10am–6pm. MAP P.93, POCKET MAP B10

The centrepiece of Chelsea's art scene, showcasing pieces by artists such as Cy Twombly and Ellsworth Kelly.

Cafés and snacks

CAFÉ GRUMPY

224 W 20th St, between Seventh and Eighth aves; three other city locations. Subway C, E to 23rd St. Mon–Fri 7am–8pm,

Sat 7.30am–8pm, Sun 7.30am–7.30pm.
MAP P.93, POCKET MAP C10

It's uncertain which will take longer, choosing a coffee – the selections described as if they were wines – or getting your fix, as each cup comes made to order. But you'll be able to taste the difference; it's as good as it gets. The original *Grumpy* is over in Brooklyn's Greenpoint.

LOBSTER PLACE

75 Ninth Ave, between 15th and 16th sts. Subway A, C, E to 14th St. Mon–Sat 9.30am–9pm, Sun 10am–8pm.
MAP P.93, POCKET MAP C11

A Chelsea Market fishmonger with a sandwich window at the back; take your chowder (small portion $4.75), fresh sushi meal or picnic box ($13.50–20.50) up to the High Line for lunch. There's also a seafood restaurant, *Cull and Pistol*, attached.

ROCKET PIG

463 W 24th St, between W Ninth and Tenth aves. Subway C, E to 23rd St ☎ 212 645 5660. Daily: winter 11am–5pm, rest of year 11am–6pm. MAP P.93, POCKET MAP C10

They do one thing – with perhaps a couple of small diversions – a messy, smoked pork sandwich ($14 for regular, $9 for a "shorty"), whose accoutrements (red onion jam, for one) help make it a signature nouveau sandwich.

Restaurants

CO.

230 Ninth Ave, at W 24th St. Subway C, E to 23rd St ☎ 212 243 1105. Mon 5–10pm, Tues & Wed 11.30am–10pm, Thurs & Fri 11.30am–11pm, Sat 11am–11pm, Sun 11am–10pm. MAP P.93, POCKET MAP C10

Fashionable new-wave pizzeria. Start with the crostini ($5–6) and an escarole salad ($10), then share a few of the oddly shaped pizzas, like shiitake and rosemary ($18), and meatball ($18).

COLICCHIO & SONS

85 Tenth Ave, at W 15th St. Subway A, C, E to 14th St, L to Eighth Ave ☎ 212 400 6699. Mon & Tues 5.30–10pm, Wed &Thurs noon–3pm & 5.30–10pm, Fri noon–3pm & 5.30–11pm, Sat 11am–3pm & 5.30–11pm, Sun 11am–3pm & 5.30–9pm. MAP P.93, POCKET MAP A17

Celebrity chef Tom Colicchio strikes again, offering a menu of small-to-medium plates with unusual combinations like pasta with lobster, chilli and bottarga. *The Tap Room* at the front has a more casual, warmer vibe than the back dining room.

COOKSHOP

156 Tenth Ave, at 20th St. Subway C, E to 23rd St ☎ 212 924 4440. Mon–Fri 8am–4pm & 5.30–11.30pm, Sat 10.30am–4pm & 5.30–11.30pm, Sun 10am–4pm & 5.30–10pm. MAP P.93, POCKET MAP C10

Part of the Marc Meyer stable, with ever-busy street-side tables and a menu of seasonal, contemporary American fare – dishes always showcase the food's provenance; entrées might include pheasant pasta, grilled rabbit from the Hudson Valley and Vermont suckling pig (most $25–30); there are interesting brunch options and inventive Bloody Marys, too.

THE OLD HOMESTEAD

56 Ninth Ave, between W 14th and 15th sts. Subway A, C, E to 14th St ☎ 212 242 9040. Mon–Thurs noon–10.30pm, Fri noon–11.30pm, Sat 1–11.30pm, Sun 1–9.30pm. MAP P.93, POCKET MAP A17

Steak. Period. But really gorgeous steak, served in an almost comically old-fashioned walnut dining room by waiters in black vests. Huge portions, but expensive – roughly $44–56.

THE RED CAT

227 Tenth Ave, between W 23rd and 24th sts. Subway C, E to 23rd St ☎ 212 242 1122. Mon–Fri noon–2.30pm & 5–11pm, Sat 11.45am–2.45pm & 5–11pm, Sun 11.45am–2.45pm & 5–10pm. MAP P.93, POCKET MAP B10

Superb service, a fine American–Mediterranean kitchen, diverse wine list and cosy atmosphere all make for a memorable dining experience.

ROCKING HORSE

182 Eighth Ave, between W 19th and 20th sts. Subway C, E to 23rd St, #1 to 18th St ☎ 212 463 9511. Mon–Thurs noon–11pm, Fri noon–midnight, Sat 11am–midnight, Sun 11am–11pm. MAP P.93, POCKET MAP C11

The high-end Mexican cuisine served at *Rocking Horse* is very inventive – seared salmon with chilli ($23), chipotle lamb shank ($27) – while the mojitos and margaritas pack a punch.

TIA POL

205 Tenth Ave, between W 22nd and 23rd sts. Subway C, E to 23rd St ☎ 212 675 8805. Mon 5.30–11pm, Tues–Thurs noon–11pm, Fri noon–midnight, Sat 11am–midnight, Sun 11am–10.30pm. MAP P.93, POCKET MAP B10

The narrow space in this popular tapas bar-restaurant is frequently full. Graze on bar snacks like

THE OLD HOMESTEAD

croquetas ($4/$8) or choose heartier octopus salad ($14) and shrimp *al ajillo* ($12); wash it all back with the easy-drinking house-made sangria ($9 glass).

UNTITLED

99 Gansevoort St, at Washington St. Subway: A, C, E, L to 14th St–Eighth Ave ☎ 212 570 3670, ⓦ www.untitledatthewhitney.com. Mon–Fri 11.30am–2.30pm & 5.30–10pm, Sat 11am–2.30pm & 5.30–10pm, Sun 11am–2.30pm & 5.30–9pm. MAP P.93, POCKET MAP A17

The main restaurant at the Whitney is more than just a place for refined salads and snacky avocado toast ($15); it offers lovely New American cooking – think braised lamb or steamed black bass ($28–31).

Bars

BARRACUDA

275 W 22nd St, between Seventh and Eighth aves. Subway C, E, #1 to 23rd St. Daily 4pm–4am. MAP P.93, POCKET MAP C10

A favourite bar in New York's gay scene, and pretty laidback for Chelsea, though drag shows and DJs perk things up in the later hours.

EL QUINTO PINO

401 W 24th St at Ninth Ave. Subway C, E to 23rd St. Mon 5pm–midnight, Tues–Fri noon–3.30pm & 5pm–midnight, Sat & Sun 11.30am–3pm & 5pm–1am. MAP P.93, POCKET MAP C10

Nibble on pork cracklings ($6) and an uncanny sea urchin sandwich ($15) in this elegant tapas bar. There's also a dining room at the back and a good selection of Spanish wines.

HALF KING

505 W 23rd St, between Tenth and Eleventh aves. Subway C, E to 23rd St. Mon–Fri 11am–4am, Sat & Sun 9am–4am. MAP P.93, POCKET MAP B10

This popular Irish pub, owned

THE JOYCE

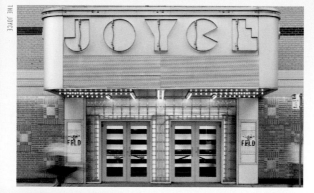

by a small group of writers/artists, features decent food and regular literary events.

PETER McMANUS CAFÉ

152 Seventh Ave, at 19th St. Subway #1 to 18th St. Mon–Sat 11am–4am, Sun noon–4am. MAP P.93, POCKET MAP C11

Unlike many Irish pubs in the city, this is the real deal, moving to this location in 1936 and appearing in episodes of *Seinfeld* and *Law & Order*. The worn oak bar adds character, along with the in-house ale, decent burgers and old-style telephone booths inside.

SID GOLD'S REQUEST ROOM

165 W 26th St, between Sixth and Seventh aves. Subway #1 to 28th St. Mon–Fri 5pm–2am, Sat 7pm–2am. MAP P.93, POCKET MAP D10

The place for a sing-a-long, some old-school cocktails and snacks, and the stylings of local music legend Joe McGinty. Fabulously retro.

Clubs and music venues

CIELO

18 Little W 12th St, at Ninth Ave. Subway A, C, E to 14th St 🕿 212 645 5700, ⓦ www .cieloclub.com. Mon & Wed–Sat 10pm–4am.

$20–25. MAP P.93, POCKET MAP A17

Expect velvet rope-burn at this super-exclusive place: there's only room for 250 people. Don't miss DeepSpace Mondays, a reggae and dub party hosted by the French DJ François K.

G LOUNGE

225 W 19th St, between Seventh and Eighth aves. Subway #1 to 18th St 🕿 212 929 1085, ⓦ glounge.com. Daily 4pm–4am. MAP P.93, POCKET MAP C11

At Chelsea's friendliest gay lounge, it's all about Martinis and preening. Go on weeknights when things are less hectic.

THE JOYCE

175 Eighth Ave, at W 19th St. Subway #1 to 18th St; C, E to 23rd St 🕿 212 691 9740, ⓦ www.joyce.org. MAP P.93, POCKET MAP C11

Touring companies both local and from around the world keep this Art Deco-style theatre in brisk business.

UPRIGHT CITIZENS BRIGADE THEATRE

307 W 26th St, between Eighth and Ninth aves. Subway C, E to 23rd St 🕿 212 366 9176, ⓦ www.ucbtheatre.com. Cover free to $10. MAP P.93, POCKET MAP C10.

Consistently hilarious sketch-based and improv comedy, seven nights a week. You can sometimes catch *Saturday Night Live* members in the ensemble.

Union Square, Gramercy Park and the Flatiron District

For a glimpse of well-preserved nineteenth-century New York, it's definitely worth a jaunt around the more genteel parts of the east-side neighbourhoods that surround Union Square and Gramercy Park. Madison Square Park and the decidedly anorexic Flatiron Building anchor the amorphous area of the Flatiron District, which veers up and down Broadway and takes in a number of elegant facades; things take on more of a high-rise, Midtown flavour the closer you get to the Empire State Building. Some of the best and most expensive restaurants in the city call this stretch home; wander east to the high 20s around Lexington Avenue, a little Indian area called Curry Hill, for wallet relief in the kosher vegetarian restaurants and *chaat* cafés frequented by taxi drivers.

UNION SQUARE

Bordered by Broadway, Park Avenue S, 14th and 17th sts. Subway L, N, Q, R, #4, #5, #6 to Union Square. MAP P.101, POCKET MAP D11

Founded as a park in 1813, **Union Square** lies between E 14th and E 17th streets, interrupting Broadway's diagonal path. The park was the site of many political protests and workers' rallies between the Civil War and the early twentieth century. Later, the area evolved into an elegant theatre and shopping district. The leafy and bench-lined square is best known for its **Farmers' Market**, held Monday, Wednesday, Friday

UNION SQUARE

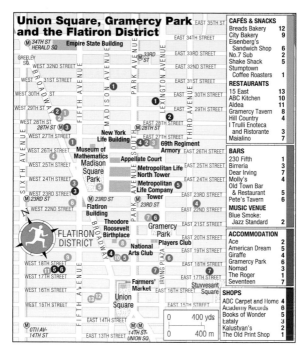

Map content:

Union Square, Gramercy Park and the Flatiron District

CAFÉS & SNACKS
Breads Bakery	12
City Bakery	9
Eisenberg's Sandwich Shop	6
No.7 Sub	2
Shake Shack	5
Stumptown Coffee Roasters	1

RESTAURANTS
15 East	13
ABC Kitchen	10
Aldea	11
Gramercy Tavern	8
Hill Country	4
I Trulli Enoteca and Ristorante	3
Maialino	7

BARS
230 Fifth	3
Birreria	1
Dear Irving	7
Molly's Old Town Bar & Restaurant	4
Pete's Tavern	6

MUSIC VENUE
Blue Smoke: Jazz Standard	2

ACCOMMODATION
Ace	2
American Dream	5
Giraffe	4
Gramercy Park	6
Nomad	3
The Roger	1
Seventeen	7

SHOPS
ABC Carpet and Home	4
Academy Records	6
Books of Wonder	5
Eataly	3
Kalustyan's	2
The Old Print Shop	1

and Saturday from 8am to 6pm; there's tons of local produce, cheese, meat, even wine. Craft vendors, none too special, line the southwest side, though they're taken over by a popular holiday market as Christmas approaches.

IRVING PLACE

Subway L, N, Q, R, #4, #5, #6 to Union Square. MAP P.101, POCKET MAP E11

This graceful six-block stretch was named after author Washington Irving, though the claims that he lived at no. 49 are spurious; he did, at the least, frequently visit a nephew who lived in the area. Regardless, it's a lovely walk from the Con Ed building at the south end up to Gramercy Park; the intersection with 19th Street – and that side street itself – is especially evocative.

THEODORE ROOSEVELT BIRTHPLACE

28 E 20th St, between Park Ave S and Broadway. Subway N, R, #6 to 23rd St ☎ 212 260 1616. Tues-Sat 9am–5pm, tours on the hour 10am–4pm (except noon). Free. MAP P.101, POCKET MAP D10

Theodore Roosevelt's birthplace was restored in 1923 to the way it would have been when he was born there in 1858; the family moved uptown when he was fourteen. The rather sombre mansion contains mostly original furnishings – a brilliant chandelier in the parlour and "Teedie's" crib – viewable on an obligatory guided tour; it doesn't take more than fifteen minutes to see it all. You might spend as much time in the attached galleries looking at hunting trophies and documents from Roosevelt's life.

GRAMERCY PARK

Irving Place, between 20th and 21st sts.
Subway #6 to 23rd St. MAP P.101, POCKET MAP E10

A former "little crooked swamp", **Gramercy Park** is one of the city's prettiest squares. The city's last private park, it is accessible only to those rich or fortunate enough to live here – or those staying at the nearby *Gramercy Park Hotel* (see p.178). Inside the gates stands a statue of the actor Edwin Booth, brother of Lincoln's assassin, John Wilkes Booth. The private **Players Club**, at 15 Gramercy Park, was founded by Booth and sits next door to the prestigious **National Arts Club** at no. 16, another members-oriented place, though you can sneak inside in the afternoons for the free art exhibits. The brick-red structure at no. 34 was one of the city's very first building cooperatives.

THE FLATIRON BUILDING

At Broadway, Fifth Ave and 23rd St. Subway N, R to 23rd St. MAP P.101, POCKET MAP D10

Set on a triangular, or iron-shaped, plot of land, the lofty, elegant 1902 **Flatiron Building** is covered with terracotta Medusa heads and other striking ornamentation. The uncommonly thin, tapered shape of this Daniel Burnham-designed skyscraper (tall for the time, at 307ft) caused consternation regarding its stability and wind-tunnel effects, but it has more than survived the years – it's become a New York symbol.

MADISON SQUARE PARK

E 23rd and 26th sts and Madison Ave and Broadway. Subway N, R to 23rd St. MAP P.101, POCKET MAP D10

Perhaps because of the stateliness of its buildings and the park-space in the middle,

Madison Square possesses a grandiosity that Union Square has long since lost. Next to the Art Deco Metropolitan Life Company's building and clock tower on the eastern side, the Corinthian-columned marble facade of the Appellate Division of the **New York State Supreme Court** is resolutely righteous with its statues of Justice, Wisdom and Peace, though the chamber where arguments are heard (Tues–Thurs 2pm) is well-nigh Rococo in its detail. The grand structure behind that, the 1928 **New York Life Building**, was the work of Cass Gilbert, creator of the Woolworth Building (see p.42).

There are plenty of places to sit and relax in and around the park, including a pedestrianized triangle on its western side. In the southeast corner is the original outpost of Danny Meyer's popular *Shake Shack* (see p.105), and at the northwest corner of 23rd and Broadway, the celebrity-chef-owned Eataly (see p.104).

MUSEUM OF MATHEMATICS

11 E 26th St, between Fifth and Madison aves. Subway N, R, #6 to 23rd St or 28th St ☎ 212 542 0566, ⓦ www.momath.org. Daily 10am–5pm. $15, kids 12 and under $9. MAP P.101, POCKET MAP D10

Somewhere between a high-minded institution and an interactive romper room, the **Museum of Mathematics** debuted in late 2012 with the goal of making maths fun and accessible to kids – and adults. Featuring roughly thirty exhibits on two floors, the gallery puts a focus on experience and engagement over understanding, with the idea that the latter will naturally follow; highlights include the square-wheeled tricycle and the Human Tree exhibit.

69TH REGIMENT ARMORY

68 Lexington Ave, between 25th and 26th sts. Subway #6 to 23rd or 28th sts ⓦ www.sixtyninth.net. MAP P.101, POCKET MAP E10.

The lumbering but landmarked **69th Regiment Armory** building, with its mansard roof and arched drill shed, was the site of the famous Armory Show of 1913, which brought modern art to New York; it was also, briefly, a very early home to the Knicks' basketball team. These days it retains its original function as the headquarters of the National Guard's "Fighting Sixth-Ninth", though its drill hall is still used for events and exhibitions.

THE EMPIRE STATE BUILDING

Fifth Ave and 34th St. Subway B, D, F, M, N, Q, R to 34th St ☎ 212 736 3100, ⓦ www.esbnyc.com. Daily 8am–2am, last trip 1.15am. $32, $26 for ages 6 to 12, additional $20 for ticket to 102nd-floor Observatory. MAP P.101, POCKET MAP D9

The 1931 **Empire State Building**, easily the city's most evocative symbol, was New

THE EMPIRE STATE BUILDING

York's tallest skyscraper for years until being topped by the original World Trade Center; after 9/11 it was the tallest once more, before being overtaken again by the new One World Trade Center in 2012. It stands at 102 floors and 1454ft – toe to TV mast – but its height is deceptive, rising in stately tiers with steady panache. Standing on Fifth Avenue below, it's easy to walk by without seeing it. From elsewhere, it can seem ubiquitous, especially at night, when it's lit in various colours.

Admire the immaculately restored Art Deco lobby and ceiling before the elevators take you to the main **86th-floor Observatory**. The views from the outside walkways here are as stunning as you'd expect; on a clear day visibility is up to eighty miles. A second set of elevators can take you to the smallish **102nd-floor Observatory**, at the base of the radio and TV antennas; the extra price makes it more for completists.

Shops

ABC CARPET AND HOME

888 Broadway, at E 19th St. Subway N, R to 23rd St. Mon–Wed & Fri–Sat 10am–7pm, Thurs 10am–8pm, Sun 11am–6.30pm. MAP P.101, POCKET MAP D11

Six floors of antiques and country furniture, knick-knacks, linens and, of course, carpets. The grandiose, museum-like setup is half the fun.

ACADEMY RECORDS

12 W 18th St, between Fifth and Sixth aves. Subway F, M to 14th St. Daily 11am–7pm. MAP P.101, POCKET MAP D11

Used, rare and hard-to-find music is the focus; this outlet has an exceptional selection for classical music fans.

BOOKS OF WONDER

18 W 18th St, between Fifth and Sixth aves. Subway #1 to 18th St, F, M to 14th St, L, N, Q, R, #4, #5, #6 to Union Square. Mon–Sat 10am–7pm, Sun 11am–6pm. MAP P.101, POCKET MAP D11

There's no better place in the city for kids' books; helpful staff, regular story times and frequent author readings make coming here a pleasure.

EATALY

200 Fifth Ave, at W 23rd St. Subway N, R to 23rd St, #6 to Astor Place. Market daily 9am–11pm, retailer hours vary. MAP P.101, POCKET MAP D10

This vast and wildly popular Mario Batali venture is part Italian café/restaurant complex, part food market. There is an incredible range of delicious wine, cheese, meat, bread and seafood for sale, sourced locally or flown in from Italy, and a wide choice of places to stop and try the tempting offerings – plus a rooftop beer bar (see p.107). Keep an eye out for tastings, classes and tours.

KALUSTYAN'S

KALUSTYAN'S

123 Lexington Ave, between E 28th and 29th sts. Subway #6 to 28th St. Mon–Sat 10am–8pm, Sun 11am–7pm. MAP P.101, POCKET MAP E10

This heavenly scented store has been selling a variety of Indian food products, spices and hard-to-find ingredients since 1944. Today its selection covers a range of foods from around the globe. The building was once home to President Chester A. Arthur.

THE OLD PRINT SHOP

150 Lexington Ave, between 29th & 30th sts. Subway #6 to 28th St. Sept–May Tues–Fri 9am–5pm, Sat 9am–4pm, June–Aug Mon–Thurs 9am–5pm, Fri 9am–4pm. MAP P.101, POCKET MAP E10

This fascinating and long-established shop is by far the best place to find yourself a great old map of a New York neighbourhood, a rare first-edition art book or a historic print from an old edition of *Harper's Weekly*.

Cafés and snacks

BREADS BAKERY

18 E 16th St, between Broadway and Fifth Ave. Subway L, N, Q, R, #4, #5, #6 to 14th St-Union Sq. Mon–Fri 6.30am–9pm, Sat 6.30am–8pm, Sun 7.30am–8pm. MAP P.101, POCKET MAP D11

You can't go wrong with the fresh-made breads, quiches or sandwiches, but it's the chocolate babka that draws raves as the city's best.

CITY BAKERY

3 W 18th St, between Fifth and Sixth aves. Subway F, M to 14th St. Mon–Fri 7.30am–7pm, Sat 8am–7pm, Sun 9am–6pm. MAP P.101, POCKET MAP D11

A smart stop for a satisfying lunch or a sweet-tooth craving. The vast array of pastries is head and shoulders above most in the city. Try a cookie or pretzel croissant with a hot chocolate.

EISENBERG'S SANDWICH SHOP

174 Fifth Ave, between E 22nd and 23rd sts. Subway N, R to 23rd St. Mon–Fri 6.30am–8pm, Sat 9.30am–6pm, Sun 9am–4pm. MAP P.101, POCKET MAP D10

A colourful luncheonette, this slice of NY life serves great tuna sandwiches ($7.50), matzoh ball soup ($4) and old-fashioned fountain sodas ($2).

NO. 7 SUB

1177 Broadway, between 28th and 29th sts, in the Ace Hotel. Subway N, R to 28th St ☎ 212 532 1680. Mon–Fri 8am–10.30am & 11.30am–5pm. MAP P.101, POCKET MAP D10

Part of the dazzling array of foodstuffs associated with the *Ace* hotel, this sandwich vendor deals up esoteric combinations that aren't done justice by their lists of ingredients (sample: broccoli, lychee muchim, feta, fried shallots). The menu changes, but you should do well whatever you choose ($7.75 half, $11.75 whole).

SHAKE SHACK

Madison Square Park, near Madison Ave and E 23rd St; other locations across the city. Subway N, R, #6 to 23rd St. Daily 11am–11pm. MAP P.101, POCKET MAP D10

Danny Meyer's leafy food kiosk has become a phenomenon, with a long wait for tables pretty much all day (try to avoid prime lunch and evening hours) and spawning Upper West Side and Soho offshoots, as well as a spot at the Mets' Citi Field. Folks come for perfectly grilled burgers and frozen custard shakes; everything is under $9.

STUMPTOWN COFFEE ROASTERS

18 W 29th St, between Broadway and Fifth Ave, in the Ace Hotel. Subway N, R to 28th St. Mon–Fri 6am–8pm, Sat & Sun 7am–8pm. MAP P.101, POCKET MAP D10

One of the country's most renowned coffee roasters brings its brews to a hip hotel; you'll have your latte methodically made by knowledgeable baristas. Cash only.

EISENBERG'S SANDWICH SHOP

Restaurants

15 EAST

15 E 15th St, between Fifth Ave and Broadway. Subway L, N, Q, R, #4, #5, #6 to 14th St-Union Square ☎212 647 0015. Mon–Fri noon–1.30pm & 6–10.30pm, Sat noon–1.30pm & 6–11pm. MAP P.101, POCKET MAP C17

The attention given to both cooked dishes (slow-poached octopus, sea urchin risotto) and fresh sushi/sashimi (chef's selection $65) elevates this stylish Japanese restaurant.

ABC KITCHEN

35 E 18th St, between Park Ave S and Broadway. Subway L, N, Q, R, #4, #5, #6 to 14th St-Union Square ☎212 475 5829. Mon–Wed noon–3pm & 5.30–10.30pm, Thurs noon–3pm & 5.30–11pm, Fri noon–3pm & 5.30–11.30pm, Sat 11am–3pm & 5.30–11.30pm, Sun 11am–3pm & 5.30–10pm. MAP P.101, POCKET MAP D11

Inside the ABC store (see p.104), this upscale resto from Jean-Georges Vongerichten focuses on market-fresh, seasonal ingredients. Get the crab toast ($16).

ALDEA

31 W 17th St, between Fifth and Sixth aves. Subway F, M to 14th St ☎212 675 7223. Tues–Thurs 5.30–10pm, Fri & Sat 5.30–11pm. MAP P.101, POCKET MAP D11

In a cool, relaxed dining room, Portuguese-accented dishes come exquisitely prepared and full of flavour. Prices are reasonable (entrees $24–36, prix fixe $79).

GRAMERCY TAVERN

42 E 20th St, between Broadway and Park Ave S. Subway N, R,#6 to 23rd St ☎212 477 0777. Main dining room: Mon–Thurs noon–2pm & 5.30–10pm, Fri noon–2pm & 5.30–11pm, Sat noon–1.30pm & 5.30–11pm, Sun 5.30–10pm; Front tavern: noon–11pm, later at weekends. MAP P.101, POCKET MAP D10

One of NYC's best restaurants; its neo-colonial decor, exquisite New American cuisine and perfect service make for a memorable meal. The seasonal tasting menus are well worth the steep prices ($125; three-course prix fixe $98), but you can also drop in for a drink or cheaper meal in the casual front room.

HILL COUNTRY

30 W 26th St, between Broadway and Sixth Ave. Subway N, R to 28th St, F to 23rd St ☎212 255 4544. Daily noon–2am, though kitchen closes 10pm Sun–Wed, 11pm Thurs and midnight Fri & Sat. MAP P.101, POCKET MAP D10

This Texas-style pioneer serves some of the best barbecue in the city, especially the moist, fatty brisket ($27/lb). Grab a table, then order your meats (all priced by the pound) and sides from the counters.

I TRULLI ENOTECA AND RISTORANTE

122 E 27th St, between Lexington and Park aves. Subway #6 to 28th St ☎212 481 7372. Mon–Thurs noon–3pm & 5.30–10.30pm, Fri noon–3pm & 5.30–11pm, Sat 5–11pm, Sun 5–10pm; Enoteca daily 3–10.30pm (food to takeout Mon–Thurs 11am–3pm). MAP P.101, POCKET MAP E10

Choose between the lovely restaurant serving quality southern Italian food and the impressive wine bar next door, which has a limited menu.

MAIALINO

Gramercy Park Hotel, 2 Lexington Ave. Subway #6 to 23rd St ☎212 777 2410. Mon–Thurs 7.30–10am, noon–2pm & 5.30–10.30pm, Fri 7.30–10am, noon–2pm & 5.30–11pm, Sat 10am–2.30pm & 5.30–11pm, Sun 10am–2.30pm & 5.30–10.30pm. MAP P.101, POCKET MAP E10

Danny Meyer's attractive Roman trattoria, looking out on Gramercy Park, is both rustic and refined. Much of the focus is on the hog (which gives the place its name) – the special is roast suckling pig. Reservations recommended, though the bar is open all day.

Bars

230 FIFTH

230 Fifth Ave. Subway N, R, #6 to 23rd St.
Mon–Fri 4pm–4am, Sat & Sun 10am–4am.
MAP P.101, POCKET MAP D10

Classy lounge bar with the
biggest roof garden in the
city – blankets and heaters are
provided in winter. Drinks and
snacks are reasonably priced for
the experience (Martinis from
$14; no cover). No sneakers/
trainers or T-shirts for men.

BIRRERIA

Eataly, 200 Fifth Ave, at 23rd St. Subway N, R,
#6 to 23rd St ☎ 212 937 8910. Mon–Wed &
Sun 11.30am–10pm, Thurs–Sat 11.30am–11pm.
MAP P.101, POCKET MAP D10

A sprawling rooftop bar, *Birreria*
is a modern twist on the beer
garden with handcrafted ales and
home-made sausages on offer.

DEAR IRVING

55 Irving Plaza, between E 17th and 18th
sts. Subway L, N, Q, R, #4, #5, #6 to 14th
St-Union Square. Mon–Thurs 5pm–2am,
Fri–Sat 5pm–3am, Sun 5pm–1am.
MAP P.101, POCKET MAP E11

Up a flight of stairs and behind
an innocuous door, this
speakeasy-lounge offers
expertly made cocktails and
attentive service.

MOLLY'S

287 Third Ave, between E 22nd and 23rd sts.
Subway #6 to 23rd St. Daily 11am–4am.
MAP P.101, POCKET MAP E10

While the city trends move
toward gastropubs and
handcrafted cocktails, the
friendly bartenders at *Molly's*
pour the best pints of Guinness.

OLD TOWN BAR & RESTAURANT

45 E 18th St, between Broadway and Park
Ave S. Subway L, N, Q, R, #4, #5, #6 to 14th
St-Union Square. Mon–Fri 11.30am–2am,
Sat noon–2am, Sun 1pm–midnight.
MAP P.101, POCKET MAP D11

PETE'S TAVERN

This atmospheric and spacious
bar is popular with publishing
types, models and
photographers. Great burgers.

PETE'S TAVERN

129 E 18th St, at Irving Place. Subway L, N, Q,
R, #4, #5, #6 to 14th St Union Square. Mon–
Thurs & Sun 11am–2am, Fri & Sat 11am–4am.
MAP P.101, POCKET MAP E11

Former speakeasy that claims
to be the oldest bar in New
York – it opened in 1864. These
days it inevitably trades on its
history, though its well-worn
counter and outdoor seating
are convivial enough.

Clubs and music venues

BLUE SMOKE: JAZZ STANDARD

116 E 27th St, between Park and Lexington
aves. Subway #6 to 28th St ☎ 212 576 2232,
Ⓦ www.jazzstandard.com. Sets at 7.30pm
and 9.30pm Mon–Thurs & Sun, with an extra
set at 11.30pm Fri & Sat. Cover $20–35.
MAP P.101, POCKET MAP E10

This gourmet club books all
flavours of jazz and serves
sublime BBQ, the best in-club
grub in town.

Midtown

The largely corporate and commercial area east of Sixth Avenue all the way to the river, from the 40s through the 50s, is known as Midtown. You'll find the city's sniffiest boutiques, best Art Deco facades and exemplary Modernist skyscrapers scattered primarily along E 42nd and E 57th streets and Fifth, Madison and Park avenues. Fifth is the grand sight- and store-studded spine of Manhattan; the sidewalks nearly reach a standstill at Christmas, with shoppers stalled at elaborate window displays. Cornelius Vanderbilt's Beaux Arts train station, Grand Central Terminal, anchors Park Avenue, while major museums and city symbols such as the Museum of Modern Art, Rockefeller Center and the United Nations dot the rest of the landscape.

THE MORGAN LIBRARY AND MUSEUM

225 Madison Ave, between E 36th and 37th sts. Subway #6 to 33rd St ☎ 212 685 0008, Ⓦ www.themorgan.org. Tues–Thurs 10.30am–5pm, Fri 10.30am–9pm, Sat 10am–6pm, Sun 11am–6pm. $18, free Fri 7–9pm. MAP P.109, POCKET MAP D9

The uplifting **Morgan Library** in Murray Hill was originally built to hold the fruits of financier J.P. Morgan's collecting sprees during frequent trips abroad; he claimed keen interest in "all the beautiful things in the world", in this case, illuminated manuscripts, paintings, prints and furniture. A stunning Renzo Piano-designed gathering space brings together Morgan's library, annex and Morgan Jr's nineteenth-century brownstone.

The collection of nearly 10,000 drawings and prints, including works by Da Vinci, Degas and Dürer, is augmented by the rare literary manuscripts of Dickens, Jane Austen and Thoreau, as well

GRAND CENTRAL TERMINAL

as hand-written correspondence between Ernest Hemingway and George Plimpton and musical scribblings by everyone from Haydn to Dylan. Morgan's personal library and study, part of the just-restored McKim building at the core of the complex, are also on view.

GRAND CENTRAL TERMINAL

E 42nd St, between Lexington and Vanderbilt aves. Subway S, #4, #5, #6, #7 to 42nd St-Grand Central ☎ 212 935 3960 or ☎ 212 883 2420 for tours, ⓦ www .grandcentralterminal.com.
MAP P.109, POCKET MAP E6

Grand Central Depot opened in 1871 under the direction of Cornelius Vanderbilt, but the current masterly piece of urban planning that replaced it, **Grand Central Terminal**, was built in 1913. With a basic iron frame and dramatic Beaux-Arts skin, the main train station's

concourse is a sight to behold – 470ft long and 150ft high, it boasts a barrel-vaulted ceiling speckled like a Baroque church with a painted representation of the winter night sky. The station's more esoteric reaches include a lower concourse brimming with takeout options as well as the landmark *Oyster Bar and Restaurant* (see p.120). Daily tours ($25; 75min) of the station begin at 12.30pm from the main information booth; a 12.30pm tour on Fridays (free; 90min) takes in some of the neighbouring area as well and starts across the street in the glass atrium of 120 Park Avenue. You can also embark on an informative, self-guided audio tour (daily 9am–6pm; $9) by picking up a device at one of the windows marked "GCT Tour", on the main concourse.

A must-visit only for those obsessed by global goings-on, the **United Nations complex** comprises the glass-curtained Secretariat, the curving sweep of the General Assembly and, connecting them, the low-rising Conference Wing. Tours – bring ID for security purposes and arrive early – take in the UN conference chambers and its constituent parts. Even more revealing than the stately rooms are its thoughtful exhibition spaces and country gifts on view.

THE MET LIFE BUILDING

200 Park Ave, between E 44th and E 45th sts. Subway S, #4, #5, #6, #7 to 42nd St-Grand Central. MAP P.109, POCKET MAP E8

The unsubtle bulk of the **Met Life Building**, looming over the southern end of Park Avenue before its interruption by Grand Central, steals the thunder of many of the more delicate structures around it. Bauhaus guru Walter Gropius had a hand in the design, and the critical consensus is that he could have done better. As the headquarters of the now-defunct Pan Am airline, the building, in profile, was meant to suggest an aircraft wing. The blue-grey mass certainly adds drama to the cityscape, even as it seals the avenue at 44th Street.

WALDORF ASTORIA HOTEL

301 Park Ave, between E 49th and E 50th sts. Subway #6 to 51st St. MAP P.109, POCKET MAP E8

The solid mass of the 1931 **Waldorf Astoria Hotel** helps contribute to the conspicuous wealth of Park Avenue. Even if you're not lucky enought to be staying here (see p.179), duck inside the block-long lobby to stroll through vintage Deco grandeur, sweeping marble and hushed luxury, which continues

THE CHRYSLER BUILDING

405 Lexington Ave, between E 42nd and E 43rd sts. Subway S, #4, #5, #6, #7 to 42nd St-Grand Central. Lobby Mon–Fri 8am–6pm. MAP P.109, POCKET MAP E8

One of Manhattan's best-loved structures, the **Chrysler Building** dates from a time (1928–30) when architects married prestige with grace and style. The car-motif friezes, jutting gargoyles and arched stainless-steel pinnacle give the solemn Midtown skyline a welcome whimsical touch. The lobby, once a car showroom, is all you can see of the building's interior – still worth it to get a look at the walls covered in African marble, murals depicting aeroplanes, machines and the brawny builders who worked on the tower, and showy elevator doors with inlaid wood.

THE UNITED NATIONS

First Ave, at E 46th St. Subway S, #4, #5, #6, #7 to 42nd St-Grand Central ☎ 212 963 8687, ⓦ www.visit.un.org. Guided tours (45min) Mon–Fri 9.30am–4.45pm. $20, $11 children 5–12. MAP P.109, POCKET MAP F8

downstairs in the grand circular bar of the *Bull and Bear*.

ST BARTHOLOMEW'S CHURCH

325 Park Ave, at E 51st St. Subway #6 to 51st St ⓦwww.stbarts.org. Daily 9am–6pm, choir service Sun 11am. MAP P.109, POCKET MAP E8

The Episcopalian **St Bartholomew's Church** is a low-slung Romanesque hybrid with portals designed by McKim, Mead, and White. Adding immeasurably to the street, it gives the lumbering skyscrapers a much-needed sense of scale. Due to the fact that it's on some of the city's most valuable real estate, the church fought against developers for years and ultimately became a test case for New York City's landmark preservation law.

THE SEAGRAM BUILDING

375 Park Ave, between E 52nd and E 53rd sts. Subway E, M Lexington Ave/53rd St, #6 to 51st St. MAP P.109, POCKET MAP E7

Designed by Mies van der Rohe with Philip Johnson, the 1958 **Seagram Building** was the seminal curtain-wall skyscraper. Its floors are supported internally, allowing for a skin of smoky glass and whisky-bronze metal. Every interior detail – from the fixtures to the lettering on the mailboxes – was specially designed. The plaza, an open forecourt designed to set the building apart from its neighbours, was such a success that the city revised the zoning laws to encourage other high-rise builders to supply similar public spaces.

More Midtown monoliths

The city, especially Midtown, is filled with far too many landmark, innovative or just plain unusual buildings to list in these pages. If you're interested in the subject of architecture, try to catch the following in addition to the ones described in this chapter: the **Ford Foundation Building**, 320 E 43rd St, between First and Second aves, whose atrium is one of New York's great indoor/outdoor experiences; Philip Johnson's **Lipstick Building**, 885 Third Ave, between E 53rd and 54th sts, named for its curved, telescoping shape; and the right-angle steel and glass slabs of the **Lever House**, 390 Park Ave, also between E 53rd and 54th sts.

CITIGROUP CENTER

601 Lexington Ave, between E 53rd and E 54th sts. Subway #6 to 51st St.
MAP P.109, POCKET MAP E7

Opened in 1978, the chisel-topped **Citigroup Center** (formerly the Citicorp Center) is one of Manhattan's most conspicuous landmarks. The slanted roof was designed to house solar panels to provide power for the building, and it adopted the distinctive building-top as a corporate logo. Inside lies small **St Peter's Church**, known as "the Jazz Church" for being the venue of many a jazz musician's funeral; jazz vespers are held on Sundays at 5pm.

THE SONY BUILDING

550 Madison Ave, between E 55th and E 56th sts. Subway E, M to 5th Ave/53rd St or Lexington Ave/53rd St. MAP P.109, POCKET MAP D7

Philip Johnson's 38-storey **Sony Building** (1978–84) follows the Postmodernist theory of eclectic borrowing from historical styles: a Modernist skyscraper sandwiched between a Chippendale top and a Renaissance base. Even though the first floor is well worth ducking into to soak in the brute grandeur, some speculate Johnson should have followed the advice of his teacher, Mies van der Rohe: "It's better to build a good building than an original one."

THE NEW YORK PUBLIC LIBRARY

E 42nd St and Fifth Ave. Subway B, D, F, M, #4, #5, #6 to 42nd St ☎ 917 275 6975, ⓦ www.nypl.org. Mon & Thurs–Sat 10am–6pm, Tues & Wed 10am–8pm, Sun 1–5pm (except in summer), building tours Mon–Sat 11am & 2pm, Sun 2pm.
MAP P.109, POCKET MAP D8

This monumental Beaux Arts building, faced in brilliant white marble (and recently restored for the library's centennial), is the headquarters of the largest public-library system in the world. Plenty of folks meet at the **NYPL**'s steps, framed by two majestic

NEW YORK PUBLIC LIBRARY

reclining lions, to while away the time; head inside to explore the place on your own or to take a free guided tour. The latter gives a good all-round picture of the building, taking in the **Map Room** and evocative **Periodicals Room**, with its stunning faux-wood ceiling and paintings of old New York. The undisputed highlight, however, is the large, coffered 636-seat **Reading Room** on the third floor, which was restored in 2016. Authors Norman Mailer and E.L. Doctorow worked here, as did Leon Trotsky during his brief sojourn in New York just prior to the 1917 Russian Revolution. It was also here that Chester Carlson came up with the idea for the Xerox copier and Norbert Pearlroth whiled away the better part of 52 years researching columns for "Ripley's Believe It or Not." More than anything, you may find the building familiar from its roles in all kinds of movies, including *Ghostbusters* and *Breakfast at Tiffany's*.

BRYANT PARK

BRYANT PARK

Sixth Ave, between W 40th and 42nd sts.
Subway B, D, F, M to 42nd St
☎ 212 768 4242, ⓦ www.bryantpark.org.
Daily 7am–10pm, later May–Sept
MAP P.109, POCKET MAP D8

Right behind the public library, **Bryant Park** is a grassy, square block filled with slender trees, flowerbeds, a small carousel and inviting chairs. It officially became a park in 1847 and is named after a newspaper editor – William Cullen Bryant of the *New York Post*, also famed as a poet and instigator of Central Park. Bryant Park was the site of the first American World's Fair in 1853, with a Crystal Palace, modelled on the famed London Crystal Palace, on its grounds –

an edifice that burned down in 1858. Summertime brings a lively scene to the park all day long: free jazz and yoga classes, table tennis and free outdoor movies on Monday evenings; come winter there's a holiday market and an ice-skating rink (roughly Nov–Feb; free entry, skate rentals extra). A tiny carousel ($3) operates year-round.

DIAMOND ROW

W 47th St, between Fifth and Sixth aves.
Subway B, D, F, M to 47–50th St-Rockefeller
Center. MAP P.109, POCKET MAP D8

You'll know **Diamond Row** by the diamond-shaped lamps mounted on pylons at either end. This strip, where you can get jewellery fixed at reasonable prices, features wholesale and retail shops chock-full of gems and was first established in the 1920s. These stores are largely managed by Hasidic Jews, and the workaday vibe feels more like the Garment District or the old Lower East Side than a part of tourist Midtown.

ROCKEFELLER CENTER

From Fifth to Sixth aves, between W 48th and W 51st sts. Subway B, D, F, M to 47–50th St/Rockefeller Center ☎212 332 6868, ⓦwww.rockefellercenter .com. Tours daily 10am–7.30pm, every 30min, $20 (☎212 698 2000 ext 5).
MAP P.109, POCKET MAP D8

The heart of Midtown's glamour, **Rockefeller Center** was built between 1932 and 1940 by John D. Rockefeller Jr, son of the oil magnate, and is one of the finest pieces of urban planning anywhere, balancing office space with cafés, underground concourses and rooftop gardens that work together with a rare intelligence and grace. At its centre, the **Lower Plaza** holds a sunken restaurant in the summer months. It's a great place for afternoon cocktails beneath Paul Manship's golden *Prometheus* sculpture. In winter this area becomes an ice rink for skaters, and every Christmas since 1931, a huge tree has been on display above the statue; its lighting, with accompanying musical entertainment, draws throngs in early December.

THE GE BUILDING

30 Rockefeller Plaza, between W 49th and W 50th sts. Subway B, D, F, M to 47–50th St/Rockefeller Center. NBC studio tours daily 8.30am–5pm, ⓦwww.thetouratnbc studios.com. ☎212 664 3700. $33, children 6–12 $29. Tapings ☎212 664 3056, ⓦwww .nbc.com/tickets-and-nbc-studio-tour.
MAP P.109, POCKET MAP D8

Perhaps the apogee of Art Deco styling, the **GE Building** (or **30 Rock**) rises 850ft, its symmetrical monumental lines matching the scale of Manhattan itself. In the GE lobby, José Maria Sert's murals, *American Progress* and *Time*, are in tune with the 1930s Art Deco ambience – though paintings by Diego Rivera were scrapped after the artist refused to remove an image glorifying Lenin. Among the building's many offices are the **NBC Studios**, which produce the long-running comedy hit *Saturday Night Live* and *The Tonight Show Starring Jimmy Fallon*. Studio tours and tapings of select shows (limited availability) should satisfy most curiosity seekers.

City views

Top of the Rock and the Empire State Building are the obvious places to go for panoramic views of New York, but you can save a bit of money and find unique angles on the city at any of the following:

The mid-point of **Brooklyn Bridge** (p.42), to see the Financial District.

The **High Line** (p.92), for a look up Tenth Avenue.

General Worth Square next to Madison Square Park (p.102), for a look at the Flatiron, Metlife tower, the park and a lot of whizzing traffic.

The Roof Garden Café at the Met (p.145), for views of Central Park.

Empire Fulton Ferry in Dumbo (p.161), for glimpses of the Brooklyn and Manhattan bridges.

TOP OF THE ROCK OBSERVATION DECK

30 Rockefeller Plaza at W 50th St. Subway B, D, F, M to 47–50th St/Rockefeller Center ☎ 212 698 2000, Ⓦ www.topoftherocknyc .com. Daily 8am–midnight, last elevator at 11pm. $32, children 6–12 $26. MAP P.109, POCKET MAP D8

It's a lot to pay for a view, but what a view. Arguably as grand as that from the Empire State Building (with the added bonus of being to able to see the Empire State), the panorama from the top of the **GE Building** lets you examine the layout of Central Park and how built-up downtown is compared to uptown, offers a vertiginous look at St Patrick's Cathedral and looks out to the George Washington Bridge and beyond. The film that introduces a bit of history on Rockefeller Center is missable; just head to the elevator that whisks you up to floor 67, with additional decks on floors 69 and 70 accessible by stairs.

RADIO CITY MUSIC HALL

1260 Sixth Ave, at W 50th St. Subway B, D, F, M to 47–50th St/Rockefeller Center. Tickets ☎ 1 866 858 0008, tours ☎ 212 247 4777, Ⓦ www.radiocity.com. Daily 11am–3pm. Tour $26.95, children 12 and under $19.95, ticket prices for concerts vary. MAP P.109, POCKET MAP D8

Heralded by one of the most familiar marquees in New York, the world-famous concert hall **Radio City** is the last word in 1930s luxury. If you're not taking in a show – greats such as Sinatra used to grace the stage here, but these days it's better-known for its "Christmas Spectacular" than for any major bookings – you'll need to join one of the hour-long "Stage Door" behind-the-scenes walking tours to see it. The staircase is resplendent, with the world's largest chandeliers, while the huge auditorium looks like an extravagant scalloped shell. The movable parts of the stage hold some fascination, and there's a brief meeting with (and photo of) a Rockette too.

RADIO CITY MUSIC HALL

ST PATRICK'S CATHEDRAL

50th St and Fifth Ave. Subway B, D, F, M to 47–50th St/Rockefeller Center ☎ 212 753 2261, ⓦ www.saintpatricks cathedral.org. Daily 6.30am–8.45pm, services throughout the day. MAP P.109, POCKET MAP D6

Designed by James Renwick and completed in 1888, **St Patrick's Cathedral** is the result of a painstaking academic tour of the Gothic cathedrals of Europe – perfect in detail, yet rather lifeless in spirit, with a sterility made all the more striking by the glass-black **Olympic Tower** next door, an exclusive apartment block where Jackie Kennedy Onassis once lived.

PALEY CENTER FOR MEDIA

25 W 52nd St, between Fifth and Sixth aves. Subway B, D, F, M to 47–50th St/Rockefeller Center, E, M to Fifth Ave/53rd St ☎ 212 621 6800, ⓦ www.paleycenter.org/visit. Wed–Sun noon–6pm, Thurs noon–8pm. $10, under 14 $5. MAP P.109, POCKET MAP D7

The former Museum of Television and Radio still largely centres on its extensive archive of American TV and radio broadcasts, so if you want to view episodes of beloved but short-lived series like *Freaks and Geeks* or old classics like *Dragnet* or the *Honeymooners*,

this is the place. An excellent computerized reference system lets you have a show at your fingertips in no time.

THE MUSEUM OF MODERN ART

11 W 53rd St between Fifth and Sixth aves. Subway B, D, F, M to 47–50th St/ Rockefeller Center, E, M to Fifth St/53rd St ☎ 212 708 9400, ⓦ www.moma.org. Mon, Wed, Thurs, Sat & Sun 10.30am–5.30pm, Fri 10.30am–8pm. $25, children 16 and under free, free Fri 4–8pm. MAP P.109, POCKET MAP D7

The Museum of Modern Art – **MoMA** to its friends – offers the finest and most complete account of late nineteenth- and twentieth-century art you're likely to find in the world. More than 100,000 paintings, sculptures, drawings, prints, photographs, architectural models and design objects make up the collection, along with a world-class film archive. Note that the specifics below represent what is typically on display. Pieces rotate with some regularity, though the biggest names can always be found.

The core is the **Paintings and Sculpture galleries**, and if this is your priority, head straight for the fifth floor – to

ST PATRICK'S CATHEDRAL

Painting and Sculpture 1, which starts with Cézanne, Gauguin and the Post-Impressionists of the late nineteenth century, takes in Picasso, Braque and Matisse (who has his own dedicated room, highlighted by the self-referential *Red Studio* and odd perspective of *The Dance*), moves through De Chirico, Duchamp and Mondrian, and finishes up with the surrealists Miró, Magritte and Dalí.

Painting and Sculpture 2, on the fourth floor, displays work from the 1940s to 1980s and inevitably has a more American feel, with works by Abstract Expressionists Pollock, Rothko and Barnett Newman, as well as lots of familiar work from the modern canon – Jasper Johns' *Flag*, Robert Rauschenberg's mixed media paintings, Warhol's soup cans and Roy Lichtenstein's cartoons.

The third-floor **Photography galleries** rotate frequently, but holdings include photos of Paris by Cartier-Bresson and Richard Avedon's penetrating portraits of cultural icons. **Architecture and Design**, on the same floor, hosts revolving exhibits showcasing every aspect of design from the mid-nineteenth century on. **The Drawing galleries**, also on this floor, feature a glittering array of twentieth-century artists – Lucien Freud, Robert Rauschenberg and his old roommate Willem de Kooning, among many others. Finally, the spacious second-floor galleries give MoMA the chance to feature contemporary art (1980s to present) in all media.

If you need to refuel, the second-floor café, *Café 2*, serves

very good, slickly presented Italian-style food. *Terrace 5*, on the fifth floor, is a more formal option, and provides nice views of the ground-level sculpture garden (which opens early, perfect for a morning stroll). A swanky restaurant, *The Modern*, sits on the first floor.

TRUMP TOWER

725 Fifth Ave, between 56th and 57th sts. Subway F to 57th St. MAP P.109, POCKET MAP D7

New York real-estate developer (and, at time of press, would-be US president) Donald Trump's outrageously overdone high-rise and atrium, **Trump Tower**, is just short of repellent to many – though perhaps not to those who frequent the boutiques on the lower floors. Perfumed air, polished marble panelling and a five-storey waterfall are calculated to knock you senseless. The building is clever, a neat little outdoor garden is squeezed high in a corner, and each of the 230 apartments above the atrium provides views in three directions.

Shops

APPLE STORE

767 Fifth Ave, between 58th and 59th sts;
other locations. Subway N, R to 5th
Ave/59th St. Daily 24hr. MAP P.109,
POCKET MAP D7

There are now eight Apple
stores in town, though this is
the only 24hr one – and
purportedly the biggest
moneymaking retail outfit on
Fifth Avenue. A giant glass cube
rises from the sidewalk to
herald the entrance; descend the
spiral staircase within to see the
latest in gadgets and to take part
in free demos and workshops.

BERGDORF GOODMAN

754 and 745 Fifth Ave, at 58th St. Subway F
to 57th St, N, R to Fifth Ave/59th St.
Mon–Sat 10am–8pm, Sun 11am–7pm.
MAP P.109, POCKET MAP D7

This venerable department store
caters to the city's wealthiest
shoppers and, in an unusual
setup, flanks Fifth Avenue.
Haute couture designers fill both
buildings, one for men, one for
women. Its holiday windows are
among the flashiest in town.

BLOOMINGDALE'S

1000 Third Ave, at E 59th St. Subway N, R,
#4, #5, #6 to 59th St. Mon–Sat
10am–8.30pm, Sun 11am–7pm. MAP P.109,
POCKET MAP E7

One of Manhattan's most
famous department stores,
packed with designer clothiers,
perfume concessions and
housewares.

SAKS FIFTH AVENUE

611 Fifth Ave, at 50th St. Subway E, M to
53rd St, B, D, F, M to 47–50th St/Rockefeller
Center. Mon–Sat 10am–8.30pm, Sun
11am–7pm. MAP P.109, POCKET MAP D8

Every bit as glamorous as it was
when it opened in 1922, Saks
remains virtually synonymous
with style and quality.

TIFFANY'S

TANNEN'S MAGIC

45 W 34th St, Suite 608, between Fifth and
Sixth aves. Subway B, D, F, M, N, Q, R to 34th
St-Herald Square. Mon–Fri 11am–6pm, Sat &
Sun 10am–4pm. MAP P.109, POCKET MAP D9

Your kids will never forget a
visit to the largest magic shop
in the world, full of props,
tricks and magic sets, and staff
who can demonstrate tricks.

TIFFANY & CO.

727 Fifth Ave, at E 57th St. Subway N, R, W
to Fifth Ave/59th St. Mon–Sat 10am–7pm,
Sun noon–6pm. MAP P.109, POCKET MAP D7

Tiffany's soothing green marble
and weathered wood interior is
perhaps best described by
Truman Capote's fictional Holly
Golightly: "It calms me down
right away… nothing very bad
could happen to you there."

Cafés and snacks

LUCID CAFÉ

311 Lexington Ave, at 38th St. Subway #4,
#5, #6, #7 to 42nd St-Grand Central. Mon–Fri
7am–5pm, Sat 8am–5pm, Sun 8am–3pm.
MAP P.109, POCKET MAP E9

You'd do well to grab one of the two window seats and enjoy a strong shot of espresso ($2.75) or a cortado ($3.75) alongside a buttery croissant at this tiny, charming spot.

THE PLAZA FOOD HALL

1 W 58th St, Concourse Level of The Plaza. Subway N, Q, R to Fifth Ave-59th St. Mon–Sat 8am–9.30pm, Sun 11am–6pm. MAP P.109, POCKET MAP D7

On the lower level of this venerable hotel, outlets of *No. 7 Sub* (see p.105), *Luke's Lobster* and others have set up shop; there's also the Todd English Food Hall (daily 11am–10pm) within the food hall, where the celebrity chef offers raw shellfish, wood-fired pizza and grilled meats.

Restaurants

AI FIORI

400 Fifth Ave, between 36th and 37th sts in the Langham Place hotel. Subway B, D, F, M, N, Q, R to 34th St-Herald Square; #6 to 33rd St ☎ 212 613 8660. Mon–Thurs 7–10.30am, noon–2.15pm & 5.30–10pm, Fri 7–10.30am, noon–2.15pm & 5–10pm, Sat 8–10.30am, 11.45am–2.30pm & 5–10.15pm, Sun 8–10.30am, 11am–2.15pm & 5.30–9pm. MAP P.109, POCKET MAP D9

The decor and atmosphere are unmemorable, but the elegant French-Italian dishes are anything but. Splurge on the four-course prix-fixe menu ($97), which allows you to choose your dishes (butter-poached lobster, for example) from the outstanding regular menu.

AQUAVIT

65 E 55th St, between Madison and Park aves. Subway #6 to 51st St ☎ 212 307 7311. Mon–Thurs 11.45am–2.30pm & 5.30–10pm, Fri 11.45am–2.30pm & 5.30–10.30pm, Sat 5.30–10.30pm. MAP P.109, POCKET MAP D7

Go for a blowout in the main dining room (three courses run to about $95) or a more casual meal in the bar-lounge. Either way, you'll sample Scandi food at its finest: silky gravlax, herring, Swedish meatballs and, of course, a home-made version of the eponymous spirit.

CHO DANG GOL

55 W 35th St, between Fifth and Sixth aves. Subway B, D, F, M, N, Q, R to 34th St ☎ 212 695 8222. Daily 11.30am–10pm. MAP P.109, POCKET MAP D9

Korean restaurants proliferate on 32nd Street between Fifth and Sixth; this one, a little off the path, specializes in home-made tofu every which way. There's more, though, like simmered pork belly served as part of a spicy lettuce wrap.

HATSUHANA

17 E 48th St, between Fifth and Madison aves. Subway #6 to 51st St ☎ 212 355 3345; another branch at 237 Park Ave. Mon–Fri noon–2.30pm & 5.30–10pm, Sat 5–10pm. MAP P.109, POCKET MAP D8

A longtime favourite of local sushi lovers, this place is not cheap but won't break the bank – and the freshness of the fish compensates in any case.

AQUAVIT

KEENS STEAKHOUSE

72 W 36th St, between Fifth and Sixth aves. Subway B, D, F, M, N, Q, R to 34th St-Herald Square ☎ 212 947 3636. Mon–Fri 11.45am–10.30pm, Sat 5–10.30pm, Sun 5–9.30pm. MAP P.109, POCKET MAP D9

This 130-year-old chophouse is a classic; the bustling pub makes a great place for a Martini and junior-sized mutton chop ($29.50), or you can go all out on the larger cuts served in the rambling dining room.

LA GRENOUILLE

3 E 52nd St, between Fifth and Madison aves. Subway E, M to Fifth Ave-53rd St ☎ 212 752 1495. Tues–Fri noon–2.30pm & 5–10.30pm, Sat 5–10.30pm. MAP P.109, POCKET MAP D7

The haute French cuisine here has melted hearts and tantalized palates since 1962. All the classics are done to perfection, and the service is gracious. Its prix-fixe lunch is $60, and dinner is $138 per person. Jacket required.

THE MODERN

9 W 53rd St. Subway E, M to Fifth Ave-53rd St ☎ 212 333 1220. Mon–Fri noon–2pm & 5–10.30pm, Sat 5–10.30pm, Bar Room only on Sun 11.30am–9.30pm. MAP P.109, POCKET MAP D7

MoMA's fine-dining offering is elegant without trying too hard. Seasonal ingredients are artfully combined to yield unexpected dishes: say, chorizo-crusted codfish with white cocoa-bean purée. Four-course set meals cost from $128. The *Bar Room at the Modern* offers more casual dining.

OYSTER BAR

Lower level, Grand Central Terminal, at 42nd St and Park Ave. Subway S, #4, #5, #6, #7 to 42nd St-Grand Central ☎ 212 490 6650. Mon–Sat 11.30am–9.30pm. MAP P.109, POCKET MAP E8

Down in the vaulted cellars of Grand Central, the fabled (and

OYSTER BAR

just restored) *Oyster Bar* draws Midtown office workers for lunch and seafood-lovers for dinner, who choose from a staggering list of daily catches including barramundi and steamed Maine lobster. Prices are moderate to expensive, but you can always choose chowder, a pan roast or a sandwich from the counter.

SARGE'S DELI

548 Third Ave, between 36th and 37th sts. Subway #6 to 33rd St ☎ 212 679 0442. Daily 24hr. MAP P.109, POCKET MAP E9

Want a classic NYC deli without the hype of the overtouristed spots? Come for a pile of pastrami (or whatever you like) at this friendly Murray Hill place that's run by a former police officer.

Bars

CAMPBELL APARTMENT

Grand Central Terminal, southwest balcony, E 42nd St. Subway S, #7,#4, #5, #6 to 42nd St-Grand Central ☎ 212 953 0409. Mon–Thurs noon–1am, Fri noon–2am, Sat 2pm–2am, Sun 2pm–midnight. MAP P.109, POCKET MAP E8

Once home of businessman John W. Campbell, who oversaw the construction of Grand Central, this majestic built to look like a thirteenth-century Florentine palace – was sealed up for years. Now, it's one of New York's most distinctive bars – although at time of press it had changed hands and was temporarily closed. Check in advance.

KING COLE BAR

2 E 55th St, between Fifth and Madison aves, in the St Regis Hotel. Subway E, M to Fifth Ave-53rd St, F to 57th St. Mon–Sat 11.30am–1am, Sun noon–midnight.
MAP P.109, POCKET MAP D7

Dress smart and be prepared to spend at the reputed home of the Bloody Mary (here known as the Red Snapper), but sipping a cocktail under the Maxfield Parrish mural at the bar, you'll surely feel like a million bucks.

PJ CLARKE'S

915 Third Ave, at E 55th St. Subway #6 to 51st St, E, M to Lexington Ave/53rd St

📞 212 317 1616. Daily 11.30am–4am.
MAP P.109, POCKET MAP E7

One of the city's most famous watering holes, *PJ Clarke's* alehouse serves good beers, but only Guinness comes in a pint serving. Tables with red-and-white-checked cloths await diners in the back, where you can choose from a classic American menu. You may recognize it as the setting of the film *The Lost Weekend*.

SALVATION TACO

145 E 39th St, between Lexington and Third aves, inside Pod Hotel. Subway #4, #5, #6, #7 to 42nd St-Grand Central 📞 212 865 5800, 🌐 www.salvationtaco.com. Daily 7am–2am.
MAP P.109, POCKET MAP E9

Hard to know what to label it – café, restaurant, gastrocantina – but *Salvation Taco*, in all its garishly hued, folk-art aesthetic glory, is best as a bar for daring cocktails (around $13) and inventive snacks, like a tostada with pig's ears and cheeks ($13).

PJ CLARKE'S

Times Square and the Theater District

The towering signs and flashing lights of Times Square, the blocks just north of 42nd Street where Seventh Avenue intersects with Broadway, bring a whole new meaning to the term "sensory overload". More than 300,000 people pass through daily, and on New Year's Eve hundreds of thousands more come to watch the apple drop at midnight. The seedy days are gone, but ostentatious displays of media and commercialism still reign. The adjoining Theater District and its million-dollar Broadway productions draw crowds, while Hell's Kitchen to the west offers innumerable restaurants as well as some gritty nightlife. You may wind up spending a decent amount of time here – it's a major hotel base and you'll probably want to take in a show or two – but there are few, if any, must-see sights (other than the sheer spectacle).

TIMES SQUARE

Broadway, Seventh Ave and 42nd St. Subway
N, Q, R, #1, #2, #3 to Times Square-42nd St
Ⓦ www.timessquarenyc.org. MAP P.123,
POCKET MAP D8

If not always so in the public imagination, **Times Square** is now a largely sanitized universe of popular consumption. It takes its name from the *New York Times* offices built in 1904 (the current *Times* building, a Renzo Piano creation, is at Eighth Avenue between 40th and 41st streets); publisher Adolph Ochs staged a New Year's celebration here in honour of their opening. This

TIMES SQUARE

tradition continues today: hundreds of thousands arrive early to pack the streets, party (as best they can without being able to purchase or publicly consume alcohol) and watch the giant Waterford Crystal Ball drop on One Times Square. The neon, so much a signature of the square, was initially confined to the theatres and spawned the term "the Great White Way", but myriad ads for hundreds of products now form one of the world's most garish nocturnal displays.

HELL'S KITCHEN

MAP P.123, POCKET MAP C8

Between 34th and 59th streets west of Eighth Avenue, **Hell's Kitchen** mostly centres on the engaging slash of restaurants, bars, ethnic delis and food shops of Ninth Avenue (which has begun to extend farther west) –

the staging set for the excellent **Ninth Avenue International Food Festival** (Øninthavenue foodfestival.com) each May. Once one of New York's most violent and lurid neighbourhoods, it was first populated by Irish and Eastern European immigrants, who were soon joined by Greeks, Puerto Ricans and blacks. The rough-and-tumble area was popularized in the 1957 musical *West Side Story*. But things have changed quite a bit: the odd tatty block is now countered by trim residential streets, and construction and renovation of luxury apartments and hotels occurs at sometimes breakneck speed. Along with other gentrifiers, there's now a substantial gay community, with nearly as many gay bars and nightspots as in Chelsea or the East Village.

CAFÉS & SNACKS		SHOPS	
Bouchon Bakery	1	B&H Photo Video	5
Donna Bell's		Drama Book Shop	3
Bake Shop	10	Empire Coffee and	
Gazala's Place	11	Tea Company	2
Margon	13	Gotham West	
The Pennsy	15	Market	1
		Hell's Kitchen	
RESTAURANTS		Flea Market	4
The Burger Joint	7		
Chez Napoleon	8		
Don Antonio			
by Starita	9		
Esca	14		
Joe Allen	12		
Le Bernardin	6		
Petrossian	2		
Pure Thai			
Cookhouse	5		
Totto Ramen	7		
Yakitori Totto	4		

BARS	
Aldo Sohm Wine Bar	7
Ardesia	6
Flaming Saddles	4
Jimmy's Corner	12
Kashkaval Garden	2
Rudy's Bar & Grill	10
Russian Vodka Room	5
Sake Bar Hagi	8

CLUBS & MUSIC VENUES	
Birdland	11
Dizzy's Club	
Coca-Cola	1
Don't Tell Mama	3
New York City Center	2

ACCOMMODATION	
414	5
Ameritania at	
Times Square	3
Casablanca	7
Distrikt	8
Hotel 41@	
Times Square	9
Ink48	4
Knickerbocker	6
Le Parker	
Meridien	2
Room Mate Grace	6
Salisbury	1

Times Square and the Theater District

The Theater District

West of Broadway and north of 42nd Street, the Theater District helps light up Times Square. Of the great old palaces still in existence, the **New Amsterdam**, at 214 W 42nd St, and family-oriented **New Victory**, at 209 W 42nd St, have been refurbished to their original splendour. **The Lyceum**, at 149 W 45th St, has its original facade, while the **Shubert Theater**, at 225 W 44th St, has a magnificent landmark interior that belies its simple outward appearance.

If you want to see a **show**, check out the TKTS booth at 47th Street in Times Square (there are other booths at the South Street Seaport and 1 Metro Center), which sells half-price, same-day tickets for Broadway shows (Mon & Wed–Sat 3–8pm, Tues 2–8pm for evening shows, also Wed, Thurs & Sat 10am–2pm, Sun 11am–3pm for matinees). The booth has available at least one pair of tickets for each performance of every Broadway and off-Broadway show, at 20 to 50 percent off (plus a $4.50 per ticket service charge). Also, many theatre box offices sell greatly reduced "standing room only" tickets the day of the show. See also ⓦwww.tdf.org.

THE INTREPID SEA, AIR & SPACE MUSEUM

Pier 86, at W 46th St and Twelfth Ave. Subway A, C, E to 42nd St, C, E to 50th St ☎ 212 245 0072, ⓦ www.intrepidmuseum.org. April–Oct Mon–Fri 10am–5pm, Sat & Sun 10am–6pm; Nov–March daily 10am–5pm. $24, ages 7–17 $19, add $7/$5 for Space Shuttle Pavilion. MAP P.123, POCKET MAP B8

This impressive, 900ft-long old aircraft carrier has picked up capsules from the Mercury and Gemini space missions and made several trips to Vietnam. It holds an array of modern and vintage air- and seacraft, including the A-12 Blackbird, the world's fastest spy plane, and the USS *Growler*, the only guided missile submarine open to the public. Interactive exhibits dominate the interior hangar, but make sure to explore further into the bowels of the carrier, where you can see the crew's dining and sleeping quarters, the anchor room and lots of navigational gadgets. The museum is also home to the retired *Concorde* and, in its new Space Shuttle Pavilion, *Enterprise* (just a test vehicle – it never made it to outer space).

INTREPID SEA, AIR & SPACE MUSEUM

CARNEGIE HALL

ED SULLIVAN THEATER

1697 Broadway, between 53rd and 54th sts. Subway B, D, E to Seventh Ave. For taping information Ⓦ www.showclix.com/event/TheLateShowWithStephenColbert. MAP P.123, POCKET MAP C7

Come afternoon, a queue can usually be seen outside this building; it's where Stephen Colbert hosts CBS's popular *Late Show*. Book well ahead (two per reservation) or join the standby line to try to catch a taping in the domed interior.

CARNEGIE HALL

154 W 57th St, at Seventh Ave. Subway N, Q, R to 57th St ☎212 903 9600, tickets ☎212 247 7800, Ⓦ www.carnegiehall.org. Tours late Sept–June usually Mon–Fri 11.30am, 12.30pm, 2pm & 3pm, Sat 11.30am & 12.30pm, Sun 12.30pm. $17, children aged under 13 $12. MAP P.123, POCKET MAP D7

One of the world's great concert venues, stately Renaissance-inspired **Carnegie Hall** was built by steel magnate Andrew Carnegie for $1 million in 1891. Tchaikovsky conducted on opening night, and Mahler, Rachmaninov, Toscanini, Frank Sinatra, Duke Ellington and Judy Garland have all played here. The superb acoustics help to ensure full houses most of the year; those craving a behind-the-scenes glimpse should take the excellent tours. The second-floor Rose Museum is free and open to the public.

COLUMBUS CIRCLE

Intersection of Broadway, Central Park West and 59th St. Subway A, B, C, D, #1 to 59th St-Columbus Circle. MAP P.123, POCKET MAP C7

A rare Manhattan roundabout that separates Midtown from the Upper West Side, **Columbus Circle** is best experienced from its centre island underneath the statue of Columbus himself, who stands uncomfortably atop a lone column. From there you can look out at the horse and carriages off Central Park and some striking buildings, like the Hearst Tower, Time Warner Center and Two Columbus Circle. Off the circle at the Central Park entrance is the **USS Maine Monument**, a large stone column with the prow of a ship jutting out from its base; a dazzlingly bright gilded statue of Columbia Triumphant tops it off. The monument is dedicated to the 260 seamen who died in an explosion that helped propel the Spanish–American War.

HEARST TOWER

300 W 57th St, at Eighth Ave. Subway A, B, C, D, #1 to 59th St-Columbus Circle. MAP P.123, POCKET MAP C7

The limestone base of the **Hearst Tower** waited for a skyscraper to top it since the Great Depression. Finally completed in 2006, the glass-and-steel geometry of the Hearst Tower sits ingeniously – and somewhat incongruously – inside the shell of that base. It's certified as one of the most environmentally friendly high-rises ever constructed and was the first skyscraper to begin construction post 9/11.

MUSEUM OF ARTS AND DESIGN

2 Columbus Circle. Subway A, B, C, D, #1 to 59th St-Columbus Circle ☎ 212 299 7777, ⓦ www.madmuseum.org. Tues–Sun 10am–6pm, Thurs & Fri 10am–9pm. $16, Thurs 6–9pm pay what you wish. MAP P.123, POCKET MAP C7

The story of the building that arcs along the south side of Columbus Circle is as interesting as the holdings of the **Museum of Arts and Design** that occupy it. Built in the 1960s to house the Gallery of Modern Art, 2 Columbus Circle was regarded as an architectural folly (and a failure as a museum), yet after years of abandonment and disrepair, the building became the subject of an epic battle over its significance and status. Noted architects like Robert A.M. Stern fought for its preservation but eventually failed, and the Museum of Arts and Design (the former American Crafts Museum) had the building totally redesigned. Gone are the portholes and white marble; in their place, slots, ceramic and glass that seem to form letter shapes on the facade. The eclectic collection inside features everything from blown-glass objets d'art to contemporary jewellery; the temporary exhibits frequently take centre stage.

TIME WARNER CENTER

10 Columbus Circle. Subway A, B, C, D, #1 to 59th St-Columbus Circle. ⓦ www .shopsatcolumbuscircle.com. MAP P.123, POCKET MAP C7

The glassy, curving **Time Warner Center**, a massive, $1.7 billion home for companies like CNN and Warner Books, with a shopping complex on its lower levels (Mon–Sat 10am–9pm, Sun 11am–7pm), opened in 2004. The timing and design make it hard not to think of it as a more modern, less-loved variation of the Twin Towers. Some of the city's priciest restaurants (*Per Se*, *Masa*) dish it out here.

TIME WARNER CENTER

Shops

B&H PHOTO VIDEO

420 Ninth Ave, at 34th St. Subway A, C, E
to 34th St. Mon–Thurs 9am–7pm, Fri
9am–2pm, Sun 10am–6pm. MAP P.123,
POCKET MAP C9

You'll find a staggering array of
cameras, camcorders, blu-ray
players and every other kind
of home electronic you might
want or need; there's a
used-goods section upstairs.
Closed on Saturdays and
Jewish holidays.

DRAMA BOOK SHOP

250 W 40th St, between Seventh and Eighth
aves. Subway A, C, E, N, Q, R, #1, #2, #3, #7
to 42nd St. Mon–Wed & Fri–Sat 10am–7pm,
Thurs 10am–8pm, Sun noon–6pm. MAP P.123,
POCKET MAP C9

A long-running shop that
stocks theatre books, scripts
and publications on all manner
of drama-related subjects.

EMPIRE COFFEE AND TEA COMPANY

568 Ninth Ave, between 41st and
42nd aves. Subway A, C, E to 42nd St.
Mon–Fri 7.30am–7pm, Sat 9am–6.30pm,
Sun 10am–6pm. MAP P.123,
POCKET MAP C8

One-hundred-year-old coffee
roaster that looks and smells
authentic. There are lots of
exotic teas, too.

GOTHAM WEST MARKET

600 Eleventh Ave, between 44th and
45th sts. Subway A, C, E to 42nd St.
Mon–Fri 7am–11pm, Sat & Sun 8am–11pm.
MAP P.123, POCKET MAP B8

One of the latest in the city's
haute food markets, this one
offers the *Ivan Ramen Slurp
Shop* as well as Blue Bottle
coffee, Ample Hills ice cream,
food counters for tacos, tapas
and charcuterie… even a bike
shop. Each place has its own
hours.

HELL'S KITCHEN FLEA MARKET

HELL'S KITCHEN FLEA MARKET

W 39th St, between Ninth and Tenth aves.
Subway A, C, E to 42nd St. Sat & Sun
9am–5pm. MAP P.123, POCKET MAP C9

While there's still an indoor flea
market in Chelsea, the outdoor
version relocated to Hell's
Kitchen; you'll find a mishmash
of home decorations, antique
jewellery, electronics and other
odds and ends.

Cafés and snacks

BOUCHON BAKERY

10 Columbus Circle, Third Floor, Time
Warner Center; another location in
Rockefeller Center. Subway A, B, C, D, #1 to
59th St–Columbus Circle. Bakery Mon–Sat
8am–9pm, Sun 8am–7pm, café Mon–Wed
11am–7pm, Thurs–Sat 10am–8pm, Sun
10am–7pm. MAP P.123, POCKET MAP C7

At this Thomas Keller
establishment you can get
something to go or sit at a table
and gaze onto the corner of
leafy Central Park, grazing on
a sandwich, decadent pastry, or
three-course $37 dinner.

DONNA BELL'S BAKE SHOP

301 W 49th St, between Eighth and Ninth Aves. Subway C, E to 50th St. Mon–Fri 6am–9pm, Sat & Sun 8am–8pm. MAP P.123, POCKET MAP C8

Tiny Southern-style bakery – cupcakes, biscuits, delicious bread pudding and some savoury dishes – opened by a TV star from the show *NCIS*. No seating.

GAZALA'S PLACE

709 Ninth Ave, between 48th and 49th sts. Subway C, E to 50th St. Mon–Thurs & Sun 11am–10.30pm, Fri & Sat 11am–11.30pm. MAP P.123, POCKET MAP C8

Supposedly the only Druze (a Middle Eastern sect) restaurant in the States – besides the outpost at 380 Columbus Ave – *Gazala's* serves lunch and dinner, but is best known for its flaky *bourekas* ($8.50), giant stuffed savoury pastries.

MARGON

136 W 46th St, between Sixth and Seventh aves. Subway B, D, F, M to 47–50th sts/ Rockefeller Center, N, Q, R to 49th St ☎ 212 354 5013. Mon–Fri 6am–5pm, Sat 7am–3pm. MAP P.123, POCKET MAP D8

This narrow Cuban lunch counter is nearly always packed; savoury Cuban sandwiches ($9 with rice and beans), garlicky *pernil* (roast pork; Wed special, $10) and brightly seasoned octopus salad ($11.50) top the choices.

THE PENNSY

2 Penn Plaza, 33rd St, at Seventh Ave. Subway 1, 2, 3, A, C, E to 34th St/Penn Station. ☎ 917 475 1830. Mon–Sat 11am–11pm, Sun 11am–8pm. MAP P.123, POCKET MAP C9

Yes, it's a posh food hall attached to workaday Penn Station. Get Pat LaFrieda steak sandwiches ($15), vegan treats from *Cinammon Snail* and craft cocktails from *The Pennsy Bar*.

Restaurants

THE BURGER JOINT

119 W 56th St, between Sixth and Seventh aves, in Le Parker Meridien. Subway F, N, Q, R to 57th St ☎ 212 708 7414. Mon–Thurs & Sun 11am–11.30pm, Fri & Sat 11am to midnight. MAP P.123, POCKET MAP D7

The secret has long been out on the retro hamburger stand hidden in a swish Midtown hotel. Good for late-night eating (burgers around $9); you might have to wait for a table, though.

CHEZ NAPOLEON

365 W 50th St, between Eighth and Ninth aves. Subway C, E to 50th St ☎ 212 265 6980. Mon–Fri noon–2pm & 5–9.30pm, Sat 5–9.30pm. MAP P.123, POCKET MAP C8

One of several highly authentic Gallic eateries that sprang up around here in the 1940s and 1950s, *Chez Napoleon*, a friendly, family-run bistro, is kind of stuck in a time warp – in a good way. There's a good-value prix fixe ($34), and the wines are well priced.

DON ANTONIO BY STARITA

309 W 50th St, between Eighth and Ninth aves. Subway C, E to 50th St ☎ 646 719 1043, ⓦwww.donantoniopizza.com. Mon–Thurs 11.30am–11pm, Fri & Sat 11.30am–midnight, Sun 11.30am–10.30pm. MAP P.123, POCKET MAP C8

The progeny of two celebrated Neopolitan pizza mavens, busy *Don Antonio* showcases a few different styles of pie; traditional margheritas ($12) share the menu with the signature Montanara Starita ($13) – which is light, smoky and chewy and comes by way of the deep fryer and the brick oven.

ESCA

402 W 43rd St, at Ninth Ave. Subway A, C, E to 42nd St-Port Authority. ☎ 212 564 7272. Mon noon–2.30pm & 5–10.30pm, Tues–Sat noon–2.30pm & 4.30–11.30pm, Sun

4.30–10.30pm. Ⓦ www.esca-nyc.com.
MAP P.123, POCKET MAP C8

Co-owned by Mario Batali, but
more the baby of chef and co-
owner Dave Pasternack, whose
passion for fresh fish is evident.
Lots of crudo ($20–25) and
whole fish grilled or salt-baked
(entrées $35–40).

JOE ALLEN

326 W 46th St, between Eighth and Ninth
aves. Subway A, C, E to 42nd St
☎ 212 581 6464. Mon–Thurs noon–11.45pm,
Wed 11.30am–11.45pm, Fri noon–midnight,
Sat & Sun 11.30am–midnight. MAP P.123,
POCKET MAP C8

The tried-and-true formula of
checked tablecloths,
old-fashioned bar-room feel, and
reliable American food at
moderate prices (entrées $19–35)
works well at this pre-theatre
spot. Make a reservation.

LE BERNARDIN

155 W 51st St, between Sixth and Seventh
aves. Subway B, D, F, M to 47–50th St/
Rockefeller Center or #1 to 50th St
☎ 212 554 1515. Mon–Thurs noon–2.30pm
& 5.15–10.30pm, Fri noon–2.30pm &
5.15–11pm, Sat 5.15–11pm. MAP P.123,
POCKET MAP D8

One of the finest and priciest
($147 prix fixe) French
restaurants in the city (though
the lounge offers an affordable
lunch menu for $49).
Award-winning chef, Eric
Ripert, offers inventive takes on
every kind of fish and seafood
imaginable. His sauces are not
to be believed.

PETROSSIAN

182 W 58th St, at Seventh Ave. Subway A, B,
C, D, #1 to 59th St/Columbus Circle ☎ 212
245 2214. Mon–Thurs & Sun 11.30am–3pm &
5–11pm, Fri & Sat 11.30am–3pm &
5.30–11pm. MAP P.123, POCKET MAP D7

Ink granite and etched mirrors
set the mood at this Art Deco
temple to decadence, where
champagne and caviar are tops.

LE BERNARDIN

More affordable options
include a $48 prix-fixe dinner.

PURE THAI COOKHOUSE

766 Ninth Ave, between 51st and 52nd sts.
Subway C, E to 50th St ☎ 212 581 0999.
Mon–Thurs noon–10.30pm, Fri & Sat
noon–11.30pm, Sun noon–10pm.
MAP P.123, POCKET MAP C7

Wok-induced smoke fills the
air at this rough-hewn Thai
spot, which does excellent
stir-fries and noodles, some a
bit more daring than elsewhere
(crab and pork dry noodles,
$13; chilli turmeric with beef,
$14).

TOTTO RAMEN

366 W 52nd St, between Eighth and Ninth
aves. Other locations in Hell's Kitchen and
Midtown. Subway C, E to 50th St ☎ 212 582
0082. Mon–Sat noon–midnight, Sun 4–11pm.
MAP P.123, POCKET MAP C8

This narrow spot (mainly
counter seating) is one of the
top places to get ramen –
preferably with char siu pork
and spicy sesame oil. The
queue forms quickly; it's
slightly easier to score a table
at the location a block further
west (464 W 51 St).

YAKITORI TOTTO

251 W 55th St, between Broadway and Eighth Ave. Subway A, B, C, D, #1 to 59th St–Columbus Circle, N, Q, R to 57th St, B, D, E to Seventh Ave ☎212 245 4555. Mon–Thurs 11.30am–2pm & 5.30pm–midnight, Fri 11.30am–2pm & 5.30pm–1am, Sat 5.30pm–1am, Sun 5.30–11pm. MAP P.123, POCKET MAP C7

This popular upstairs hideaway is perfect for late-night snacking – though you may miss out on some of the more esoteric grilled skewers (soft knee bone served rare, anyone?), which can be gone by then. Chicken heart, skirt steak and chicken thigh with scallion all burst with flavour (most $3–5 each). Reasonable set lunches, too.

Bars

ALDO SOHM WINE BAR

151 W 51st St, between Sixth and Seventh aves. Subway B, D, F, M to 47–50th Sts/ Rockefeller Center. Mon–Thurs 11.30am–3pm & 4.30–11.30pm, Fri 11.30am–3pm & 4.30pm–midnight, Sat 4.30pm–midnight. MAP P.123, POCKET MAP D8

Run by the sommelier from *Le Bernardin* (see p.129), this comfortably upscale bar offers one of the best wine lists in town, accompanied by an array of charcuterie and small bites.

ARDESIA

510 W 52nd St, between Tenth and Eleventh aves. Subway C, E to 50th St. Mon–Wed 4pm–midnight, Thurs, Fri & Sat 4pm–2am, Sun 2pm–midnight ☎212 247 9191, ⓦ www .ardesia-ny.com. MAP P.123, POCKET MAP B7

A sleek but comfortable wine bar with a bold snack menu (home-made pretzels, quail-egg toast, house-cured meats) and a diverse selection of vintages, thirty of which are available by the glass ($9–16).

FLAMING SADDLES

793 Ninth Ave, between 52nd and 53rd sts. Subway C, E to 50th St ⓦ www .flamingsaddles.com. Mon–Fri 3pm–4am, Sat & Sun noon–4am. MAP P.123, POCKET MAP C7

One of the newer LGBT hangouts in the area, this one comes with a Texas twist. There's dancing on the bar, a Western vibe and drink specials all day (and most of the night).

JIMMY'S CORNER

140 W 44th St, between Broadway and Sixth Ave. Subway B, D, F, M, N, Q, R, #1, #2, #3 to 42nd St. Mon–Sat 11.30am–4am, Sun 3pm–4am. MAP P.123, POCKET MAP D8

The walls of this long, narrow corridor of a bar, owned by an ex-fighter/trainer, make up a virtual Boxing Hall of Fame. You'd be hard pressed to find a more characterful dive – or a better jazz/r&b jukebox.

KASHKAVAL GARDEN

852 Ninth Ave, between 55th and 56th sts. Subway A, B, C, D, #1 to 59th St/Columbus Circle. Mon–Thurs noon–2am, Fri noon–3am, Sat 11am–3am, Sun 11am–1am. MAP P.123, POCKET MAP C7

This cosy wine and cheese bar serves up tasty bites, including excellent cheese and meat plates, cold tapas and fondues.

RUDY'S BAR & GRILL

627 Ninth Ave, between W 44th and 45th sts. Subway A, C, E to 42nd St–Port

JIMMY'S CORNER

Authority. Mon–Sat 8am–4am, Sun Noon–4am. MAP P.123, POCKET MAP C8

One of New York's cheapest, friendliest and liveliest dive bars, a favourite with local musicians. *Rudy's* offers free hot dogs and a great backyard.

RUSSIAN VODKA ROOM

265 W 52nd St, between Broadway and Eighth Ave. Subway C, E, #1 to 50th St. Mon–Wed & Sun 4pm–2am, Thurs–Sat 4pm–4am. MAP P.123, POCKET MAP C7

They serve more than fifty types of vodka here, including their own fruit-flavoured and sublime garlic-infused concoctions; there's also caviar and plenty of small plates. Whatever you do, don't ask for a mixer with your shot.

SAKE BAR HAGI

152 W 49th St, between Sixth and Seventh aves. Subway B, D, M, F to 47–50th St/Rockefeller Center, N, R to 49th St, #1 to 50th St ☎ 212 764 8549. Daily 5.30pm–3am. MAP P.123, POCKET MAP D8

Bustling izakaya (snack) bar, with cheap sakes and beer, plus a fine array of accompaniments like grilled fatty pork, yellowtail collar and yakitori.

Clubs and music venues

BIRDLAND

315 W 44th St, between Eighth and Ninth aves. Subway A, C, E to 42nd St–Port Authority ☎ 212 581 3080, ⓦ www.birdlandjazz.com. Cover $20–50, $10 food/drink minimum. Shows generally at 8.30pm & 11pm. MAP P.123, POCKET MAP C8

Celebrated alto saxophonist Charlie "Bird" Parker served as the inspiration for this jazz venue, which has existed in some incarnation for 65 years. The menu – with a Cajun twist – is decent.

DIZZY'S CLUB COCA-COLA

Time Warner Center, Broadway, at W 60th St, 5th floor. Subway A, B, C, D, #1 to 59th St–Columbus Circle ☎ 212 258 9595, ⓦ www.jazz.org Shows at 7.30pm, 9.30pm & 11pm. $20–45 cover, $10 minimum at tables. MAP P.123, POCKET MAP C7

Part of Jazz at Lincoln Center's home within the Time Warner Center, this room named in honour of Dizzy Gillespie is the only great jazz venue in town with a view – that of Central Park. Book a table for dinner or just drinks and enjoy hot acts.

DON'T TELL MAMA

343 W 46th St, between Eighth and Ninth aves. Subway A, C, E to 42nd St–Port Authority or 50th St ☎ 212 757 0788, ⓦ www.donttellmamanyc.com. Cover $10–25. MAP P.123, POCKET MAP C8

The lively, convivial piano bar and cabaret features rising stars. Two-drink minimum in cabaret rooms; showtimes vary.

NEW YORK CITY CENTER

131 W 55th St, at Seventh Ave. Subway B, D, E to Seventh Ave, F to 57th St, N, Q, R to 57th St–Seventh Ave ☎ 212 581 1212, ⓦ www.nycitycenter.org. MAP P.123, POCKET MAP D7

This large, restored venue – once a temple – revives long-forgotten musicals, hosts the Manhattan Theatre Club and features the Ailey American Dance Theater.

Central Park

"All radiant in the magic atmosphere of art and taste", enthused *Harper's* magazine upon the opening in 1876 of Central Park, the first landscaped park in the US. Today, few New Yorkers could imagine life without it. Set smack in the middle of Manhattan, extending from 59th to 110th streets, it provides residents (and street-weary tourists) with a much-needed refuge from the arduousness of big-city life. The two architects commissioned to transform 843 swampy acres, Frederick Law Olmsted and Calvert Vaux, were inspired by classic English landscape gardening. They designed 36 elegant bridges, each unique, and planned a revolutionary system of four sunken transverse roads to keep traffic out of sight. Although some of the open space has been turned into asphalted playgrounds, the intended sense of captured nature largely survives.

WOLLMAN MEMORIAL ICE SKATING RINK

830 Fifth Ave, at E 63rd St. Subway N, R to Fifth Ave-59th St ☎212 439 6900, ⓦwww .wollmanskatingrink.com. Oct–early April Mon & Tues 10am–2.30pm, Wed & Thurs 10am–10pm, Fri & Sat 10am–11pm, Sun 10am–9pm. Mon–Thurs $11.25, Fri–Sun $18, children $6, skate rentals $8, spectator fee $5. MAP P.133, POCKET MAP D6

Get in the rink for some of the city's most atmospheric ice skating; you're surrounded by onlookers, trees and, beyond that, a brilliant view of Central Park South's skyline. In summer, **Wollman Rink** becomes **Victorian Gardens**, a small amusement park.

CENTRAL PARK ZOO

Enter at Fifth Ave and E 64th St. Subway N, R to Fifth Ave-59th St ☎ 212 439 6500, ⓦwww.centralparkzoo.com. April–Oct Mon–Fri 10am–5pm, Sat & Sun 10am–5.30pm, Nov–March daily 10am–4.30pm. $12, ages 3–12 $7. MAP P.133, POCKET MAP D6

This small zoo contains over 150 species in largely natural-looking homes with the animals as close to the viewer as possible: the penguins, for example, swim around at eye level in Plexiglas pools. Other highlights include giant polar bears, snow leopards and a humid tropical zone filled with exotic birds. The complex also features the **Tisch Children's Zoo**, with a petting zoo.

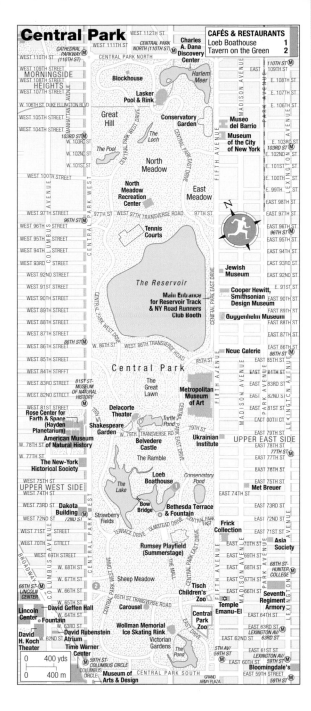

Central Park

CAFÉS & RESTAURANTS	
Loeb Boathouse	1
Tavern on the Green	2

THE CAROUSEL

Mid-park, at 64th St. Subway A, B, C, D, #1, to 59th St-Columbus Circle ☎ 212 439 6900 ext 4. Daily: April–Oct 10am–6pm; Nov–March roughly same hours, weather permitting; call ahead. $3. MAP P.133, POCKET MAP D6

Built in 1908 and moved to the park from Coney Island in 1951, this hand-carved, wooden **carousel** is one of around 150 such specimens left in the country.

THE MALL

Roughly mid-park, from 66th to 72nd sts. Subway #6 to 68th St, B, C to 72nd St. MAP P.133, POCKET MAP D6

If the weather's nice, head straight to the **Mall**, where you'll find every manner of street performer. Flanked by statues of Robert Burns and a pensive Sir Walter Scott, with Shakespeare nearby (all part of the so-called literary walk), the Mall is the park's most formal, but by no means quiet, stretch.

THE SHEEP MEADOW

Between 66th and 69th sts on the western side. Subway #1 to 66th St-Lincoln Center. Mid-April to mid-Oct dawn to dusk. MAP P.133, POCKET MAP C6

This swathe of green, named after the fifteen acres of commons where sheep grazed until 1934, is crowded in the summer with picnic blankets.

Two grass courts used for lawn bowling and croquet are found on a hill near the meadow's northwest corner; to the southeast lie volleyball courts. On warm weekends, the area between the **Sheep Meadow** and the north end of the Mall is filled with colourfully attired rollerbladers.

STRAWBERRY FIELDS

W 72nd St and Central Park W. Subway B, C to 72nd St. MAP P.133, POCKET MAP C5

This peaceful pocket of the park is dedicated to the memory of John Lennon, who was murdered in 1980 in front of his home, the **Dakota Building** (see p.148). The tragic event is memorialized with a round Italian mosaic with the word "Imagine" at its centre, donated by Lennon's widow, Yoko Ono.

BETHESDA TERRACE AND FOUNTAIN

Roughly mid-park, at 72nd St. Subway B, C to 72nd St. MAP P.133, POCKET MAP D5

The only formal element of the original Olmsted and Vaux plan, the **Bethesda Terrace** overlooks the lake; beneath the terrace is an elaborate arcade with tiled floors. The crowning centrepiece of the **Bethesda Fountain** is the *Angel of the Waters* sculpture.

STRAWBERRY FIELDS

LOEB BOATHOUSE

Mid-park, near 74th st. Subway B, C to 72nd St ☎ 212 517 2233, Ⓦ www .thecentralparkboathouse.com. April–Oct Mon–Fri 10am–6pm, Sat & Sun 9am–6pm, weather permitting; $15 for the first hour, and $3/15min after, $20 deposit required. MAP P.133, POCKET MAP D5

You can go for a Venetian-style gondola ride ($45/30min) or rent a rowing boat ($34/30min) from the **Loeb Boathouse** on the lake's eastern bank. Bicycles are also available ($9–15/hr or $45–50/day; $200 deposit and ID required).

THE GREAT LAWN

Mid-park, from 79th to 85th sts. Subway B, C to 81st or 86th sts. MAP P.133, POCKET MAP D4

The **Great Lawn** hosts free New York Philharmonic and Metropolitan Opera summertime concerts, holds eight softball fields, basketball and volleyball courts, and a running track. At the southern end, **Turtle Pond** is a fine place to view turtles and birds.

BELVEDERE CASTLE

Mid-park, at 79th St ☎ 212 772 0288. Visitor Center daily 10am–5pm. Regular walking tours, birdwatching excursions and educational programmes on offer. MAP P.133, POCKET MAP D5

The highest point in the park (and a splendid viewpoint), **Belvedere Castle**, designed by park architect Vaux and his assistant, houses the New York Meteorological Observatory's **weather centre** and the **Henry Luce Nature Observatory**.

DELACORTE THEATER

Mid-park, at 80th St. Subway B, C to 81st St ☎ 212 539 8750, Ⓦ www.publictheater.org. MAP P.133, POCKET MAP D5

This performance space is most notably home to **Shakespeare in the Park** in the summer. Tickets are free but go quickly, visit the website for details.

CONSERVATORY GARDEN

East side from 104th to 106th sts, entrance at Fifth Ave and 105th St. Subway #6 to 103rd St. MAP P.133, POCKET MAP D2

If you see nothing else above 86th Street in the park, don't miss the **Conservatory Garden**, the park's only formal garden, featuring English, Italian and French styles.

Cafés and restaurants

Besides vendors and a few cafés, there are only two eating destinations in the park. *Loeb Boathouse* (see above) offers both upscale dining and casual bar-and-grill fare. *Tavern on the Green*, at Central Park West and 67th Street (☎ 212 877 8684), is a reincarnation of a storied restaurant and focuses on seasonal food – like the Boathouse, the setting is half the point.

The Upper East Side

The defining characteristic of Manhattan's Upper East Side is wealth. While other neighbourhoods were penetrated by immigrant groups and artistic trends, the area has remained primarily a privileged enclave of the well off, with high-end shops, clean and relatively safe streets, well-preserved buildings and landmarks, most of the city's finest museums, and some of its most famous boulevards: Fifth, Madison and Park avenues. Madison Avenue is lined with designer clothes stores, while primarily residential Park Avenue is stolidly comfortable and often elegant, sweeping down the spine of upper Manhattan. It has awe-inspiring views south, as the avenue coasts down to Grand Central and the Met Life Building. Shedding its stuffy image somewhat, an influx of young professionals has sparked a mini surge in gastropubs and cocktail bars in the last few years.

FIFTH AVENUE

Subway F to Lexington Ave/63rd St, N, R to Lexington Ave/59th St, #4, #5, #6 to 59th St, #6 to 68th St, 77th St, 86th St or 96th St. MAP P.137, POCKET MAP D3–D7

The haughty patrician face of Manhattan since the 1876 opening of Central Park along which it runs, **Fifth Avenue** lured the Carnegies, Astors,

CARTIER, FIFTH AVENUE

Vanderbilts, Whitneys and others north to build their fashionable Neoclassical residences. In the late nineteenth century, fanciful mansions were built at vast expense, but lasted only ten or fifteen years before being demolished for even wilder extravagances or, more commonly, grand apartment buildings. As Fifth Avenue progresses north, it turns into the **Museum Mile**.

TEMPLE EMANU-EL

1 E 65th St, at Fifth Ave. Subway F to Lexington Ave/63rd St, #6 to 68th St ☎ 212 744 1400, ⊕ www.emanuelnyc.org. Synagogue and museum Sun–Thurs 10am–4.30pm. Free. MAP P.137, POCKET MAP D6

America's largest reform synagogue, the **Temple Emanu-El**, is a brooding, Romanesque–Byzantine cavern. The on-site museum houses a fascinating collection of Judaica.

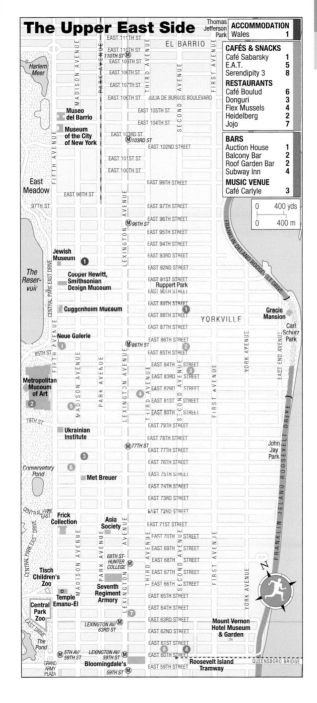

The Upper East Side

FRICK COLLECTION

1 E 70th St, at Fifth Ave. Subway #6 to 68th St ☎ 212 288 0700. ⓦ www.frick.org. Tues–Sat 10am–6pm, Sun 11am–5pm. $20; pay what you wish Sun 11am–1pm. MAP P.137, POCKET MAP D6

Built in 1914 for Henry Clay Frick, probably the most ruthless of New York's robber barons, this handsome pile is now the tranquil home of the **Frick Collection**, displaying artwork from the Middle Ages to the nineteenth century. Opened in 1935, the museum has been largely kept as it looked when the Fricks lived there. Much of the furniture is heavy eighteenth-century French, but what sets it apart from most galleries – and the reason many rate the Frick so highly – is that it strives hard to be as unlike a museum as possible. There is no wall text describing the pictures, though you can dial up info on each work using hand-held guides.

This legacy of Frick's self-aggrandizement affords a revealing glimpse into the sumptuous life enjoyed by the city's big industrialists, while the collection includes paintings by Constable, Reynolds, Hogarth, Gainsborough, Goya, Bellini, El Greco, Titian and Vermeer. The **West Gallery** holds Frick's greatest prizes: two Turners, views of Cologne and Dieppe; and a set of piercing self-portraits by Rembrandt, along with his enigmatic *Polish Rider*. Also unmissable are Holbein's famous portraits of Thomas More and Thomas Cromwell in the **Living Hall**, and Vermeer's stunning *Officer and a Laughing Girl*.

At the far end of the West Gallery you will find a tiny chamber called the **Enamel Room**, named after the exquisite set of mostly sixteenth-century Limoges enamels on display.

METROPOLITAN MUSEUM OF ART

1000 Fifth Ave, at E 82nd St. Subway #4, #5, #6 to 86th St ☎ 212 535 7710. ⓦ www.metmuseum.org. Sun–Thurs 10am–5.30pm, Fri & Sat 10am–9pm. Suggested donation $25. MAP P.137, POCKET MAP D5

The foremost art museum in America, the **Metropolitan Museum of Art** (or the Met) takes in over two million works and spans the cultures of America, Europe, Africa, the Far East, and the classical and Egyptian worlds.

You enter at the **Great Hall**, where you can consult floor plans and check tour times. From here the Grand Staircase

FRICK COLLECTION

leads to the museum's greatest attraction – the **European Painting galleries**. Dutch painting is particularly strong, embracing an impressive range of Rembrandts, Hals and Vermeers – his *Young Woman with a Water Jug* is a perfect example of his skill in composition and tonal gradation, combined with an uncannily naturalistic sense of lighting; you'll also find such masters as Goya, Velázquez, and a room of freaky, dazzling canvases by El Greco, each of which underscores the jarring modernism of his approach.

Highlights of the popular **Nineteenth-Century galleries** include stunning Rodin sculptures and a lauded collection of Impressionists; Manet, Monet, Cézanne and Renoir are all well represented, and there are mesmerizing works by Van Gogh and Gauguin nearby.

The Museum's Asian art section is justly celebrated for its Japanese screens and Buddhist statues, and the Chinese Garden Court, a serene, minimalist retreat; a pagoda, small waterfall and stocked goldfish pond landscaped with limestone rocks, trees and shrubs create a sense of peace.

Close to being a museum in its own right, the **American Wing** is a thorough introduction to the development of fine art in America, with a vast collection of paintings, period furniture, glass, silverware and ceramics. The undeniable standout of the Egyptian collection is the **Temple of Dendur**, built by the emperor Augustus in 15 BC and moved here en masse as a gift of the Egyptian government during the construction of the Aswan High Dam in 1965.

Thanks to a magnificent renovation completed in 2007, one of the largest collections of Roman and Greek art in the world occupies some of the most attractive wings of the museum; check out the wonderfully bright **Greek Sculpture Court**, a fittingly elegant setting for sixth- to fourth-century BC marble sculptures.

Whatever you do choose to see, between May and October be sure to ascend to the **Roof Garden Bar** (see p.145) for incredible views and changing contemporary sculpture exhibits.

NEUE GALERIE

1048 Fifth Ave, at E 86th St. Subway #4, #5,
#6 to 86th St ☎ 212 628 6200, Ⓦ www
.neuegalerie.org. Thurs–Mon 11am–6pm. $20.
MAP P.137, POCKET MAP D4

Dedicated to early
twentieth-century art from
Austria and Germany, the **Neue
Galerie** occupies an ornate
Beaux Arts mansion built in
1914. It's a relatively small
space and the exhibits tend to
rotate, but the collection
contains some real gems.

The galleries begin on the
second floor, where the
undoubted star is Gustav
Klimt's *Portrait of Adele
Bloch-Bauer I* (1907), a
resplendent gold portrait from
Klimt's "Golden Period". The
Bloch-Bauers were one of
Vienna's richest Jewish families;
the painting was looted by the
Nazis in 1938, but descendants
sued the Austrian government
and had the painting returned
in 2006 – the gallery is said to
have paid $135 million for it
soon after. On this floor you'll
also find exceptional work by
Egon Schiele and Max
Oppenheimer, while the third

floor is usually reserved for
rotating work of German
Expressionism: look out for
Paul Klee, Ernst Ludwig
Kirchner and Otto Dix.

GUGGENHEIM MUSEUM

1071 Fifth Ave, at E 89th St. Subway #4, #5,
#6 to 86th St ☎ 212 423 3500, Ⓦ www
.guggenheim.org. Sun–Wed & Fri
10am–5.45pm, Sat 10am–7.45pm. $18; pay
what you wish Sat 5.45–7.45pm.
MAP P.137, POCKET MAP D4

Designed by Frank Lloyd
Wright, the 1959 **Guggenheim
Museum** is better known for
the building in which it's
housed than its collection. Its
centripetal spiral ramp, which
winds all the way to its top
floor, is an exhilarating space,
and some still favour Wright's
talents over those of the artists
exhibited. Nevertheless, the
museum boasts an
awe-inspiring ensemble of art,
not least its fabulous stash of
Kandinsky paintings gathered
by Solomon Guggenheim
(1861–1949), the mining
millionaire who laid the
foundations for the museum.

Temporary exhibits, often
linked to pieces in the
permanent collection, take up
most of the galleries, but you'll
always see plenty of
Kandinsky's exuberant work:
look out particularly for the
jarring *Komposition 8* and the
abstract *Blue Mountain*.

The Level 2 and 3 annexes
also contain permanent
displays: highlights include
Picasso's haunting *Woman
Ironing*, Van Gogh's vivid
Roadway with Underpass,
Cézanne's magnificent *Man
with Crossed Arms* and *Dancers
in Green and Yellow* by Degas.
The museum also owns notable
paintings by Chagall, Gauguin,
Kirchner, Matisse and Monet,
as well as contemporary work
by artists such as Roni Horn.

NEUE GALERIE

UKRAINIAN INSTITUTE

2 East 79th St, at Fifth Ave. Subway #4, #5, #6 to 86th St ☎ 212 288 8660, Ⓦ www.ukrainianinstitute.org. Tues–Sun noon–6pm. Suggested donation $5. MAP P.137, POCKET MAP D5

Inevitably overshadowed by the Met just up the road, the Ukrainian Institute boasts a small but intriguing art collection – temporary exhibits from modern Ukrainian artists take up the second floor, but the upper levels contain some real gems. Still life from Sergei Belik, abstract work from Alexander Archipenko and paintings from David Burliuk, the one-eyed "father of Russian Futurism", plus some huge Soviet Socialist Realist canvases, saved from destruction in the 1990s by collector Jurii Maniichuk and on loan here till 2018. The opulent building was completed in 1899 and served as the home of scandal-prone oilman Harry Sinclair in the 1920s.

COOPER HEWITT, SMITHSONIAN DESIGN MUSEUM

2 East 91st St, at Fifth Ave. Subway #6 to 96th St ☎ 212 849 8400, Ⓦ www.cooperhewitt.org. Sun–Fri 10am–6pm, Sat 10am–9pm. $18. MAP P.137, POCKET MAP D4

Housed in an elegant mansion completed for millionaire industrialist Andrew Carnegie in 1902, this museum blends modern galleries with an original interior – don't miss the old Carnegie Library on the second floor, adorned with intricate Indian-style teak carvings. Much of the museum comprises temporary or rotating exhibits with a design theme, though some version of "Making Design", showcasing the permanent collection, should be on display, plus one of the largest collections of work from artists Winslow Homer and Frederic Edwin Church.

JEWISH MUSEUM

1109 Fifth Ave, at E 92nd St. Subway #6 to 96th St ☎ 212 423 3200, Ⓦ www.thejewishmuseum.org. Fri–Tues 11am–5.45pm, Thurs 11am–8pm. $15, Sat free. MAP P.137, POCKET MAP D4

With over 28,000 items, this is the largest museum of Judaica outside Israel. Highlights of the permanent exhibition, "Culture and Continuity: The Jewish Journey", include a large and rare collection of Hanukkah lamps, the oldest dating from eighteenth-century Eastern Europe and Germany; you'll also find absorbing temporary displays of works by major international Jewish artists, such as Chagall and Man Ray.

MUSEUM OF THE CITY OF NEW YORK

1220 Fifth Ave, at E 103rd St. Subway #6 to 103rd St ☎ 212 534 1672, ⓦ www.mcny.org. Daily 10am–6pm. Suggested donation $14. MAP P.137, POCKET MAP D2

Housed in a grand neo-Georgian building purpose-built in 1930, the **Museum of the City of New York** has been transformed by major renovations in recent years. Most of the galleries feature temporary exhibits – subjects delve into all sorts of New York-related topics, from affordable housing and Currier & Ives prints (the museum has one of the world's largest collections) to World Fairs and the Gilded Age. The enlightening "Timescape" audiovisual presentation (25min; 15min and 45min past the hour) on the second floor, which tackles the history of the city from the Lenape Indians to 9/11, is permanent, as is the **Activist New York gallery**, a thought-provoking journey through the city's most contentious protest movements, from defending the Quakers in the 1650s to modern debates on gay rights.

MUSEO DEL BARRIO

1230 Fifth Ave, at E 104th St. Subway #6 to 103rd St ☎ 212 831 7272, ⓦ www.elmuseo .org. Tues–Sat 11am–6pm, Sun noon–5pm. Suggested donation $9 (free every 3rd Sat of month). MAP P.137, POCKET MAP D2

Literally translated as "the neighbourhood museum", **Museo del Barrio** has largely a Puerto Rican emphasis in its traditional and contemporary collections, but the museum embraces the whole of Latin American and Caribbean cultures; its location places it on the edge of East Harlem, also known as "*El Barrio*" or Spanish Harlem. The

pre-Columbian collection includes intricately carved vomiting sticks (used to purify the body with the hallucinogen cohoba before sacred rites).

MET BREUER

945 Madison Ave, at E 75th St. Subway #6 to 77th St ☎ 212 748 8600, ⓦ www.metmuseum .org. Tues, Wed, Sat & Sun 10am–5.30pm, Thurs & Fri 10am–9pm. Suggested donation $25. MAP P.137, POCKET MAP D5

The Whitney Museum relocated to new premises in 2015 (see p.92), and its old home now serves as the **Met Breuer**, an extension of the Met displaying modern and contemporary art. Galleries show temporary exhibitions from artists such as Indian modernist Nasreen Mohamedi, photographer Diane Arbus and painter Kerry James Marshall. The Marcel Breuer-designed building originally opened in 1966; the Brutalist design was initially a controversial addition to the Upper East Side, but in a sign of how beloved the structure became, plans to wreck its integrity with a Neoclassical addition were shouted down in the late 1980s.

THE ASIA SOCIETY MUSEUM

THE ASIA SOCIETY MUSEUM

725 Park Ave, at E 70th St. Subway #6 to 68th St ☎ 212 288 6400, Ⓦ www.asiasociety. org. Tues–Sun 11am–6pm, Fri until 9pm (Sept–June only). $12, free Fri 6–9pm (Sept–June only). MAP P.137, POCKET MAP E6

A prominent educational resource on Asia founded by John D. Rockefeller 3rd, the **Asia Society** offers an exhibition space dedicated to both traditional and contemporary art from all over Asia. Exhibits are revolving, but often draw from the society's extensive permanent collection; exhibitions have included the arts of ancient Vietnam and South Indian Chola bronze sculptures. Intriguing performances, political roundtables, lectures, films and free events are frequently held.

MOUNT VERNON HOTEL MUSEUM & GARDEN

421 E 61st St, between First and York aves. Subway F to Lexington Ave/63rd St, N, R to Lexington Ave/59th St, #4, #5, #6 to 59th St ☎ 212 838 6878, Ⓦ www.mvhm.org. Tues–Sun 11am–4pm. $8. MAP P.137, POCKET MAP F7

Inside this fine stone house is a series of period rooms from the 1820s, meticulously restored by the Colonial Dames of America (an association of women who can trace their ancestry back to colonial times). The Dames were attracted by a connection with Abigail Adams Smith (daughter of President John Adams), though recent research has revealed this to be tenuous; the property was part of an estate bought by Abigail and husband in 1795, but the family soon went bankrupt, and it was only completed as a carriage house in 1799 by the new owner. The house served as a hotel between 1826 and 1833.

GRACIE MANSION

East End Ave, at E 88th St. Subway #4, #5, #6 to 86th St ☎ 311 or 212 676 3060 (outside NYC). Tours (45min) on Tues 10am. 11am, 2pm & 3pm. Free; reservations required. MAP P.137, POCKET MAP F4

One of the city's best-preserved colonial buildings, the 1799 **Gracie Mansion** has served as the official residence of the mayor of New York City since 1942; billionaire Michael Bloomberg opted not to live at the mansion, but current mayor Bill de Blasio has continued the tradition. The mansion was meticulously restored in 2002, but other than a few antiques and the bold murals in the dining room, the house itself isn't particularly compelling, and the tours are most interesting for the effusive guides and the stories of past mayors.

Cafés and snacks

CAFÉ SABARSKY

1048 Fifth Ave, at E 86th St. Subway #4, #5, #6 to 86th St. Mon & Wed 9am–6pm, Thurs–Sun 9am–9pm. MAP P.137, POCKET MAP D4

Try to get a table by the window at this sumptuous Viennese café with great pastries and coffees. Conveniently located in the Neue Galerie.

E.A.T.

1064 Madison Ave, between E 80th and E 81st sts. Subway #6 to 77th St ☎ 212 772 0022. Daily 7am–10pm. MAP P.137, POCKET MAP D5

Expensive and crowded but the food at this New York deli is excellent (celebrated restaurateur and gourmet grocer Eli Zabar is the owner). Try the soups and breads, or the heavenly mozzarella, basil and tomato sandwiches.

SERENDIPITY 3

225 E 60th St, between Second and Third aves. Subway N, R, #4, #5, #6 to 59th St. Sun–Thurs 11.30am–midnight, Fri & Sat 11.30am–1am. MAP P.137, POCKET MAP E7

Adorned with Tiffany lamps, this long-established eatery/ice-cream parlour is celebrated for its frozen hot chocolate, which is out of this world; there's a wealth of sundaes (from $9.50) too, with everything from cinnamon fudge to fresh fruit and "Forbidden Broadway" (chocolate blackout cake, ice cream, hot fudge topped with whipped cream).

Restaurants

CAFÉ BOULUD

20 E 76th St, between Madison and Fifth Ave, at the Surrey Hotel. Subway #6 to 77th St ☎ 212 772 2600. Mon–Thurs 7am–10am, noon–2.30pm & 5.45–10.30pm, Fri & Sat 7am–10am, noon–2.30pm & 5.45–11pm, Sun 8am–11am, noon–3pm & 5.45–10.30pm. MAP P.137, POCKET MAP D5

Exceptional French–American cuisine directed by celebrated chef Daniel Boulud, a slightly more casual version of his swanky *Daniel* (entrées $21–50).

DONGURI

309 E 83rd St, between First and Second aves. Subway #4, #5, #6 to 86th St ☎ 212 7373 5656. Tues–Sun 5.30–9.30pm. MAP P.137, POCKET MAP E4

Hidden Japanese gem, not far from the Met, serving exquisite sushi dinners in a tiny five-table space; superb seafood.

FLEX MUSSELS

174 E 82nd St, between Third and Lexington aves. Subway #4, #5, #6 to 86th St ☎ 212 717 7772. Mon 5.30–10pm, Tues–Thurs 5.30–11pm, Fri 5.30–11.30pm, Sat 11.30am–2.30pm & 5–11.30pm, Sun 11.30am–2.30pm & 5–10pm. MAP P.137, POCKET MAP E5

Serves mussels fresh from Prince Edward Island (Canada) with various sauces, from Dijon to Thai, ranging from $25–28. Don't miss the cornmeal-crusted clam strips ($12).

CAFÉ SABARSKY

HEIDELBERG

1648 Second Ave, between E 85th and E 86th
sts. Subway #4, #5, #6 to 86th St
☎ 212 628 2332. Mon 5–10pm, Tues–Thurs
11.30am–10pm, Fri 11.30am–11.30pm, Sat
10.30am–11.30pm, Sun 10.30am–10pm.
MAP P.137, POCKET MAP E4

The atmosphere here is
Mittel-European kitsch, with
gingerbread trim and staff
sporting traditional dirndls and
lederhosen. The food is the real
deal, too.

JOJO

160 E 64th St, between Lexington and Third
aves. Subway F to Lexington Ave/63rd St
☎ 212 223 5656. Mon–Thurs 11.45am–2.45pm
& 5.30–10.30pm, Fri 11.45am–2.45pm &
5.30–11pm, Sat 11am–3pm & 5.30–11pm,
Sun 11am–3pm & 5.30–10pm. MAP P.137,
POCKET MAP F6

Lavish townhouse restaurant
created by feted chef Jean-
Georges Vongerichten, serving
excellent French fusion cuisine
with the freshest ingredients.

Bars

AUCTION HOUSE

300 E 89th St, between First and Second
aves. Subway #4, #5, #6 to 86th St. Mon–
Thurs & Sun 7.30pm–3am, Fri & Sat
7.30pm–4am. MAP P.137, POCKET MAP E4

This is a cosier, smarter
alternative to the frat-boy pubs
that dominate this part of town.
The two quiet candlelit rooms
decked out like Victorian
parlours are perfect for couples.

BALCONY BAR & ROOF GARDEN BAR

Metropolitan Museum of Art, 1000 Fifth Ave, at
E 82nd St. Subway #4, #5, #6 to 86th St. Sun–
Thurs 10am–4.30pm, Fri & Sat 10am–8.15pm.
MAP P.137, POCKET MAP D5

It's hard to imagine a more
romantic spot to sip a glass of
wine, whether on the *Roof
Garden Bar* (open May–Oct),

THE BALCONY BAR, METROPOLITAN MUSEUM OF ART

which has some of the best
views in the city, or in the
Balcony Bar overlooking the
Great Hall (Fri–Sat 4–8.30pm).

SUBWAY INN

1140 Second Ave, at E 60th St. Subway N, R,
#4, #5, #6 to Lexington Ave/59th St. Mon–Fri
10am–4am, Sat 11am–4am, Sun noon–4am..
MAP P.137, POCKET MAP F7

A neighbourhood anomaly
since 1937, this downscale
dive bar is great for a
late-afternoon beer – and the
perfect retreat after a visit to
Bloomingdale's.

Music venue

CAFÉ CARLYLE

The Carlyle Hotel, 35 E 76th St, at Madison
Ave. Subway #6 to 77th St ☎ 212 570 7175,
Ⓦ www.rosewoodhotels.com. Mon–Sat
6.30pm–midnight. MAP P.137, POCKET MAP D5

This stalwart venue is home to
Woody Allen, who plays the
clarinet with his jazz band here
on Monday nights (Jan–June;
$165 cover). Other shows cost
$55–140, but it's free if you
book a table for dinner. Sets are
at 8.45pm (plus 10.45pm Sat).

The Upper West Side

The Upper West Side has traditionally exuded a more unbuttoned vibe than its counterpart across Central Park, though there is plenty of money in evidence, especially in the dazzling late nineteenth-century apartment buildings along the lower stretches of Central Park West and Riverside Drive, and at Lincoln Center, New York's palace of culture. This is generally less true further north, though gorgeous – and occasionally landmarked – blocks pop up in the 80s, 90s and 100s. Along the way a few museums, most significantly the Natural History Museum, are worth your time. At its northern edge, marked by the monolithic Cathedral of St John the Divine, Morningside Heights is a diverse area with a youthful buzz from Columbia University; most action revolves around Broadway.

LINCOLN CENTER FOR THE PERFORMING ARTS

W 62nd St to W 66th St, between Broadway, Amsterdam and Columbus aves. Subway #1 to 66th St-Lincoln Center ☎212 875 5000, ✆www.lincolncenter.org. MAP P.147, POCKET MAP C6

This marble assembly of early 1960s buildings, which received a substantial facelift for its 50th birthday, hosts New York's most prestigious performing arts groups. At the centre of the complex, the world-class **Metropolitan Opera House** is an impressive marble and glass building, with murals by Marc Chagall. Flanking the Met are **David Geffen Hall** (formerly Avery Fisher Hall), home to the New York Philharmonic, and Philip Johnson's elegant **David H Koch Theater**, home to the New York City Ballet. The fountain in the middle serves as a meeting place; other spaces include an arts library, multiple theatres, and parks and plazas for summer events. Informative tours (1hr–1hr 30min, 2–7 tours daily, 10.30am–4.30pm; $20; ☎212 875 5350) leave from the attractive Atrium, on Broadway between 62nd and 63rd streets.

LINCOLN CENTER

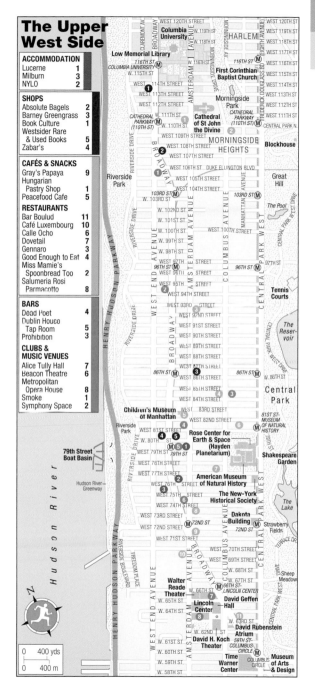

The Upper West Side

ACCOMMODATION
Lucerne	1
Milburn	3
NYLO	2

SHOPS
Absolute Bagels	2
Barney Greengrass	3
Book Culture	1
Westsider Rare & Used Books	5
Zabar's	4

CAFÉS & SNACKS
Gray's Papaya	9
Hungarian Pastry Shop	1
Peacefood Cafe	5

RESTAURANTS
Bar Boulud	11
Café Luxembourg	10
Calle Ocho	6
Dovetail	7
Gennaro	3
Good Enough to Eat	4
Miss Mamie's Spoonbread Too	2
Salumeria Rosi Parmacotto	8

BARS
Dead Poet	4
Dublin House Tap Room	5
Prohibition	3

CLUBS & MUSIC VENUES
Alice Tully Hall	7
Beacon Theatre	6
Metropolitan Opera House	8
Smoke	1
Symphony Space	2

THE UPPER WEST SIDE

13

147

THE DAKOTA BUILDING

1 W 72nd St, at Central Park West. Subway B, C to 72nd St. MAP P.147, POCKET MAP C5

An early co-op finished in 1884, this grandiose German Renaissance-style mansion is best known as the home of John Lennon and his wife Yoko Ono (who still lives here). It was outside the Dakota, on the night of December 8, 1980, that the ex-Beatle was shot.

THE NEW-YORK HISTORICAL SOCIETY

170 Central Park West, at W 77th St. Subway B, C to 81st St ☎212 873 3400, ☺www .nyhistory.org. Tues–Thurs & Sat 10am–6pm, Fri 10am–8pm, Sun 11am–5pm. $18, children 5–13 $6, Fri 6–8pm free. MAP P.147, POCKET MAP C5

The **New-York Historical Society** holds an extensive collection of books, prints, drawings, portraits and manuscripts. Among the highlights are all 435 existing original watercolours of James Audubon's landmark *Birds of America* (a selection of them is exhibited periodically). Elsewhere you'll find a broad cross section of nineteenth-century American painting, notably Thomas Cole's Course of Empire series. The **Henry Luce Center** contains cultural and historical odds and ends. The lowest level holds the

DiMenna Children's History Museum, which teaches history to children through the history *of* children.

THE AMERICAN MUSEUM OF NATURAL HISTORY

Central Park West, at W 79th St. Subway B, C to 81st St ☎212 769 5100, ☺www.amnh.org. Daily 10am–5.45pm. Suggested admission $22, children 2–12 $12.50, IMAX films, space show & special exhibits extra ($13, children $10, to cover all). MAP P.147, POCKET MAP C5

This elegant giant fills four blocks with a strange architectural melange of heavy Neoclassical and rustic Romanesque styles that was built in several stages, the first by Calvert Vaux and Jacob Wrey Mould in 1872. The museum boasts 32 million items in its holdings, superb nature dioramas and anthropological collections, interactive and multimedia displays, and an awesome assemblage of bones, fossils and models. Top billing goes to the crowded **Dinosaur Halls**. **The Hall of Diversity** focuses on both the ecological and evolutionary aspects of nature, while other delights include the massive totems in the **Hall of Northwest Coast Indians**, the taxidermal marvels in North American Mammals and the giant whale suspended

AMERICAN MUSEUM OF NATURAL HISTORY

in the **Hall of Ocean Life**.

The **Hall of Planet Earth** takes on the formation of planets, earthquake tracking and carbon dating. You can watch the earth via satellite on its **Dynamic Earth Globe**.

Housed inside a metal and glass sphere, the **Hayden Planetarium** is one of the prime features of the **Rose Center for Earth and Space**; it regularly screens a 3D movie and the space show *Dark Universe* about the past century of space discovery.

THE CATHEDRAL OF ST JOHN THE DIVINE

1047 Amsterdam Ave, at W 112th St. Subway B, C, #1 to 110th St ☎212 316 7490, tour info ☎212 932 7540, 🌐www.stjohndivine.org. Daily 7.30am–6pm. MAP P.147, POCKET MAP C2

The largest Anglican church in the world holds that title despite being only two-thirds finished. A curious mix of Romanesque and Gothic styles, **St John the Divine** was begun in 1892, but its full 601ft length was completed only in 1941, after which construction stopped, to proceed sporadically between the late 1970s and 1997. As it stands, St John is big enough to swallow Notre Dame and Chartres whole.

Inside, note the intricately carved wood Altar for Peace, the Poets' Corner, the octagonal baptistry and the triptych by Keith Haring – his final finished work. The amazing stained-glass windows include scenes from American history among biblical ones. There are regular organ recitals and highlight tours (Mon 11am & 2pm, Tues–Sat 11am & 1pm, Sun 1pm; $12), plus "vertical" tours to the roof (Wed & Fri noon, Sat noon & 2pm; $20).

COLUMBIA UNIVERSITY

Between Broadway and Morningside Drive from 114th to 120th sts. Subway #1 to 116th St. MAP P.147, POCKET MAP B1

Columbia University's campus (1754) is the oldest university in the city. Alumni include Barack Obama, Isaac Asimov, Ruth Bader Ginsburg and Kathryn Bigelow.

McKim, Mead, and White led the way in designing its new Italian Renaissance-style campus after it moved from Midtown in 1897, with the domed and colonnaded **Low Memorial Library** as the focal point. Hour-long tours (☎212 854 4900; free) of the campus leave Mon–Fri 10am–4pm from the visitors' center on the second floor of the library.

Shops

ABSOLUTE BAGELS

2788 Broadway, between 107th and 108th sts. Subway #1 to 110th St-Cathedral Parkway. Daily 6am–9pm. MAP P.147, POCKET MAP B2

This tiny shop bakes hot, fresh, chewy bagels that some claim as the best in the city. After tasting one – whether loaded with egg salad, smeared with lox spread or just au naturel – you'll find it hard to disagree.

BARNEY GREENGRASS

541 Amsterdam Ave, between W 86th and W 87th sts. Subway #1 to 86th St ☎ 212 724 4707. Tues–Fri 8.30am–4pm, Sat & Sun 8.30am–5pm, takeout counter until 6pm. MAP P.147, POCKET MAP C4

Around the dawn of time, or at least a hundred years ago, the self-styled Sturgeon King began providing Upper West Siders with a beautiful array of smoked fish, cheese blintzes and the like. Be thankful that this deli-restaurant shows no sign of letting up.

BOOK CULTURE

2915 Broadway, at 114th St. Subway #1 to 110th St. Mon–Fri 9am–11pm, Sat 10am–11pm, Sun 11am–10pm. MAP P.147, POCKET MAP B2

One of the top independent bookstores left in the city, Book Culture offers an airy space conducive to browsing and a downstairs kids' room; the original branch at 536 112th St carries mainly academic titles (on its second floor).

WESTSIDER RARE & USED BOOKS

2246 Broadway, between 80th and 81st sts. Subway #1 to 79th St. Daily 10am–10pm. MAP P.147, POCKET MAP B5

All manner of titles (especially strong on art books) are crammed floor to ceiling and

ZABAR'S

into every nook and cranny of this eclectic bookshop, which is ripe for browsing; pretty much all of them are in good shape and sold at reasonable prices. There's a related record store down on 72nd St.

ZABAR'S

2245 Broadway, at W 80th St. Subway #1 to 79th St. Mon–Fri 8am–7.30pm, Sat 8am–8pm, Sun 9am–6pm, café opens an hour earlier. MAP P.147, POCKET MAP B5

A veritable Upper West Side institution, this beloved family store offers a quintessential taste of New York: bagels, lox and all manner of *schmears*, not to mention a dizzying selection of gourmet food. An attached café means you can sample the goods right away if you wish.

Cafés and snacks

GRAY'S PAPAYA

2090 Broadway, at W 72nd St. Subway #1, #2, #3 to 72nd St ☎ 212 799 0243. Daily 24hr. MAP P.147, POCKET MAP C6

This popular hot-dog joint is an NYC institution, famous for its long-running "Recession

Special": two dogs and a drink for $4.95.

HUNGARIAN PASTRY SHOP

1030 Amsterdam Ave, between W 110th and 111th sts. Subway B, C, #1 to 110th St. Mon–Fri 7.30am–11.30pm, Sat 8.30am–11.30pm, Sun 8.30am–10.30pm. MAP P.147, POCKET MAP B2

If you're looking for a place to stop and relax near St John the Divine or Columbia, you won't do better than this simple coffee house. Sip your espresso and read all day if you like – the only problem is choosing among the home-made pastries, cookies and cakes.

PEACEFOOD CAFE

460 Amsterdam Ave. at 82nd St, another location at 41 E 11th St. Subway #1 to 79th St, B, C to 81st St ☎ 212 362 2266. Daily 10am–10pm. MAP P.147, POCKET MAP B5

A friendly stop to pick up some tasty vegan baked goods, or to linger and make a full meal of it: go for an array of roasted veg ($7.95–13.95), fried seitan panini ($14.95) or cheeseless pizza ($12.95), perhaps washed down with a gingerade ($4).

Restaurants

BAR BOULUD

1900 Broadway, between 63rd and 64th sts. Subway A, B, C, D, #1 to 59th St-Columbus Circle, #1 to 66th St-Lincoln Center ☎ 212 595 0303. Mon–Thurs 11.30am–2.30pm & 5–11pm, Fri 11.30am–2.30pm & 5pm–midnight, Sat 11am–3.30pm & 5pm–midnight, Sun 11am–4pm & 5–10pm. MAP P.147, POCKET MAP C6

Treat this Daniel Boulud restaurant like a pre- or post-theatre wine bar, and zoom in on the home-made pâtés, terrines and charcuterie, accompanied by a glass – or

bottle – from the Rhône. Full dinners (entrées $23–33, prix fixe $48) are fairly priced for the quality.

CAFÉ LUXEMBOURG

200 W 70th St between Amsterdam and West End aves. Subway #1, #2, #3 to 72nd St ☎ 212 873 7411. Mon & Tues 8am–11pm, Wed–Fri 8am–midnight, Sat 9am–midnight, Sun 9am–11pm. MAP P.147, POCKET MAP B6

Popular Lincoln Center area bistro that packs in a slightly sniffy crowd to enjoy first-rate, contemporary French food. Entrées $25–40; the brasserie menu is a bit cheaper.

CALLE OCHO

45 W 81st St, between Columbus Ave and Central Park West in the Excelsior Hotel. Subway B, C to 81st St ☎ 212 873 5025. Mon–Thurs 6–10.30pm, Fri 6–11.30pm, Sat noon–3pm & 5–11.30pm, Sun noon–3pm & 5–10pm. MAP P.147, POCKET MAP C5

Very tasty Latino fare, such as *ceviches* ($13–18) and *chimichurri* steak ($28), is served in a colourfully decked-out restaurant with a hopping bar. The mojitos are as potent as any in the city.

DOVETAIL

103 W 77th St, between Columbus and Amsterdam aves. Subway B, C to 81st St-Museum of Natural History ☎ 212 362 3800. Mon–Thurs & Sun 5.30–10pm, Fri & Sat 5–11pm. MAP P.147, POCKET MAP C5

A rare Michelin-starred (and worth it) restaurant in this area, with bold, fresh market-driven dishes like Brussels sprouts salad ($20) and steak with beef cheek lasagne ($52). Sunday "suppas" offer a great prix fixe (three courses $58) and Mondays offer a four-course vegetarian feast (also $58).

GENNARO

665 Amsterdam Ave, between W 92nd and W 93rd sts. Subway #1, #2, #3 to 96th St

GENNARO

☎212 665 5348. Daily 5–11pm.
MAP P.147, POCKET MAP C4

A rare outpost of good Italian food around these parts, though you'll have a wait for a table. Reasonably priced standouts include a warm potato, mushroom and goat cheese tart ($11.95).

GOOD ENOUGH TO EAT

520 Columbus Ave, at 85th St. Subway #1 to 86th St ☎ 212 496 0163. Mon–Thurs 8am–10.30pm, Fri 8am–11pm, Sat 9am–11pm, Sun 9am–10.30pm. MAP P.147, POCKET MAP C4

Cutesy Upper West Side restaurant known for its cinnamon-swirl French toast ($11.75), meatloaf ($18.50) and weekend brunch specials.

MISS MAMIE'S SPOONBREAD TOO

366 W 110th St, between Columbus and Manhattan aves. Subway B, C to Cathedral Parkway (110th St) ☎ 212 865 6744. Mon–Thurs 11.30am–10pm, Fri & Sat 11.30am–11pm, Sun 11.30am–9.30pm.
MAP P.147, POCKET MAP C2

Excellent soul-food restaurant with a 1950s-themed interior, addictive North Carolina ribs ($15.95) and some of the best fried chicken ($13.95) in the city.

SALUMERIA ROSI PARMACOTTO

283 Amsterdam Ave, between 73rd and 74th sts. Subway #1, #2, #3 to 72nd St
☎212 877 4800. Mon–Thurs noon–10pm, Fri noon–11pm, Sat 11am–11pm, Sun 11am–10pm. MAP P.147, POCKET MAP C5

On your left as you enter is a deli counter with a dizzying array of gorgeous cured meats. Order lots of small plates: a selection of salumi and some cheeses (each choice $6–9, platters $18–27); escarole and anchovy salad ($13); pasta ($15); meatballs (if available).

Bars

DEAD POET

450 Amsterdam Ave, between W 81st and W 82nd sts. Subway #1 to 79th St. Mon–Sat 10am–4am, Sun noon–4am.
MAP P.147, POCKET MAP B5

You'll be waxing poetic if you stay for the duration of this sweet little bar's daily specials – usually involving $4 or $5 pints. The backroom has armchairs, books and a pool table.

DUBLIN HOUSE TAP ROOM

225 W 79th St, between Broadway and Amsterdam Ave. Subway #1 to 79th St. Daily 8am–4am. MAP P.147, POCKET MAP B5.

Beneath the cool neon sign, this lively Irish pub is the place to go before or after a gig at the Beacon Theatre.

PROHIBITION

503 Columbus Ave, at W 84 St. Subway B, C to 86th St. Mon–Wed & Sun 5pm–1/2am, Thurs–Sat 5pm–4am. MAP P.147, POCKET MAP C4

Stylish bar and lounge with a funky, retro decor (check out the lamps in suspended wine bottles), decent array of draught beers and diabolical Martinis. Free live music nightly (usually from 9.30pm or 10.30pm).

Clubs and music venues

ALICE TULLY HALL

1941 Broadway at 65th St, Lincoln Center. Subway A, B, C, D, #1 to 59th St–Columbus Circle, #1 to 66th St–Lincoln Center ☎ 212 721 6500, ⓦ www.lincolncenter.org. Tickets $25–100. MAP P.147, POCKET MAP C6

A small performance hall for top chamber orchestras, string quartets and instrumentalists.

BEACON THEATRE

2124 Broadway, at W 74th St. Subway #1, #2, #3 to 72nd St ☎ 212 465 6500, tickets ☎ 1-866 858 0008, ⓦ www.beacontheatre .com. Tickets $25–100. MAP P.147, POCKET MAP B5

This beautifully restored theatre caters to a mature rock crowd. One of the more established music venues in town, plenty of big names play here.

METROPOLITAN OPERA HOUSE

Lincoln Center, Columbus Ave, at 64th St. Subway A, B, C, D, #1 to 59th St–Columbus Circle, #1 to 66th St–Lincoln Center ☎ 212 362 6000, ⓦ www.metopera.org Tickets $20–495. MAP P.147, POCKET MAP C6

Home to the world-renowned Metropolitan Opera Company from September to May. Seats are expensive and nearly impossible to get, though $20–30 standing-room tickets are available at 10am the day of a performance (call for info).

SMOKE

2751 Broadway, at W 106th St. Subway #1 to 103rd St ☎ 212 864 6662, ⓦ www.smokejazz .com. Mon–Fri 5pm–2am, Sat & Sun 11am–2am (jazz brunch sets 11.30am, 1pm & 2.30pm); evening sets typically 7pm, 9pm & 10.30pm. Cover free to $40. MAP P.147, POCKET MAP B2

This Upper West Side jazz joint is a real neighbourhood treat – nice bar, intimate seating, smooth sounds – and does creditable bistro-style dinners.

SYMPHONY SPACE

2537 Broadway, at W 95th St. Subway #1, #2, #3 to 96th St ☎ 212 864 5400, ⓦ www .symphonyspace.org. Tickets free to $50. MAP P.147, POCKET MAP B3

Performing arts centre, with regular short-story readings, as well as music performances. Known for its uninterrupted reading of James Joyce's *Ulysses* every Bloomsday (June 16).

BEACON THEATRE

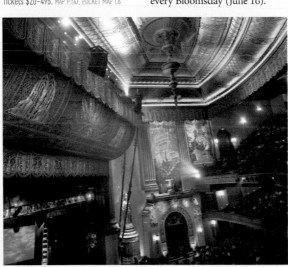

Harlem and north Manhattan

The most famous black community in America, Harlem has been the bedrock of African-American culture since the 1920s, when poets, activists and jazz blended in the Harlem Renaissance. Though it acquired a notoriety for street crime in the 1970s, it is now a neighbourhood on the rise. Indeed, Harlem's streets are as safe as any other in New York. Though most tourists still visit Harlem solely to see its wonderful Gospel choirs on Sundays, you'll also find some fabulous West African and soul-food restaurants, a vibrant local jazz scene, plenty of historic sights and some of the prettiest streets in the city. Explore African-American history at the Schomburg Center, or visit contemporary temples of black culture: the Apollo Theater and Abyssinian Baptist Church. North of Harlem lies Washington Heights and Inwood, home to the largest Dominican population in the United States.

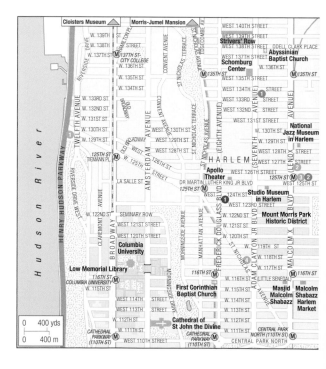

116TH STREET

Subway B, C, #2, #3, #6 to 116th St.
MAP P.154-155, POCKET MAP C1-D1

Harlem lies north of 110th St, but the first area of interest lies along **116th Street**; it's here that the spirit of the late Malcolm X is perhaps the most palpable. Look for the green onion dome of the **Masjid Malcolm Shabazz**, 102 West 116th St, at Lenox Ave; the mosque was renovated in the 1960s and named after him. Between Lenox and Fifth avenues, at no. 52, you'll pass the bazaar-like **Malcolm Shabazz Harlem Market** (daily 10am–8pm), its entrance marked by colourful fake minarets. The market's offerings include textiles, jewellery and clothing, all with a distinctly Afro-centric flavour. The stretch of 116th St between Lenox and Manhattan avenues

MURAL, HARLEM

has become a hub for West African immigrants and is unofficially known as **Little Senegal**; it's lined with shops, beauty parlours and African restaurants. There are also some African-influenced buildings nearby, including the fanciful blue-and-white Moorish-style First Corinthian Baptist Church, 1912 Powell Blvd, at 116th Street.

MOUNT MORRIS PARK HISTORIC DISTRICT

Subway #2, #3 to 116th St or 125th St.
MAP P.154-155, POCKET MAP D1

Centred on Malcolm X Blvd (aka Lenox Ave) between W 118th and 124th streets, this 16-block area, which is full of magnificent, four- to five-storey late nineteenth-century brownstones and quiet streets, was one of the first to attract residential development after the elevated railroads were constructed – it remains a relatively exclusive neighbourhood, with the likes of basketball legend Kareem Abdul-Jabbar living here (and Maya Angelou before she died).

125TH STREET

Subway A, B, C, D, #2, #3 to 125th St.
MAP P.154-155

125th Street between Broadway and Fifth Avenue is the working centre of Harlem and its main commercial drag. It's here that recent investment in the area is most obvious – note the presence of numerous chain stores and fashion retailers – spurred by the establishment of former president Bill Clinton's offices at 55 W 125th St in 2001. Looming over the whole strip is the Brutalist **Adam Clayton Powell, Jr State Office Building**, commissioned in 1972 and built on the corner of Powell Boulevard. The building was named in honour of Harlem's first black congressman, and his 12ft-high bronze **statue** was unveiled here in 2005. The **National Jazz Museum in Harlem** (Mon–Fri 11am–5pm; free; Ⓦwww.jazzmuseumin harlem.org), at 58 W 129th St between Malcolm X Blvd and Fifth Ave, organizes live jazz, and has a small exhibit of old jazz memorabilia and rare recordings.

THE STUDIO MUSEUM IN HARLEM

144 W 125th St, between Lenox and Seventh aves. Subway #2, #3 to 125th St
☏ 212 864 4500, Ⓦ www.studiomuseum.org.
Thurs–Fri noon–9pm, Sat 10am–6pm, Sun noon–6pm. $7, free Sun. MAP P.154-155

The **Studio Museum in Harlem** has over 60,000 square feet of exhibition space dedicated to showcasing contemporary African-American painting, photography and sculpture. The superb permanent collection is displayed on a rotating basis and includes works by Harlem Renaissance-era photographer James Van Der Zee.

APOLLO THEATER

THE APOLLO THEATER

253 W 125th St. Subway A, B, C, D, #2, #3 to 125th St ☎ 212 531 5300, ⓦ www .apollotheater.com. Tours (min 20 people) Mon, Tues, Thurs & Fri 11am, 1pm, 3pm, Wed 11am, Sat & Sun 11am & 1pm. $16 Mon–Fri, $18 Sat & Sun. MAP P.154–155

From the 1930s to the 1970s, the **Apollo Theater** was the centre of black entertainment in northeastern America. Almost all the great figures of jazz and blues played here along with singers, comedians and dancers. Past winners of its famous Amateur Night (still running on Wed at 7.30pm; from $20) have included Ella Fitzgerald, Billie Holiday, the Jackson Five, Sarah Vaughan, Marvin Gaye and James Brown. Hip-hop diva Lauren Hill was actually booed at her debut as a young teen. Yet the Apollo has also become the spiritual heart of black America; James Brown's casket lay in state in the theatre, and when Michael Jackson died in 2009, an official exhibit was arranged inside a few days later.

SCHOMBURG CENTER FOR RESEARCH IN BLACK CULTURE

515 Malcolm X Blvd, at W 135th St. Subway B, C, #2, #3 to 135th St ☎ 212 491 2200, ⓦ www.nypl.org/research/sc. Exhibitions Mon & Thurs–Sat 10am–6pm, Tues & Wed 10am–8pm. Free. MAP P.154–155

Primarily a research library, the **Schomburg Center** also holds enlightening temporary exhibitions held in three galleries on site – recent topics have included the struggle to end segregation in US schools. The library itself was created in 1925 by Arthur Schomburg, a black Puerto Rican obsessed with documenting black culture. Further enriching the site are the ashes of poet Langston Hughes, perhaps most famous for publishing *The*

ABYSSINIAN BAPTIST CHURCH

Negro Speaks of Rivers in 1921. The poem inspired the terrazzo and brass "cosmogram" in the atrium beyond the main entrance. Seven lines radiate out from a circle, and the last, "My soul has grown deep like the rivers", located in the centre, marks where he is interred.

ABYSSINIAN BAPTIST CHURCH

132 Odell Clark Place (W 138th St), off Adam Clayton Powell Jr Blvd. Subway #2, #3 to 135th St ☎ 212 862 7474, ⓦ www .abyssinian.org. Tourists are welcome to the Sun 11am service only (2hr 30min). Free. MAP P.154–155

With its roots going back to 1808, the **Abyssinian Baptist Church** houses one of the oldest (and biggest) Protestant congregations in the country. In the 1930s, its pastor, Reverend Adam Clayton Powell Jr, was instrumental in forcing the mostly white-owned, white-workforce stores of Harlem to employ the blacks whose patronage ensured the stores' economic survival. It's worth a trip here for its revival-style Sunday-morning services and gut-busting choir. Dress formally and remember that this is a religious service and not a show.

STRIVERS' ROW

Subway B, C, #2, #3 to 135th St. MAP P.154–155

On W 138th and 139th sts (between Adam Clayton Powell Jr and Frederick Douglass blvds), **Strivers' Row** comprises three of the finest blocks of Renaissance-influenced row houses in Manhattan. Commissioned in 1891 during a housing boom, this dignified development within the burgeoning black community came to be the most desirable place for ambitious professionals to reside at the turn of the twentieth century – hence its name. Today it remains an extremely posh residence for professionals of all backgrounds.

MORRIS–JUMEL MANSION

65 Jumel Terrace, at W 160th St between St Nicholas and Edgecombe aves. Subway C to 163rd St ☎ 212 923 8008, Ⓦ www .morrisjumel.org. Tues–Fri 10am–4pm, Sat & Sun 10am–5pm. $10. MAP P.154–155

This 1765 mansion, the oldest house in Manhattan, features proud Georgian outlines and a Federal portico, and served briefly as George Washington's headquarters before it fell to the British in 1776. Later, wine merchant Stephen Jumel bought the mansion and

refurbished it for his wife Eliza, formerly a prostitute and his mistress. On the top floor, you'll find a magnificently fictionalized account of her "scandalous" life.

CLOISTERS MUSEUM

99 Margaret Corbin Drive, Fort Tryon Park. Subway A to 190th St ☎ 212 923 3700, Ⓦ www.metmuseum.org/cloisters. Daily 10am–5.15pm; closes 4.45pm Nov–Feb. Suggested donation $25, free with same-day Met Museum entry. MAP P.154–155

This reconstructed monastic complex houses the pick of the Metropolitan Museum's medieval collection. Most prized are the mystery-shrouded **Unicorn Tapestries**, seven elaborate panels thought to have been created in the late thirteenth century in France or Belgium. Among the Cloisters Museum's larger artefacts are a monumental Romanesque hall made up of French remnants and a frescoed Spanish Fuentidueña chapel, both thirteenth century. At the centre of the museum is the **Cuxa Cloister** from a twelfth-century Benedictine monastery in the French Pyrenees; its capitals are brilliant works of art, carved with weird, self-devouring grotesque creatures.

CLOISTERS MUSEUM

Restaurants

THE CECIL

210 W 118th St, between St Nicholas Ave and Powell Blvd. Subway B, C to 116th St ☎ 212 866 1262. Mon–Thurs 5pm–midnight, Fri 5pm–1am, Sat 11am–1am, Sun 11am–10pm. MAP P.154–155, POCKET MAP C1

Stylish Afro-Asian-American brasserie (a fusion concept based on the African diaspora), featuring scrumptious oxtail dumplings and cinnamon-scented fried guinea hen.

DINOSAUR-BAR-B-QUE

700 W 125th St. Subway #1 to 125th St ☎ 212 694 1777. Mon–Thurs 11.30am–11pm, Fri & Sat 11.30am–midnight, Sun noon–10pm. MAP P.154–155

Get some of the best slow pit-smoked ribs here, smothered in a home-made sauce you'll delightfully taste for days after your meal. Or sample the "Big Ass Pork Plate" for $16.95.

RED ROOSTER

310 Malcolm X Blvd, between W 125th and W 126th sts. Subway #2, #3 to 125th St ☎ 212 792 9001. Mon–Thurs 11.30am–3.30pm & 4.30–10.30pm, Fri 11.30am–3.30pm & 4.30–11.30pm, Sat 10am–3pm & 4.30–11.30pm, Sun 10am–3pm & 4.30–10pm. MAP P.154–155

Marcus Samuelsson's restaurant brings a touch of class to Harlem with a sophisticated take on Southern comfort food. Sandwiches $15–18, with mains such as lamb and sweet potato hash at $18–37. Leave room for the "music roots" pie ($12).

SYLVIA'S RESTAURANT

328 Malcolm X Blvd, between W 126th and W 127th sts. Subway #2, #3 to 125th St ☎ 212 996 0660. Mon & Tues 11am–10.30pm, Wed–Sat 8am–10.30pm, Sun 11am–8pm. MAP P.154–155

So famous that the late Sylvia has her own package food line, this is Harlem's premier soul-food landmark. While the BBQ ribs ($25.95) are exceptional and the candied yams are justly celebrated, *Sylvia's* is a bit of a tourist trap – avoid Sundays when tour groups arrive for the Gospel brunch.

Music venues

GINNY'S SUPPER CLUB

310 Malcolm X Blvd, between W 125th and W 126th sts. Subway #2, #3 to 125th St ☎ 212 421 3821, Ⓦ www.ginnyssupperclub .com. Thurs 6pm–midnight, Fri & Sat 6pm–3am, Sun 10.30am–12.30pm. MAP P.154–155

Stylish bar and jazz venue (under *Red Rooster*), with live sets accompanied by punchy house cocktails ($13–14) and excellent soul-food plates ($16).

SHRINE BAR

2271 Powell Blvd, between 133rd and 134th sts. Subway B, #2, #3 to 135th St ☎ 212 690 7807, Ⓦ www.shrinenyc.com. Daily 4pm–4am. MAP P.154–155

Funky bar, restaurant and live music venue (mostly jazz and world music), which also hosts comedy and poetry nights; shows start at 6pm most nights, and at 1pm on Sundays.

DINOSAUR-BAR-B-QUE

The outer boroughs

New York City doesn't end with Manhattan. There are four other boroughs to explore: Brooklyn, Queens, The Bronx and Staten Island. They cover an enormous area and you'll naturally want to pick your attractions carefully, although some of the more alluring parts of Brooklyn and Queens, like Brooklyn Heights and Long Island City, are just a subway stop away from Downtown or Midtown. Staten Island is the only borough that lacks an essential must-see sight or dynamic neighbourhoods for great ethnic food – the free ferry ride back and forth, with its views of Downtown and the Statue of Liberty, is excitement enough. Otherwise, between the Bronx Zoo, Coney Island, Greek Astoria and more, you'll be torn in which direction to head.

BROOKLYN HEIGHTS

MAP P.163, POCKET MAP G15

From Manhattan, simply walk over the Brooklyn Bridge, take the left fork near the pedestrian path's end and emerge in one of New York City's most beautiful, historic and coveted neighbourhoods. This peaceful, tree-lined area was settled by financiers from Wall Street, and has been home to literary figures such as Truman Capote and Tennessee Williams. Make sure you take in the **Promenade**, a terrace with terrific views of lower Manhattan.

DUMBO

MAP P.163, POCKET MAP G15

An acronym for Down Under Manhattan Bridge Overpass, **DUMBO** is a walk downhill from Brooklyn Heights Promenade and fronts the East River. It was a busy hub for ferries and trade in the nineteenth century, but the opening of the Brooklyn Bridge (see p.42) in 1883 led to the area's demise. In the past two decades luxury condo conversions and art galleries have made it lively again. Check out the shops on Water,

WILLOW STREET, BROOKLYN

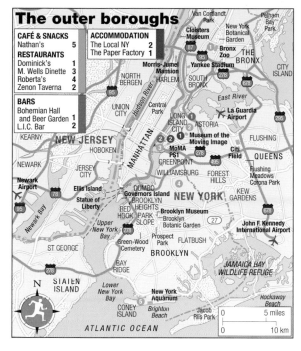

Map legend:

The outer boroughs

CAFÉ & SNACKS
Nathan's 5

RESTAURANTS
Dominick's 1
M. Wells Dinette 3
Roberta's 4
Zenon Taverna 2

BARS
Bohemian Hall
and Beer Garden 1
L.I.C. Bar 2

Main, Washington and Front streets before drinking in the views from the water's edge.

BROOKLYN BRIDGE PARK

Subway #2, #3 to Clark St, A, C to High St
Ⓦ www.brooklynbridgepark.org.
MAP P.163, POCKET MAP F15

The latest attempt to reimagine New York's waterfront, **Brooklyn Bridge Park** begins around Fulton Ferry Landing and runs alongside Brooklyn Heights down to Atlantic Avenue. **Empire Fulton Ferry** boasts Jane's Carousel (May–Sept Mon & Wed–Sat 11am–7pm, Oct–April Thurs–Sun 11am–6pm; $2) and brilliant views of the bridges, while Pier 6 has a cool water-play area, a huge sandpit, steep slides, and ferries to Governors Island (see p.40). Pier 2 has a pop-up pool and

skating area, while **St Ann's Warehouse** (see p.173) occupies a historic building. There's also boating, beach volleyball and outdoor movies.

BLDG 92

Flushing Ave, at Carlton Ave, in the Brooklyn Navy Yard Ⓣ 718 907 5992, Ⓦ www.bldg92 .org. Wed–Sun noon–6pm. Free, Navy Yard tours (2hr) $30. MAP P.163, POCKET MAP H14

Another waterfront redevelopment success, the industrial park of once-derelict Brooklyn Navy Yard has become an attraction in its own right. Visit **BLDG 92** to get acquainted with the yard's history; the centre, a modular, energy-efficient glass structure attached to an 1857 brick house, holds a museum with three floors of exhibitions (an 11-tonne anchor hangs down to greet you as you enter).

NEW YORK TRANSIT MUSEUM

Intersection of Boerum Place and Schermerhorn St, downtown Brooklyn. Subway #2, #3, #4, #5 to Borough Hall, A, C, F, R to Jay Street-MetroTech ☎ 718 694 1600, Ⓦ www.mta.info/mta/museum. Tues–Fri 10am–4pm, Sat & Sun 11am–5pm. $7, children 2–17 $5. MAP P.163, POCKET MAP G16

Housed in an abandoned 1930s subway station, the **Transit Museum** offers more than one hundred years' worth of transportation history and memorabilia, including antique turnstiles, and more than twenty restored subway cars and buses that you can hop on and off of. It's an excellent place for kids.

RED HOOK

MAP P.163

This waterfront district, a former shipping centre, was once one of the more rough-and-tumble in the city, but now holds artists' galleries, unique restaurants, converted warehouses and, to some folks' chagrin, twin retail giants in IKEA and Fairway. Cut off from the subway system, **Red Hook** can be reached by water taxi or bus, a worthwhile venture to hit the **Red Hook Ball Fields** on summer weekends, where you can sample Latin American street food and watch soccer, or to take in fabulous views of the Statue of Liberty and lower Manhattan from the piers, while snacking on a key lime pie from *Steve's Authentic Key Lime Pies* (204 Van Dyke St).

THE BROOKLYN MUSEUM

200 Eastern Parkway, Prospect Heights, Brooklyn. Subway #2, #3 to Eastern Parkway ☎ 718 638 5000, Ⓦ www.brooklynmuseum.org. Wed & Fri–Sun 11am–6pm, Thurs 11am–10pm, first Sat of every month 11am–11pm. Suggested donation $16, aged 19 and under free. MAP P.161

One of the largest museums in the country, the **Brooklyn Museum** boasts 1.5 million objects and five floors of exhibits in its McKim, Mead, and White-designed Neoclassical home. A changing selection of Rodin sculptures greets you inside the door, while another exhibition showcases some detailed African carvings. The third floor holds arguably the museum's crown jewel in its delicately carved "Brooklyn Brown Head", one of 1200 pieces in the Ancient Egyptian Art section. A flight up, Judy Chicago's *Dinner Party* installation marks an important moment in feminist art, while the fifth floor tops things off with the big-name-driven but uneven "American Identity" exhibit. The Visible Storage Study Center on the same level is packed with Tiffany lamps, antique furniture and paintings that the museum doesn't have room to display elsewhere.

BROOKLYN BOTANIC GARDEN

Entrance on Eastern Parkway, next to Brooklyn Museum. Subway #2, #3 to Eastern Parkway, B, Q, S to Prospect Park ☎ 718 623 7200, Ⓦ www.bbg.org. Mid-March to Oct Tues–Fri 8am–6pm, Sat & Sun 10am–6pm, Nov to mid-March Tues–Fri 8am–4.30pm, Sat & Sun 10am–4.30pm. $12 (free winter weekends), children under 12 free. MAP P.161

Brooklyn

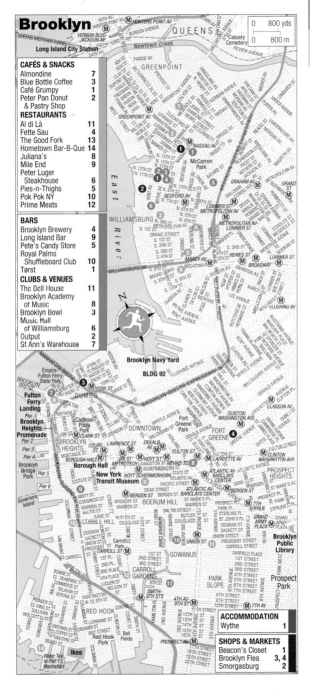

CAFÉS & SNACKS

Almondine	7
Blue Bottle Coffee	3
Café Grumpy	1
Peter Pan Donut & Pastry Shop	2

RESTAURANTS

Al di Là	11
Fette Sau	4
The Good Fork	13
Hometown Bar-B-Que	14
Juliana's	8
Mile End	9
Peter Luger Steakhouse	6
Pies-n-Thighs	5
Pok Pok NY	10
Prime Meats	12

BARS

Brooklyn Brewery	4
Long Island Bar	9
Pete's Candy Store	5
Royal Palms Shuffleboard Club	10
Tørst	1

CLUBS & VENUES

The Bell House	11
Brooklyn Academy of Music	8
Brooklyn Bowl	3
Music Hall of Williamsburg	6
Output	2
St Ann's Warehouse	7

ACCOMMODATION

Wythe	1

SHOPS & MARKETS

Beacon's Closet	1
Brooklyn Flea	3, 4
Smorgasburg	2

The **Brooklyn Botanic Garden** is one of the most enticing park spaces in the city and a relaxing place to unwind after a couple of hours in the museum next door. Though smaller, it is more immediately likeable than its more celebrated cousin in the Bronx (see p.167). Some 12,000 plants from around the world occupy 52 acres of manicured terrain. Highlights are mostly seasonal, but include the Rose Garden, Japanese Garden, Cherry Esplanade (April is a great time for this) and Celebrity Path, honouring Brooklyn's famous sons and daughters.

PROSPECT PARK

Flatbush Ave and Prospect Park West, Brooklyn. Subway #2, #3 to Grand Army Plaza, F to 7th Ave or 15th St, B, Q to Prospect Park ☎718 965 8951, ⓦwww.prospectpark.org. MAP P.163

Energized by their success with Central Park, architects Olmsted and Vaux landscaped 526-acre **Prospect Park** in the early 1860s, completing it just

PROSPECT PARK

as the finishing touches were being put to Grand Army Plaza outside (home to an excellent farmers' market Sat 8am–4pm). Focal points include the Lefferts Homestead, an eighteenth-century colonial farmhouse that is open free of charge at weekends; the Prospect Park Zoo (April–Oct Mon–Fri 10am–5pm, Sat and Sun 10am–5.30pm; Nov–March daily 10am–4.30pm; $8); the new lakeside development, with enclosed and open-air skating rinks; the carousel (late March to mid-Nov Thurs–Sun noon–5pm; $2); and the ninety-acre Long Meadow, which cuts through the centre.

CONEY ISLAND

Subway D, F, N, Q to Coney Island-Stillwell Ave or F, Q to W 8th St-NY Aquarium ⓦ www.coneyisland.com. Boardwalk open year-round, rides are seasonal (roughly April–Sept). MAP P.161

Generations of working-class New Yorkers came to relax at one of Brooklyn's farthest points: **Coney Island**, which at its height accommodated 100,000 people daily. It's now down-and-out and the Astroland amusement park has shut, replaced by **Luna Park** (mid-April to Oct, days and hours vary), which complements the 90-year-old Wonder Wheel, the almost-that-old wooden roller coaster, the Cyclone and the newish Thunderbolt, a steel coaster. Other summertime highlights include the Fourth of July Hot Dog Eating Contest at *Nathan's* (see p.169) and the annual Mermaid Parade (3rd or 4th Sat in June).

NEW YORK AQUARIUM

Surf Ave and West 8th St. Subway F, Q to West 8th St-NY Aquarium ☎718 265 3474,

Ⓦwww.nyaquarium.com. June–Aug daily 10am–6pm, Sept–May 10am–4.30pm. $11.95. MAP P.161

The seashell-shaped New York Aquarium sits on Coney Island's boardwalk. It's still in the midst of a long rehab due to 2012's Hurricane Sandy, but you can see rays and piranhas, watch the sea lion show, enjoy seal feedings and more – including, due in 2018, a flashy new shark exhibit.

WILLIAMSBURG

WILLIAMSBURG

MAP P.163, POCKET MAP J11

With easy access to Manhattan and excellent waterfront views, it's not hard to see why **Williamsburg** has become one of the city's most happening spots – especially for live music and late-night carousing. The L train to Bedford Avenue will land you on the main stretch; vintage shops, plenty of galleries and artisanal-food purveyors can be found on surrounding blocks.

McCarren Park separates northern Williamsburg from the fashionable Polish enclave of **Greenpoint**, and the park serves as a big hangout, with summer concerts. Its historic pool, restored in 2012, briefly becomes an ice rink in winter. Further out, Bushwick also has its share of restaurants and rock clubs.

ASTORIA

MAP P.161, POCKET MAP J3

Developed in 1839 and named after John Jacob Astor, **Astoria**, Queens is known for two things: film-making (Paramount had a studio here between 1920 and 1928), and its vibrant Greek population.

Greek Astoria stretches from Ditmars Boulevard to Broadway, and from 31st Street across to Steinway Street, though plenty of Moroccans, Egyptians, Brazilians and others have moved in; it makes for a foodie haven, evidenced in the patisseries, fresh seafood restaurants and kebab stands.

THE MUSEUM OF THE MOVING IMAGE

35th Ave, at 37th St, Astoria, Queens. Subway N, Q to 36th St, M, R to Steinway St ☎718 784 0077, Ⓦwww.movingimage.us. Wed–Thurs 10.30am–5pm, Fri 10.30am–8pm, Sat & Sun 11.30am–7pm. $15, children 3–7 $7, Fri 4–8pm free. MAP P.161, POCKET MAP J5

Part of the old Paramount complex, the **Museum of the Moving Image** tells the fascinating story of cinema through state-of-the-art theatres, hands-on exhibits and vintage props. The museum's core collection, "Behind the Screen", holds old movie cameras and special-effects equipment; sketches and set models from *The Silence of the Lambs*; and enough *Star Wars* action figures to make an obsessed fan drool with envy. The film series and temporary exhibitions are an equal lure.

ISAMU NOGUCHI GARDEN MUSEUM

9-01 33rd Rd, at Vernon Blvd, Long Island City, Queens. Subway N, Q to Broadway, F to

Queensbridge–21st St ☎ 718 204 7088,
Ⓦ www.noguchi.org. Wed–Fri 10am–5pm,
Sat & Sun 11am–6pm. $10.
MAP P.161, POCKET MAP G5

While hard to reach, the **Isamu Noguchi Garden Museum** easily repays curiosity. The museum is devoted to the "organic" sculptures, drawings, modern dance costumes and Akari light sculptures of the prolific Japanese-American abstract sculptor Isamu Noguchi (1904–88), whose studio was here. His pieces, in stone, bronze and wood, exhibit a sublime simplicity.

MoMA PS1

22–25 Jackson Ave, at 46th Ave, Long Island
City. Subway #7 to 45 Rd-Courthouse Square;
E, M to Court Square-23rd St, #7 to Court
Sqaure, G to 21st St ☎ 718 784 2004, Ⓦ www
.momaps1.org. Thurs–Mon noon–6pm.
Suggested admission $10 (free with same-day
MoMA ticket). MAP P.161, POCKET MAP H8

MoMA PS1 is one of the oldest and biggest organizations in the United States devoted exclusively to contemporary art and to showing leading emerging artists. Since its founding in 1971, this public school-turned-exhibition space has hosted some of the city's most exciting art displays. Summertime's Warm Up series (Sat afternoon) is a DJ-led dance-and-art party.

FLUSHING MEADOWS CORONA PARK

Between the Van Wyck Expressway and
Grand Central Parkway, east of 111th St
Subway #7 to 111th St or Mets-Willets Point.
Ⓦ www.nycgoparks.org. MAP P.161

Sprawling **Flushing Meadows Corona Park** contains a multitude of Queens cultural institutions and sports venues. Baseball's Mets play at **Citi Field**; the US Open Tennis Championships are held at the **Billie Jean King National Tennis Center**; the **Queens Museum** holds the awe-inspiring city scale model *Panorama of the City of New York*; and the **New York Hall of Science** holds good fun for kids. Elsewhere in the park are holdovers from the 1964–65 World's Fair.

ROCKAWAY BEACH

Subway A (rush hour) to Rockaway Park-Beach
116th St or the A to Broad Channel, transfer to
the S (Rockaway Shuttle – all times of day),
which also takes you to Rockaway Park-Beach
116th St; there are numerous other stops the
length of the peninsula and summer ferries from
Pier 11 (Wall Street) in Manhattan. MAP P.161

The spit of **Rockaway** stretches for ten miles southwest of Brooklyn; its namesake beach, celebrated by the Ramones in song, runs along the shore from Beach 9th Street to Beach 149th

BRONX ZOO

heroes are enshrined with plaques and monuments, and tours (daily except home game days 11am–1.40pm, every 20min; $20; ☎ 646 977 8687) take in these, the dugout, the clubhouse and batting cages.

BRONX ZOO

Main gate on Fordham Rd. Subway #2, #5 to East Tremont Ave/West Farms Square ☎ 718 220 5100, Ⓦ www.bronxzoo.com. April–Oct Mon–Fri 10am–5pm, Sat & Sun 10am–5.30pm, Nov–March daily 10am–4.30pm. $16.95, children 3–12 $12.95; special rides and attractions extra, though discount for Total Experience tickets; Wed "pay what you wish". MAP P.161

The largest urban zoo in the United States, which first opened its gates in 1899, houses over six thousand animals and was one of the first institutions of its kind to realize its inhabitants both looked and felt better out in the open. The "Wild Asia" exhibit is an almost forty-acre wilderness through which tigers, elephants and deer roam relatively free, visible from a monorail (May–Oct; $5). The lemurs of Madagascar and the Congo Gorilla Forest are also highlights.

NEW YORK BOTANICAL GARDEN

Entrance across the road from the zoo's main gate. Subway B, D, #4 to Bedford Park Blvd, though Metro-North from Grand Central to Botanical Garden Station is easier ☎ 718 817 8700, Ⓦ www.nybg.org. Tues–Sun 10am–6pm. All garden $25, children 2–12 $10; grounds only $13, children 2–12 $2. MAP P.161

The late nineteenth century **New York Botanical Garden** is a brilliant companion piece to the zoo opposite. Near the main entrance, the Enid A. Haupt Conservatory, a landmark crystal palace, showcases jungle and desert ecosystems, a palm court and a fern forest, among other seasonal displays. Close by are herb and perennial gardens.

Street. Hotspots like the hip *Playland Motel*, *Tacoway Beach* and the *Rockaway Beach Surf Club* have recently popped up; there are places to rent boards and take surf lessons (the surfing sections are at 67th–69th sts and 87th–92nd sts); and excellent coffee and meals can be enjoyed from *Cuisine by Claudette*. Thing get lively for the **Riis Park Beach Bazaar**, 157 Rockaway Beach Blvd (summer Mon–Fri noon–8pm, Sat & Sun 11am–9pm; Ⓦ riisparkbeachbazaar.com). free music programming, food vendors and beachy sports.

YANKEE STADIUM

161st St and River Ave. Subway B, D, #4 to Yankee Stadium ☎ 212 926 5337, Ⓦ newyork.yankees.mlb.com. Tickets $20–300. MAP P.161

Yankee Stadium is home to the New York Yankees, 27-time World Series champs and the most famous franchise in sports. Babe Ruth, Lou Gehrig, Joe DiMaggio and dozens more have formed a continuous line of superstars to the present day, though longtime franchise face Derek Jeter just retired. A brand-new stadium, inaugurated for the 2009 season, replaced the "House That Ruth Built"; the team's

Shops and markets

BEACON'S CLOSET

74 Guernsey St, between Nassau and Norman aves, Greenpoint, Brooklyn; other locations in Park Slope and the Village. Subway L to Bedford Ave. W www.beaconscloset.com. Daily 11am–8pm. MAP P.163, POCKET MAP H10

This huge clothing exchange is great for finding excellent deals on vintage designer duds or making a bit of cash if you've got used stuff in good condition to spare.

BROOKLYN FLEA

176 Lafayette Ave, between Clermont and Vanderbilt aves, Fort Greene (April–Nov Sat 10am–5pm); Manhattan Bridge Archway Plaza, DUMBO (April–Nov Sun 10am–5pm), and other locations. Subway C to Lafayette Ave, G to Clinton-Washington aves, F to York St W brooklynflea.com. MAP P.163, POCKET MAP J15 & G15

The Fort Greene version is bigger, but at both you'll find all manner of knick-knacks and vintage clothes, housewares and jewellery, as well as superb artisan food. The flea also runs Smorgasburg (see below).

BEACON'S CLOSET

SMORGASBURG

East River State Park, Williamsburg: Sat 11am–6pm, Prospect Park: Sun 11am–6pm. Subway L to Bedford Ave and B, Q to Prospect Park W www.smorgasburg.com. MAP P.163, POCKET MAP H11

From April to November, these two scenic parks brim with gourmet food vendors; come wintertime, they move indoors (in Industry City, in Brooklyn's Sunset Park). Come armed with cash and be prepared to join the queues for favourites like the salteñas (similar to empanadas) from Bolivian Llama Party. There are additional versions at other locations; check the website for the latest.

Cafés and snacks

ALMONDINE

85 Water St, Dumbo, Brooklyn. Subway A, C to High St, F to York St. Mon–Sat 7am–7pm, Sun 10am–6pm. MAP P.163, POCKET MAP F15

It just might be the best bakery in the city, with its exquisite chocolate cakes and fruit tarts, buttery croissants and tasty salami sandwiches. Eat in or, better yet, take it to the nearby park between the bridges.

BLUE BOTTLE COFFEE

160 Berry St, between Fourth and Fifth sts, seven other locations in the city. Subway L to Bedford Ave. Daily 7am–7pm. MAP P.163, POCKET MAP H12

The first of a half dozen or so city outposts of a well-regarded San Francisco coffee roaster. A cross between a café and a lab, the java used for iced coffee drips in giant bulbous tubes. Filters are lined up to make coffee to order and a working roastery fills the back.

CAFÉ GRUMPY

193 Meserole Ave, at Diamond St, Greenpoint, Brooklyn. Subway G to Nassau Ave. Mon–Fri 7am–7.30pm, Sat & Sun 7.30am–7.30pm. MAP P.163, POCKET MAP J10.

As celebrated in the TV show *Girls*, this is the original location in a minichain of ultracool coffee culture. A half dozen others are scattered around town.

NATHAN'S

1310 Surf Ave, at Schweiker's Walk, Coney Island, Brooklyn. Subway D, F, N, Q to Coney Island-Stillwell Ave ☎ 718 333 2202. Mon–Thurs & Sun 9am–midnight, Fri & Sat 9am–2am. MAP P.161

Home of the "famous Coney Island hot dog", served since 1916, *Nathan's* is a bona fide New York experience. It holds an annual Hot Dog Eating Contest on July 4.

PETER PAN DONUT & PASTRY SHOP

727 Manhattan Ave, between Norman and Meserole aves, Greenpoint. Subway G to Nassau Ave. Mon–Fri 4.30am–8pm, Sat 5am–8pm, Sun 5.30am–7pm (donuts at 8am). MAP P.163, POCKET MAP H10

Old-school counter with formica and swivel stools. Perch on one and order delectable crullers, chocolate cake donuts… or any other variety.

Restaurants

AL DI LÀ

248 Fifth Ave, at Carroll St, Park Slope, Brooklyn. Subway R to Union St ☎ 718 783 4565. Mon–Thurs noon–3pm & 6–10.30pm, Fri noon–3pm & 6–11pm, Sat 11am–3.30pm & 5.30–11pm, Sun 11am–3.30pm & 5–10pm. MAP P.163

Venetian country cooking at its finest at this husband-and-wife-run restaurant. Standouts include beet ravioli ($12),

Swiss chard gnocchi ($16) and braised rabbit ($29). Expect an hour-long wait (no reservations).

DOMINICK'S

2335 Arthur Ave, at 187th St, the Bronx. Subway B, D to Fordham Rd ☎ 718 733 2807. Mon & Wed–Sun noon–9.30pm. MAP P.161

All you could hope for in a Belmont neighbourhood Italian: great, rowdy atmosphere, communal seating, wonderful food and low(ish) prices. Stuffed baby squid, veal *parmigiana* and chicken *scarpariello* are standouts. Cash only.

FETTE SAU

354 Metropolitan Ave, at Havemeyer St, Williamsburg, Brooklyn. Subway L to Bedford Ave, G to Metropolitan Ave ☎ 718 963 3404. Mon–Fri 5pm–1am, Sat & Sun noon–1am. MAP P.163. POCKET MAP J12

The industrial-chic vibe (it's in an old auto repair shop) of this barbecue specialist fits the neighbourhood. Order your meat by the pound (beef brisket, pork shoulder or pork belly $16), tack on a couple of sides (burnt end baked beans $5.25) and wash it down with a microbrew ($6 pints).

NATHAN'S

THE GOOD FORK

391 Van Brunt St, Red Hook, Brooklyn. Subway F, G to Smith-9th sts ☎718 643 6636. Tues–Fri 5.30–10.30pm, Sat 10am–3pm & 5.30–10.30pm, Sun 10am–3pm & 5.30–10pm. MAP P.163

Though it's a neighbourhood restaurant at heart (in an out-of-the-way spot), it's worth making the effort for the inventive cocktails, delectable dumplings ($10) and Korean-inspired take on steak and eggs ($29).

HOMETOWN BAR-B-QUE

454 Van Brunt St, at Reed St, Red Hook. Subway F, G to Smith-9th St, then bus #61. Tues–Thurs noon–11pm, Fri & Sat noon–midnight, Sun noon–10pm. MAP P.163

Reckoned by some as the best purveyor of 'cue in the city, Hometown does justice to pulled pork ($22/lb) and brisket ($28/lb). Lively roadhouse atmosphere.

JULIANA'S

19 Old Fulton St, between Front and Water Sts, Dumbo. Subway F to York St, A, C to High St ☎718 596 6700. Mon–Fri 11.30am–11pm, Sat & Sun 11am–11pm. MAP P.163, POCKET MAP F22

Patsy Grimaldi sold the naming rights to his famous *Grimaldi's* (right next door), and has come out of retirement to open this coal-oven pizzeria. He's still got the touch. Pies only ($17–32).

M. WELLS DINETTE

22–25 Jackson Ave, between 46th Rd and 46th Ave, Long Island City. Subway G, #7 to Court Square, E, M to Court Square-Ely ☎718 786 1800. Mon & Thurs–Sun noon–6pm. MAP P.161, POCKET MAP H8

In a faux-schoolroom in MoMA PS1 (see p.166), this adventurous café serves up a revolving menu of dishes like foie gras and oats, beef tartare and a spaghetti sandwich.

MILE END

97A Hoyt St, between Pacific and Atlantic, Boerum Hill, Brooklyn ☎718 852 7510. Subway F, G to Bergen, A, C, G to Hoyt-Schermerhorn. Mon–Wed 8am–4pm & 5–10pm, Thurs & Fri 8am–4pm & 5–11pm, Sun 10am–4pm & 5–10pm. MAP P.163, POCKET MAP H16

This cosy Montréal-style Jewish deli serves tasty breakfast all day and smoked meat sandwiches that rival any in town, along with takes on Old World home cooking – for example, chicken and *latkes* (potato pancakes). A real treat.

PETER LUGER STEAK HOUSE

178 Broadway, at Driggs Ave, Williamsburg, Brooklyn. Subway J, M, Z to Marcy Ave ☎718 387 7400. Mon–Thurs 11.45am–9.45pm, Fri & Sat 11.45am–10.45pm, Sun 12.45–9.45pm. MAP P.163, POCKET MAP J13

Catering to carnivores since 1873, *Peter Luger's* may just be the city's finest steakhouse. The service is surly and the decor plain, but the porterhouse steak – essentially the only cut served – is divine. Make sure to order the bacon starter, too. It's expensive; tabs can easily run to $100 or so per person.

PIES-N-THIGHS

166 S 4th St, at Driggs Ave. Subway J, M, Z to Marcy Ave, Williamsburg, Brooklyn ☎347 529 6090. Mon–Fri 9am–4am & 5pm–midnight, Sat & Sun 10am–4pm & 5pm–midnight. MAP P.163, POCKET MAP J12

M. WELLS DINETTE

Tucked in a bright corner location, *P-n-T* do exemplary Southern-style food: great chicken biscuits (a scone with a fried chicken filling; $7.50), expertly fried chicken ($13 with waffles, $14.50 with a side) and a changing rotation of pies (key lime is a favourite; slices $4.50–5.50). Cash only.

POK POK NY

127 Columbia St, between Kane and Degraw sts, Brooklyn. Subway F, G to Bergen St. ☎ 718 923 9322. Mon–Fri 5.30–10pm, Sat & Sun noon–10pm. MAP P.163

Come early or reserve a table at this renowned northern Thai specialist, courtesy of Portland transplant Andy Ricker; the cocktails are strong and the food – grilled eggplant salad ($15), sticky wings ($15) – their perfect accompaniment.

PRIME MEATS

465 Court St, at Luquer St, Carroll Gardens, Brooklyn. Subway F, G to Carroll St ☎ 718 254 0327. Thurs 11am–1am, Fri 11am–midnight, Sat 10am–midnight, Sun 10am–11pm. MAP P.163

Popular spot serving up excellent steaks ($36 for a NY strip), burgers ($23) and handmade sausage ($12–18) in a room that feels decades old.

ROBERTA'S

261 Moore St, at Bogart St. Subway L to Morgan Ave, Bushwick ☎ 718 417 1118. Mon–Fri 11am–midnight, Sat & Sun 10am–midnight. MAP P.161

Slightly in the middle of nowhere (ever-burgeoning Bushwick), this acclaimed spot serves up some of the city's best pies in an unassuming building – though the courtyard is nice, and the place hides a super-upscale restaurant within a restaurant, *Bianca* (☎ 347 799 2807; book a month ahead).

BROOKLYN BREWERY

ZENON TAVERNA

34-10 31st Ave, Astoria, Queens. Subway N, Q to 30th Ave, R, M to Steinway St ☎ 718 956 0133. Daily noon–11pm. MAP P.161, POCKET MAP J4

Charred octopus ($17), grilled meatballs ($10) and taramasalata dip will get your meal off on the right foot at the super-friendly Greek-Cypriot tavern; whole fish or one of the lamb specials ($22–25) keep it headed in the right direction.

Bars

BOHEMIAN HALL AND BEER GARDEN

29-19 24th Ave between 29th and 30th sts, Astoria, Queens. Subway N, Q to Astoria Blvd. ☎ 718 274 4925. Mon–Thurs 5pm–1am, Fri 5pm–3am, Sat noon–3am, Sun noon–midnight. MAP P.161, POCKET MAP J3

This Czech bar is the real deal, catering to old-timers and serving a good selection of pilsners as well as hard-to-find brews. Out the back, there's a very large beer garden, complete with picnic tables, trees, burgers and sausages, and a bandshell for polka groups. Great fun in good weather and worth the trip.

BROOKLYN BREWERY

79 N 11th St, Williamsburg, Brooklyn. Subway L to Bedford Ave. Fri 6–11pm, Sat noon–8pm, Sun noon–6pm. MAP P.163, POCKET MAP H11

Check out this stellar Williamsburg microbrewery, which hosts events year-round; hang out in their tasting room at weekends or take a free tour (Mon–Thurs 5pm, $15; Sat & Sun 1pm, free).

L.I.C. BAR

45–58 Vernon Blvd, at 46th Ave, Long Island City, Queens. Subway #7 to Vernon Blvd-Jackson Ave or 45th Rd-Courthouse Square, G to 21st St ☎ 718 786 5400. Mon–Fri 4pm–2am, Sat & Sun 1pm–2am. MAP P.161, POCKET MAP G8

A friendly, atmospheric place for a beer, burger and free live music (Mon, Wed, Sat & Sun); hunker down at the old wooden bar or in the pleasant garden.

LONG ISLAND BAR

110 Atlantic Ave, at Henry St, Cobble Hill, Brooklyn. Subway #2, #3, #4, #5 to Borough Hall. Mon–Thurs 5.30pm–midnight, Fri & Sat 5.30pm–2am, Sun 11am–midnight. MAP P.163, POCKET MAP G16

A recently revived relic whose vintage sign leads the way to a room with meticulously made cocktails and, in the fried cheese curds ($12), one of the best bar snacks going.

PETE'S CANDY STORE

709 Lorimer St, between Frost and Richardson sts, Williamsburg, Brooklyn. Subway L to Lorimer St, G to Metropolitan Ave. Mon–Thurs 5pm–2am, Fri & Sat 4pm–4am, Sun 4pm–2am. MAP P.163, POCKET MAP J11

This terrific little spot to tipple was once a real candy store. There's free live music every night, a reading series, Scrabble and Bingo nights, pub quizzes and some well-poured cocktails.

ROYAL PALMS SHUFFLEBOARD CLUB

514 Union St, between Third Ave and Nevins St, Gowanus. Subway R to Union St. Tues–Wed 6pm–midnight, Thurs & Fri 6pm–2am, Sat noon–2am, Sun noon–midnight. MAP P.163

Perhaps it was inevitable for such a place to pop up, considering every other trend to hit (or be spawned by) Brooklyn, but this cheerful multipurpose spot does offer tropical cocktails, food trucks, DJs and, of course, courts for the eponymous sport ($40/hr).

TØRST

615 Manhattan Ave, between Nassau and Driggs aves, Greenpoint, Brooklyn. Subway G to Nassau Ave. Mon–Wed & Sun noon–midnight, Thurs–Sat noon–2am. MAP P.163, POCKET MAP J10

A shiny new temple for beer drinkers, Tørst boasts reclaimed wood and a sleek metal bar, behind which some twenty draughts sit hooked up to the "flux capacitor", which allows bartenders to monitor and adjust the gas and carbonation. The results: flawless 8oz or 14oz pours. An upscale restaurant, *Luksus*, shares the premises.

PETE'S CANDY STORE

Clubs and venues

THE BELL HOUSE

149 7th St, between Second and Third aves, Gowanus, Brooklyn. Subway F, G, R to Fourth Ave-9th St ☎ 718 643 6510, ⓦ www.thebellhouseny.com. MAP P.163

A converted printing house in up-and-coming Gowanus provides the setting for indie band performances and wacky events – cookoffs, Burt Reynolds' film celebrations and so on. The front-room bar (daily 5pm–4am) is a pleasantly spacious place to drink.

BROOKLYN ACADEMY OF MUSIC

30 Lafayette St between Ashland Place and St Felix St, Brooklyn. Subway #2, #3, #4, #5, B, Q to Barclays-Atlantic Ave, D, M, N, R to Pacific St ☎ 718 636 4100, ⓦ www.bam.org. MAP P.163, POCKET MAP J16

America's oldest performing arts academy (1859) and one of the most daring producers in New York is worth crossing the river for, especially to catch African dance, European theatre troupes and rare movie screenings.

BROOKLYN BOWL

61 Wythe Ave, between 11th and 12th sts, Williamsburg. Subway L to Bedford Ave ⓦ www.brooklynbowl.com. Mon–Thurs 6pm–2am, Fri 6pm–4am, Sat noon–4am, Sun noon–2am. Shows $5–20 or more. MAP P.163, POCKET MAP H11

A converted warehouse with live concerts, DJ sets and, oh yeah, bowling. Roots drummer Questlove typically spins Thursday nights.

MUSIC HALL OF WILLIAMSBURG

66 N 6th St, at Kent, Williamsburg, Brooklyn. Subway L to Bedford Ave ☎ 718 486 5400, ⓦ www.musichallofwilliamsburg.com. Tickets

BROOKLYN ACADEMY OF MUSIC

$15–30. MAP P.163, POCKET MAP H11

A large performance space with excellent acoustics. Set in an old factory this is one of the city's best spots for live music and indie-rock.

OUTPUT

78 Wythe St at 12th St, Williamsburg. Subway L to Bedford Ave ⓦ outputclub.com. Wed–Sat 10pm–6am. Cover free–$30 (buy in advance). MAP P.163, POCKET MAP H11

A club with a big sound system in a smallish industrial space, where you can groove out to techno and ambient music. The focus is more on dancing than being part of the scene.

ST. ANN'S WAREHOUSE

45 Water St, at Dock St, Dumbo. Subway A, C to High St, F to York St ☎ 718 254 8779, ⓦ stannswarehouse.com. MAP P.163, POCKET MAP F22

This waterfront theatre, recently transplanted to what was once the crumbling Tobacco Warehouse, puts on avant-garde performances – plays, puppetry, concerts and the like.

ACCOMMODATION

Hotels

Accommodation prices in New York City are extremely high: many hotels charge more than $200 a night for a double room; $400–500 in high season can be common. The traditional centre of hotel life is midtown Manhattan, but more and more new places are being built below 34th Street. Booking ahead is near essential, and at certain times of the year – early to mid-autumn or the weeks leading up to Christmas – the city can seem sold out. There's hardly such a thing as a fixed room price. Rates in this chapter refer to the cost of the cheapest double room at peak times; be aware that prices can change on a daily basis, depending on a hotel's occupancy and other factors subject to the whims of the booking computer. For some places, rates might be up to half as much as what's listed here, depending on when you check; booking online – whether directly with the hotel or through a third-party travel site – can save lots of money, too. Taxes add 14.75 percent to your bill, plus $3.50 per night in "occupancy tax" and room fees.

Financial District

RITZ-CARLTON > 2 West St, Battery Park. Subway #1 to Rector St, #4, #5 to Bowling Green ☎ 212 344 0800, Ⓦ www.ritzcarlton.com. MAP P.34–35, POCKET MAP C24 The views of New York Harbor and the Statue of Liberty don't get much better than from this elegant high-rise hotel. It features a lively bar, 425-square-foot rooms with soothing muted tones – all with dazzling vistas and "bath butlers" to draw baths and provide warm towels. Weekend discounts. **$595.**

Soho and Tribeca

COSMOPOLITAN > 95 W Broadway, at Chambers St. Subway A, C, #1, #2, #3 to Chambers St ☎ 1-888 895 9400 or 212 566 1900, Ⓦ www.cosmohotel .com. MAP P.45, POCKET MAP C21 Great Tribeca location, with smart, well-maintained rooms at reasonable prices, this is one of the best of the conventional hotels downtown. **$409.**

CROSBY STREET HOTEL > 79 Crosby St, between Spring and Prince sts. Subway N, R to Prince St, #6 to Spring St ☎ 212 226 6400, Ⓦ www.firmdale .com. MAP P.45, POCKET MAP D19 It's expensive, but you get bright and spacious rooms set around a courtyard on the edge of trendy Soho, with luxurious bathrooms, floor-to-ceiling windows and contemporary art throughout. Rooms on the higher floors have spectacular views. Afternoon tea ($38) is served all day in the drawing room. **$680.**

SMYTH TRIBECA > 85 W Broadway, between Warren and Chambers sts. Subway A, C, #1, #2, #3 to Chambers St ☎ 212 587 7000, Ⓦ www .thompsonhotels.com. MAP P.45, POCKET MAP C21 One of the trendier boutiques in this part of town, with plush, contemporary design and furnishings with classical and Art Deco touches; iPod docking station, plasma TV and large bathroom (with Kiehl products) included. **$459.**

TRIBECA GRAND HOTEL > 2 Sixth Ave, between White and Walker sts. Subway #1 to Franklin St ☎1-877 519 6600 or 212 519 6600, ⓦwww.tribecagrand.com. MAP P.45, POCKET MAP C20 Craving anonymity, the Tribeca Grand is unlabelled and tucked behind a brick facade. The lounge is perfect for drinks and the rooms are stylish, yet understated, though each bathroom boasts a phone and built-in TV. **$479.**

The Lower East Side

BLUE MOON > 100 Orchard St, between Delancey and Broome sts. Subway F to Delancey St, J, M, Z to Essex St ☎212 533 9080, ⓦwww.bluemoon-nyc.com. MAP P.63, POCKET MAP E19 Five-storey Lower East Side tenement transformed into a luxurious boutique, with rooms named after 1930s and 1940s celebrities and decked out with period iron-frame beds and the odd antique – rooms on the 6th, 7th and 8th floors also come with fabulous views across the city. Continental breakfast and wi-fi included. **$295.**

HOTEL 91 > 91 E Broadway. Subway F to E Broadway ☎212 266 6800, ⓦwww.thehotel91.com. MAP P.63, POCKET MAP F21 Funky Lower East Side boutique, with a slight Asian theme – orchids grace every room, and a statue of Buddha sits in the lobby. Rooms are compact but well equipped, with LCD TVs and marble bathrooms. Free wi-fi. **$245.**

The East Village

BOWERY HOTEL > 335 Bowery, at E 3rd St. Subway #6 to Bleecker St ☎212 505 9100, ⓦwww.theboweryhotel.com. MAP P.70-71, POCKET MAP D18 This fabulous, but pricey, boutique property oozes sophistication and tempts guests with iPod docks, floor-to-ceiling windows, marble tubs with a view and a hip lounge bar. **$545.**

The West Village

LARCHMONT > 27 W 11th St, between Fifth and Sixth aves. Subway F, M, L to 14th St ☎212 989 9333, ⓦwww.larchmonthotel.com. MAP P.82-83, POCKET MAP C17 This budget hotel, with a terrific location on a tree-lined street in Greenwich Village, has small but nice clean rooms – it's a bargain, but the bathrooms are shared. Slightly more expensive at weekends. **$135.**

Chelsea and the Meatpacking District

CHELSEA PINES INN > 317 W 14th St, between Eighth and Ninth aves. Subway A, C, E to 14th St ☎1-888 546 2700 or 212 929 1023, ⓦwww.chelseapinesinn.com. MAP P.93, POCKET MAP A17 Housed in an old brownstone, this super-friendly hotel offers clean, comfortable, shabby-chic rooms, all done with a movie motif and recently renovated. Long popular with a gay and lesbian clientele. Best to book in advance. **$269.**

HÔTEL AMERICANO > 518 W 27th St, between Tenth and Eleventh aves. Subway #1 to 28th St ☎212 216 0000, ⓦwww.hotel-americano.com. MAP P.93, POCKET MAP B10 The first venture outside of Mexico by boutique developers Grupo Habita, the eye-catching *Americano* sits right on the High Line, with a sleek, modern style all its own. Some evidence: Japanese-style platform beds, showers looking out onto the skyline and separate elevators for guest and public use. **$445.**

THE JANE > 113 Jane St, at West St. Subway A, C, E, to 14th St, L to Eighth Ave. ☎212 924 6700, ⓦwww.thejanenyc.com. MAP P.93, POCKET MAP A17. Equipped with a hip bar-club, this chic place has small rooms inspired by ship's cabins. Bunk-bed rooms (shared bathroom) are a good deal, but there are also pricier captain's cabins (en suite). Bunks **$145**, Captain's **$325.**

MARITIME > 88 Ninth Ave, between W 16th and 17th sts. Subway A, C, E, L to 14th St-Eighth Ave. ☎212 242 4300, ⓦwww.themaritimehotel.com.

MAP P.93, POCKET MAP C11. The nautical theme runs through this contemporary hotel, and rooms come with porthole windows – as well as complimentary bike use and access to a top-notch gym and rooftop bar. **$425.**

Union Square, Gramercy Park and the Flatiron District

ACE > 20 W 29th St, at Broadway. Subway N, R to 28th St ☎212 679 2222, ⓦwww.acehotel.com/newyork. MAP P.101, POCKET MAP D10 Capturing the spirit of old New York, yet fully modern, the *Ace Hotel* sets a new standard for bohemian chic. A whole host of different room styles are on offer (including cheaper bunks), with retro-style fridges, guitars, muted tones and cool artwork. **$402.**

GIRAFFE > 365 Park Ave, at 26th St. Subway #6 to 28th St ☎ 212 685 7700, ⓦ www.hotelgiraffe.com. MAP P.101, POCKET MAP E10 A small, boutique hotel with a personal touch, the *Giraffe* offers deluxe rooms with tiny terraces and all the amenities; there's a wine and cheese hour (daily 5–8pm) in the lobby with live music accompaniment. **$442.**

GRAMERCY PARK > 2 Lexington Ave, at E 21st St. Subway #6 to 23rd St ☎ 212 920 3300, ⓦwww.gramercyparkhotel.com. MAP P.101, POCKET MAP E10 An Ian Schrager overhaul gave new life to this once bohemian hotel, located in a prime Gramercy spot with access to the private park. The rooms are bold and luxurious. **$599.**

NOMAD > 1170 Broadway, at W 28th St. Subway N, R to 28th St ☎212 796 1500 or 1 855 796 1505, ⓦwww.thenomadhotel.com. MAP P.101, POCKET MAP D10 A competitor for the same crowd as the nearby *Ace* (see above), with a celebrated on-site restaurant, the welcoming *NoMad* offers stylish, spacious rooms with damask patterns, Iranian rugs, clawfoot tubs, king-size beds and a mishmash of tasteful art on the walls – different in each space. A definite cut above. **$525.**

THE ROGER > 131 Madison Ave, at 31st St. Subway #6 to 33rd St ☎1 888 448 7788 or 212 448 7000, ⓦwww.therogernewyork.com. MAP P.101, POCKET MAP D9. Full of cleanliness and sharp contrasts, *The Roger* has a comfortable lobby and well-appointed rooms. Some come with small terraces with views of the Empire State Building. **$450.**

SEVENTEEN > 225 E 17th St, between Second and Third aves. Subway L, N, Q, R, #4, #5, #6 to 14th St-Union Square ☎212 475 2845, ⓦwww.hotel17ny.com. MAP P.101, POCKET MAP E11 *Seventeen*'s rooms feature a/c, cable TV and wi-fi, though all share baths. It's clean, friendly and nicely situated on a pleasant tree-lined street minutes from Union Square and the East Village. **$150.**

Midtown

70 PARK AVENUE HOTEL > 70 Park Ave, at 38th St. Subway S, #4, #5, #6, #7 to 42nd St-Grand Central ☎1-877 707 2752 or 212 973 2400 ⓦwww.70parkave.com. MAP P.109, POCKET MAP E9 This classy boutique hotel is adorned with re-creations of classical friezes and frescoes, and original lighting and furnishing design featuring rich woods and muted earth tones. Extras include a 24hr fitness centre, flat-screen TVs, wi-fi and a nightly wine reception. Pet-friendly. **$427.**

AFFINIA SHELBURNE > 303 Lexington Ave, between E 37th and E 38th sts. Subway #4, #5, #6, #7 to 42nd St-Grand Central ☎212 689 5200, ⓦwww.affinia.com. MAP P.109, POCKET MAP E9 Luxurious hotel in the most elegant part of Murray Hill. Many rooms have kitchenettes ($30 extra), its restaurant *Rare* specializes in gourmet burgers, and there's a rooftop bar. **$370.**

ALGONQUIN > 59 W 44th St, between Fifth and Sixth aves. Subway B, D, F, M to 42nd St ☎ 212 840 6800, ⓦ www.algonquinhotel.com. MAP P.109, POCKET MAP D8 At New York's classic literary hangout, you'll find a resident cat named Matilda, suites with silly names and a whole lot of style and tradition. The bedrooms have been refurbished to good effect. **$479.**

CHAMBERS > 15 W 56th St, between Fifth and Sixth aves. Subway F to 57th St ☏ 1 866 204 5656 or 212 974 5656, ⓦ www.chambershotel.com. MAP P.109, POCKET MAP D7 Designed by architect David Rockwell, *Chambers* is well placed for Central Park and MoMA, though you can just sit and admire the 500 original works in the hallways. Modern, tasteful rooms approximate a New York apartment, as do the mezzanine lounge spaces. A *Momofuku* offspring, *Má Pêche*, is on-site. **$575.**

IROQUOIS > 49 W 44th St, between Fifth and Sixth aves. Subway B, D, F, M to 42nd St ☏ 1 800 332 7220 or 212 840 3080, ⓦ www.iroquoisny.com. MAP P.109, POCKET MAP D8 A former haven for rock bands, this reinvented "boutique" hotel has comfortable, tasteful rooms with Italian marble baths and a health centre, library and an upscale French restaurant. One of the hotel's noted visitors is immortalized in the suite named after him: James Dean lived here 1951–53 (room #803). **$489.**

LIBRARY > 299 Madison Ave, at E 41st St. Subway #4, #5, #6, #7 to 42nd St-Grand Central ☏ 212 983 4500, ⓦ www.libraryhotel.com. MAP P.109, POCKET MAP D8 The *Library's* unusual concept has each floor devoted to one of the ten major categories of the Dewey Decimal System. Coloured in shades of brown and cream, the rooms are average-sized but nicely appointed, with big bathrooms. The hotel throws wine and cheese get-togethers weekday evenings. **$392.**

THE MANSFIELD > 12 W 44th St, between Fifth and Sixth aves. Subway B, D, F, M to 42nd St ☏ 1 800 255 5167 or 212 277 8700, ⓦ www.mansfieldhotel .com. MAP P.109, POCKET MAP D8 One of the loveliest, friendliest hotels in the city, the *Mansfield* is both grand and intimate. With its recessed floor spotlighting, copper-domed salon, clubby library and nightly jazz, there's a charming, quirky feel about the place. **$325.**

THE METRO > 45 W 35th St, between Fifth and Sixth aves. Subway B, D, F, M,

N, Q, R to 34th St ☏ 1 800 356 3870 or 212 947 2500, ⓦ www.hotelmetronyc .com. MAP P.109, POCKET MAP D9 A very stylish hotel, with minimal Hollywood theming, a delightful seasonal rooftop terrace, clean rooms, wi-fi and free continental breakfast. **$364.**

MORGANS > 237 Madison Ave, between E 37th and E 38th sts. Subway #6 to 33rd St ☏ 1 800 334 3408 or 212 686 0300, ⓦ www.morganshotel .com. MAP P.109, POCKET MAP D9 Still one of the chicest flophouses in town; rooms come in soothing neutral tones (save for some checkerboard accents) and maple panelling, with specially commissioned photographs by the late Robert Mapplethorpe. **$419.**

POD > 230 E 51st St, between Second and Third aves. Subway #6 to 51st St ☏ 212 355 0300, ⓦ www.thepodhotel .com. MAP P.109, POCKET MAP E8 This pleasant budget hotel is one of the best deals in Midtown. All 370 "pods" (solo, double, bunk, queen or "odd"; reminiscent of a ship's quarters) come with a/c, iPod docks, free wi-fi and flat-screen TVs, though some share baths. The open-air roof deck is a bonus, with stunning views. **$299.**

ROGER SMITH > 501 Lexington Ave, at E 47th St. Subway #6 to 51st St ☏ 1 800 445 0277 or 212 755 1400, ⓦ www.rogersmith.com. MAP P.109, POCKET MAP E8 Lots of style and personality: individually decorated rooms and bold artwork on display in the common areas. Breakfast is included. **$424.**

THE STRAND > 33 W 37th St, between Fifth and Sixth aves. Subway B, D, F, M, N, Q, R to 34th St-Herald Square ☏ 212 448 1024, ⓦ www.thestrandnyc.com. MAP P.109, POCKET MAP D9 The rooms, some of which have views of the Empire State Building, are fresh and comfortable, but it's the soothing lobby and lovely roof-deck bar that help this hotel stand out. **$499.**

WALDORF ASTORIA > 301 Park Ave, at E 50th St. Subway #6 to 51st St ☏ 1 800 925 3673 or 212 355 3000,

Ⓦwww.waldorfnewyork.com.
MAP P.109, POCKET MAP E8 One of the great names among New York hotels and restored to its 1930s glory, the *Waldorf* is a wonderful place to stay if you can afford it or someone else is paying. Even if you can't, it's worth dropping by for a look at the lobby (see p.110) and a drink at the mahogany bar downstairs. **$549.**

Times Square and the Theater District

414 > 414 W 46th St, between Ninth and Tenth aves. Subway C, E to 50th St ⓣ 212 399 0006 or 1-866/414-HOTEL, Ⓦ www.414hotel.com. MAP P.123, POCKET MAP C8 Popular with Europeans but welcoming to all, this guesthouse, which has larger-than-ordinary rooms in two townhouses, makes a nice camp a bit removed from Times Square's bustle. The backyard garden is a wonderful place to enjoy your morning coffee. **$329.**

AMERITANIA AT TIMES SQUARE > 54 230 W 54th St, at Broadway. Subway B, D, E to Seventh Ave ⓣ 855 767 5050 or 212 247 5000, Ⓦ www.ameritanianyc.com. MAP P.123, POCKET MAP C7. One of the coolest-looking hotels in the city, with well-furnished rooms with marble bathrooms; there's a bar/restaurant off the high-tech, funky lobby. **$369.**

CASABLANCA > 147 W 43rd St, between Sixth Ave and Broadway. Subway B, D, F, M, #1, #2, #3 to 42nd St ⓣ 1 888 922 7225 or 212 869 1212, Ⓦ www.casablancahotel.com. MAP P.123, POCKET MAP D8 Moorish tiles, ceiling fans and *Rick's Café* are all here in this unusual and understated theme hotel. While the feeling is 1940s Morocco, the rooms are all up to date. **$395.**

DISTRIKT > 342 W 40th St, between Eighth and Ninth aves. Subway A, C, E to 42nd St-Port Authority ⓣ 1-888 444 5610 or 212 706 6100, Ⓦ www .distrikthotel.com. MAP P.123, POCKET MAP C9 With a city neighbourhood theme, the welcoming *Distrikt* has nice-sized

rooms done in classy muted browns and beiges; choose one of the upper floors (eg "Harlem") for the best views. The street outside is on the unsalubrious side. **$375.**

INK48 > 653 Eleventh Ave, between 47th and 48th sts. Subway C, E to 50th St ⓣ 877 843 8869 or 212 757 0088 Ⓦ www.ink48.com. MAP P.123, POCKET MAP B8 Located on an industrial strip, this old printing press has been re-made into a dashing hotel; all rooms face outwards – many to the Hudson – for splendid views (best from upper-floor corner rooms), and have modern decor and lofty ceilings. The rooftop bar, *Press Lounge*, is a plus, as is the spa. Dog-friendly. **$409.**

KNICKERBOCKER >6 Times Square, Broadway, at 42nd St. Subway #1, #2, #3, N, Q, R to Times Sq-42nd St. ⓣ 1 855 86K NICK, Ⓦ www .theknickerbocker.com. MAP P.123, POCKET MAP D8. This century-old Beaux Arts landmark, once a high-society hotel built by John Jacob Astor, was reopened in 2015. The largish rooms are elegantly appointed but not overdone. **$399**

LE PARKER MERIDIEN > 119 W 56th St, between Sixth and Seventh aves. Subway F to 57th St ⓣ 212 245 5000 or 800 543 4300, Ⓦwww.parkermeridien.com. MAP P.123, POCKET MAP D7. This hotel maintains a shiny, clean veneer, with spacious, modern rooms, a huge fitness centre, rooftop swimming pool and 24hr room service. The tucked-away, ground-floor *Burger Joint* (see p.128) is a fun place for a bite to eat. **$514.**

ROOM MATE GRACE > 125 W 45th St, between Sixth and Seventh aves. Subway B, D, F, M, #1, #2, #3 to 42nd St ⓣ 212 354 2323, Ⓦ www.room-matehotels .com. MAP P.123, POCKET MAP D8 You won't find many hotels like this one, with a lobby that more closely resembles a concession stand; a tiny glassed-in pool overlooked by a louche loungey bar; different, funky retro wallpaper on each floor; and ultra-modern rooms with platform beds. **$379.**

SALISBURY > 123 W 57th St, between Sixth and Seventh aves. Subway F, N, Q, R to 57th St ☎ 212 246 1300, Ⓦ www .nycsalisbury.com. MAP P.123, POCKET MAP D7 Good service, large rooms with kitchenettes and proximity to Central Park are the attractions here. **$339.**

The Upper East Side

WALES > 1295 Madison Ave, between E 92nd and E 93rd sts. Subway #6 to 96th St ☎ 866 925 3746 or 212 876 6000, Ⓦwww.hotelwalesnyc.com. MAP P.137. POCKET MAP D4 Just steps from "Museum Mile", this Carnegie Hill hotel has hosted guests for over a century. Rooms are attractive with antique details, thoughtful in-room amenities and some views of Central Park. There's also a rooftop terrace and free continental breakfast. **$370.**

The Upper West Side

LUCERNE > 201 W 79th St, at Amsterdam Ave. Subway B, C to 81st St; #1 to 79th St ☎ 1 800 492 8122 or 212 875 1000, Ⓦwww.thelucernehotel .com. MAP P.147, POCKET MAP B5 This beautifully restored 1904 brownstone, with its extravagantly Baroque red terracotta entrance, charming rooms and friendly staff, is just a block from the American Museum of Natural History and close to the liveliest stretch of Columbus Avenue. **$350.**

MILBURN > 242 W 76th St, between Broadway and West End. Subway #1 to 79th St ☎ 1 800 833 9622 or 212 362 1006, Ⓦwww.milburnhotel .com. MAP P.147, POCKET MAP B5 Once past the classic feel of the lobby, the rooms are less showy but are on the large side, all with kitchenettes. It's a good choice for families, and the hotel offers free use of a swimming pool one block away. **$259.**

NYLO > 2178 Broadway, at 77th St. Subway #1 to 79th St ☎ 1 800 509 7598 or 212 362 1100, Ⓦ www .nylo-nyc.com. MAP P.147, POCKET MAP B5 Sizeable rooms, community balconies and no-nonsense design make this updated hotel a solid option. **$340.**

Harlem

ALOFT HARLEM > 2296 Frederick Douglass Blvd, at W 124th St. Subway A, B, C, D to 125th St ☎ 212 49 4000, Ⓦwww.aloftharlem.com. MAP P.154–155. The first hotel to open in the neighborhood since the 1960s has a bright, stylish interior and airy, loft-inspired rooms with platform beds. **$269**

Williamsburg

WYTHE > 80 Wythe Ave, at N 11th St. Subway L to Bedford St ☎ 718 460 8000, Ⓦwww.wythehotel.com MAP P.163, POCKET MAP H11 This old factory has been smartly converted into a chic boutique hotel; various industrial touches have been preserved and emphasized, whether exposed brick or floor-to-ceiling warehouse-style windows. "Baby queens" and bunks offer a good deal, though you may want to pay extra for more space and the Brooklyn or Manhattan-side views from higher floors. **$375.**

Long Island City

PAPER FACTORY > 37-06 36th St, at 37th Ave, Long Island City, Queens. Subway R, M to 36th St, N, Q to 36th Ave ☎ 718 392 7200, Ⓦwww .paperfactoryhotel.com. MAP P.161, POCKET MAP J6. A stylish hotel in an increasingly popular part of town, the *Paper Factory* was, indeed, once an exemplar of its name. Rooms have a certain rough-hewn chic, and many rooms come with views of the neighbourhood or Manhattan skyline. **$229.**

Hostels

Hostels can offer savings as well as a sociable vibe, but there are, relatively speaking, limited options in the city – at least that fit the bill in terms of quality and prime location. Wherever the case, book ahead: reservations are usually essential.

AMERICAN DREAM > 168 E 24th St, between Third and Lexington aves. Subway #6 to 23rd St ☎ 212 260 9779, Ⓦ www.americandreamhostel.com. MAP P.101, POCKET MAP E10 A great location helps this clean, hospitable hostel be a good option for a short-term budget stay; complimentary wi-fi and continental breakfast. Prices increase at weekends. **Shared rooms $60–85/person, singles $95–110.**

CHELSEA INTERNATIONAL HOSTEL > 251 W 20th St, between Seventh and Eighth aves. Subway C, E, #1 to 23rd St ☎ 212 647 0010, Ⓦwww.chelseahostel.com. MAP P.93, POCKET MAP C10 In the heart of Chelsea, this is a smart downtown choice. Guests must leave a $10 key deposit. No curfew; passport required and advance reservations near essential. **Shared rooms $45–80/person, private doubles $145–175.**

HOTEL 41 @ TIMES SQUARE > 206 W 41st St, between Seventh and Eighth aves. Subway A, C, E to 42nd St-Port Authority or N, Q, R, S, #1, #2, #3, #7 to Times Square-42nd St ☎ 212 703 8600, Ⓦ www.hotel41ny.com. MAP P.123, POCKET MAP C9 Not strictly a hostel, but they have rooms for up to three people with single beds. You won't find much cheaper if you want to be right in the middle of the madness. Rooms come with high-speed Internet access and free continental breakfasts. **Doubles $140, triples $210.**

THE LOCAL NY > 1302 44th Ave, Long Island City, Queens. Subway E, M to Court Sq-23rd St ☎347 738 5251, Ⓦwww.thelocalny.com. MAP P.163, POCKET MAP G7 This newish hostel has basic but bright rooms and a café-bar; the surrounding neighbourhood is a nice change of pace. **Dorms $59, private double $180.**

B&Bs and apartments

Bed-and-breakfast accommodation can be a good way of staying right in the centre of Manhattan at an affordable price. But don't expect to socialize with your temporary landlord/lady – chances are you'll have a self-contained room and hardly see them. Reservations are normally arranged through an agency such as those listed below; book well in advance. Try Craigslist (Ⓦ newyork.craigslist.org) for everything from apartment swaps to short-term rentals; more holiday apartment listings can be found on HomeAway (Ⓦ homeaway.com), Vacation Rentals by Owner (Ⓦ www.vrbo.com) and Airbnb (Ⓦ www.airbnb.com).

B&B agencies

AFFORDABLE NEW YORK CITY >
21 E 10th St ☎ 212 533 4001, ⓦ www
.affordablenewyorkcity.com. Detailed
descriptions are provided for this
established and customer-oriented
network of 120 properties (B&Bs and
apartments). Cash or travellers' cheques
only; four- and five-night minimums.
**B&B accommodation from $95 (shared
bathroom) and $135 (private bathroom),
unhosted studios $170–250 and
one-bedroom apartments $175–300.**

CITY LIGHTS BED & BREAKFAST >
Box 1562 First Ave, NY 10028 ☎212 737
7049, ⓦwww.citylightsbedandbreakfast
.com. More than 400 carefully screened
B&Bs (and short-term apartment rentals)
on its books, with many of the hosts
involved in theatre and the arts. Minimum
stay two nights, with some exceptions.
Reserve well in advance. **Hosted doubles
$80–175, unhosted apartments
$135–300 and up.**

COLBY INTERNATIONAL > 21 Park
Ave, Eccleston Park, Prescot L34 1QY,
England, UK ☎ 0151 292 2910,
ⓦ www.colbyinternational.com.
Excellent B&B accommodations arranged
from the UK. Book at least a fortnight
ahead in high season. **Singles from
$120 (per room); most studios and
apartments are more like $215–250
per night.**

B&B and apartment
properties

COLONIAL HOUSE INN > 318 W
22nd St, between Eighth and Ninth
aves. Subway C, E to 23rd St
☎212 243 9669 or 800 689 3779,
ⓦwww.colonialhouseinn.com.
MAP P.93, POCKET MAP C10 You
won't mind that this B&B is a little
worn around the edges (though it has
recently been updated) – its attractive
design and association with Gay Men's
Health Crisis make for a feel-good
accommodation experience. Only deluxe
rooms include en-suite bathrooms, while
some rooms even have refrigerators and
fireplaces, and sleep four. Continental
breakfast included. **Doubles $130,
suites up to $300.**

JONES STREET GUESTHOUSE >
31 Jones St, between Bleecker and
W 4th sts. Subway A, B, C, D, E, F, M
to W 4th St, #1 to Christopher St,
contact via email only,
ⓦwww.jonesstreetguesthouse.com.
MAP P.82–83, POCKET MAP B18 Rare
B&B in the heart of the West Village,
just off Bleecker; two nicely renovated
en-suite rooms, spotlessly clean, with
friendly owners in the apartments
above (their duplex can also be rented)
– closest you'll get to "living like a
local". Breakfast is courtesy of a $5 per
person voucher at nearby *Doma*. Free
wi-fi. **Single $240, double $260.**

Favourite places to stay

There's something for every
taste in the city, though
even if you find the perfect
accommodation for you, you'll
probably still register some
surprise at the (small) size of the
room. Here are just a few of our
favourites:

Best place for downtown chic:
Blue Moon, p.177

**Best place to blow the expense
account**: *Waldorf Astoria*, p.179

**Best place for a romantic
getaway**: *Gramercy Park*, p.178

**Best place to be in the heart of
it all**: *The Mansfield*, p.179

Best place for a modest budget:
Cosmopolitan, p.176

**Best place for a room with a
view**: *Ink48*, p.180.

**Best place for mixing function
with form**: *Nomad*, p.178

Arrival

By air

New York City is served by three major airports: most international flights use John F. Kennedy, or **JFK** (☎ 718 244 4444), in Queens, and **Newark Liberty** (☎ 973 961 6000), in New Jersey, which has easier access to Lower Manhattan. Most domestic arrivals touch down at **LaGuardia** (☎ 718 533 3400), also in Queens, or at Newark. All three share a website at ⓦ www.panynj.gov.

Getting into the city

From JFK, the NYC Airporter (☎ 212 875 8200, ⓦ www.nyairporter.com) runs **buses** to Grand Central Terminal, Port Authority Bus Terminal and Penn Station (every 20–30min 5am–11.30pm; 1hr 30min; $17 one-way, $30 round-trip). The **AirTrain** (24hr daily; ☎ 1-877 535 2478, ⓦ www.panynj.gov; $5) runs between JFK and the Jamaica and Howard Beach subway stations in Queens; at Jamaica you can connect to the E, J or Z subway lines, and at Howard Beach to the A line, into Manhattan (from both stations: 1hr; $2.75). Alternatively, the **Long Island Railroad** (LIRR) runs faster trains from the Jamaica station to Penn Station (35min; $15 peak).

From LaGuardia, New York Airport Service buses (see above) take up to one hour to get to Grand Central and Port Authority (every 20–30min 7.30am–11pm; $14 one-way, $26 round-trip). Alternatively, for $2.75 (with **MetroCard**), take the #M60 bus to 106th St in Manhattan, where you can transfer to downtown-bound subway lines.

From Newark, **Newark Airport Express Bus** (☎ 877 863 9275, ⓦ www.coachusa.com) runs buses to Grand Central Station, Port Authority Bus Terminal and Penn Station (every 30min–1hr, 24hr; $16 one-way, $28 round-trip). For train services, take the short **AirTrain** (every 3–15min; 24hr) ride to Newark Airport Train Station and connect with frequent NJ Transit or Amtrak trains heading into the city (every 20–30min 4.30am–2.30am; $13). The AirTrain costs $5.50, but if you buy a NJ Transit or Amtrak ticket before leaving the system, the AirTrain ticket is included.

Taxis are available at all airports: reckon on paying $25–37 from LaGuardia to Manhattan, a flat rate of $52 from JFK and $50–70 from Newark; you'll also be responsible for the turnpike and tunnel tolls – an extra $8 or so – as well as a fifteen- to twenty-percent tip for the driver. Note that bridges between Brooklyn/Queens and Manhattan are free, but the Queens Midtown Tunnel has a toll of $8. You should only use official yellow taxis that wait at designated ranks – just follow the signs out of the terminal.

By bus or train

Greyhound and most other long-distance **bus** lines (with the exception of the Chinatown buses, which arrive in Chinatown, and Mega Bus/Bolt Bus which drop off on the streets of Midtown) terminate at the Port Authority Bus Terminal, W 42nd St and Eighth Ave.

Amtrak trains come in to Penn Station, at Seventh Avenue and W 33rd St. From either Port Authority or Penn Station, multiple subway lines will take you where you want to go.

Getting around

Buses

Bus and subway information

☎718 330 1234 (daily 6am–10pm).
New York's **bus system** is clean and
usually efficient. It is often extremely
slow in peak hours, but it can be your
best bet for travelling crosstown. Pay
on entry with a **MetroCard** ($2.75,
express $6.50) or exact fare in coins;
you can transfer for free from subway
to bus, bus to subway, or from bus to
bus, in one direction within two hours.

City tours

Big Onion Walking Tours

☎212 439 1090, ⓦwww.bigonion
.com. Excellent walking tours by
guides with advanced degrees in
American history ($20).

Circle Line Pier 83, at the end of W
42nd St at the West Side Highway,
☎212 563 3200, ⓦwww.circleline42
.com. Boat cruises around Manhattan
($37 1hr 30min, $42 2hr30min).

Gray Line ☎1 800 669 0051, ⓦwww
.newyorksightseeing.com. Double-
decker hop on, hop-off buses touring
the main sights (around $49 for 24hr).

Big Apple Jazz Tours ☎212 439
1090, ⓦwww.bigapplejazz.com.
Fabulous introduction to the Harlem
jazz scene, minibus tours take in
clubs and jazz history (from $99).

Hush Hip Hop Tours ☎212 391
0900, ⓦwww.hushtours.com. Bus
tours of hip-hop haunts, given by
legends such as Grandmaster Caz
and Rahiem ($55–75).

Liberty Helicopter Tours Pier 6 on
South St, between Broad St and
Coenties Slip ☎212 967 6464 or ☎1
800 542 9933, ⓦwww.liberty
helicopters.com. Helicopter tours
($185 for 12–15min to $250 for
16–20min/person).

Cycling

New York's bike share scheme is
dubbed **Citi Bike** (ⓦwww
.citibikenyc.com; 24hr Pass is $9.95,
the 7-Day Pass is $25). Pay at any
bike station kiosk with a credit card.
Trips of less than thirty minutes are
free with your pass.

The subway

The fastest way to get around is the
user-friendly **subway**, open 24hr. A
number or letter identifies each
train and route, and most routes in
Manhattan run uptown (north) or
downtown (south), rather than
crosstown. Every trip, whether on
express or local lines, costs $2.75
if you pay by **MetroCard**, available
at station booths or debit/credit
card capable vending machines
(you'll pay $3 for a single ticket
without a MetroCard). MetroCards
can be purchased in any amount
from $5.50 to $80; a $20 purchase
gives you $22.50 on your card.
Unlimited-ride cards – the best
deal if you intend to be on the go
– allow unlimited travel for a
certain period of time: a 7-day pass
costs $31 and a 30-day pass is
$116.50 (there is no one-day pass).

Taxis

Taxis are reasonably priced – $3 upon
entry and $0.50 for every 1/5 mile, with
a $0.50 surcharge 8pm–6am, and a $1
surcharge Mon–Fri 4–8pm. Most
drivers take up to four passengers,
refuse bills larger than $20, and ask for
the nearest cross street to your
destination. It's customary to tip ten to
twenty percent. **Boro Taxis** are
painted light green and serve areas
not commonly covered by yellow cabs
(northern Manhattan and the outer
boroughs). They follow the same rates
and rules as yellow cabs.

Directory A-Z

Cinema

For first-run movies and block-busters, head to megaplexes such as AMC Empire 25 at 234 W 42nd St, between Seventh and Eighth aves (🕿 1 888 262 4386), or Regal Union Square at 850 Broadway and 13th St (🕿 212 253 6266). Good places for indie flicks, old classics and documentaries are IFC Center, 323 6th Ave, at W 3rd St (🕿 212 924 7771, 🌐 www.ifccenter.com), Film Forum at 209 W Houston St and 6th Ave (🕿 212 727 8110, 🌐 www.filmforum.org), the Paris Theater at 4 W 58th St (🕿 212 688 3800, 🌐 www.citycinemas.com) and the Walter Reade Theater at the Lincoln Center, 165 W 65th St, at Broadway (🕿 212 875 5601, 🌐 www.filmlinc.org). Tickets at most cinemas are around $15 (buy online at 🌐 www.movietickets.com).

Consulates

Australia, 34/F, 150 E 42nd St, (🕿 212 351 6500, 🌐 www.newyork.consulate.gov.au).
Canada, 1251 6th Ave, at 50th St (🕿 212 596 1628, 🌐 www.can-am.gc.ca/new_york).
Ireland, 17/F, 345 Park Ave, between 51st and 52nd sts (🕿 212 319 2555, 🌐 www.can-am.gc.ca/new-york).
New Zealand, 295 Madison Ave, at 41st St (🕿 212 832 4038).
South Africa, 333 E 38th St, between First and Second aves (🕿 212 213 4880, 🌐 www.dfa.ie/irish-consulate/newyork).
UK, 845 3rd Ave, between 51st and 52nd sts (🕿 212 745 0200, 🌐 www.gov.uk).

Emergency numbers For Police, Fire or Ambulance dial 🕿 911.

Crime

In two words: don't worry. New York has come a long way in recent years. While the city can sometimes feel dangerous, the reality is somewhat different. New York is America's safest city with a population over one million. Take the normal precautions and you should be fine; carry bags closed and across your body, don't let cameras dangle, keep wallets in front – not back – pockets, and don't flash money around. You should also keep a firm grip on your tablet or phone on the subway (these are occasionally snatched just as the doors close). Mugging can and does happen, but rarely during the day. Avoid wandering empty streets or the subway late at night (especially alone). If you are unlucky enough to be mugged, try to stay calm and hand over the money.

Electricity

110V AC with two-pronged plugs. Unless they're dual voltage (most mobile phones, cameras, tablets and laptops are), all Australian, British, European, Irish, New Zealand and South African appliances will need a voltage transformer as well as a plug adaptor (hair-dryers are the most common problem for travellers).

Gay and lesbian New York

There are few places in America where gay culture thrives as it does in New York. Chelsea, Hell's Kitchen, the Villages, the Lower East Side and Park Slope are the biggest hubs of gay life. If you're looking for local resources, check out *Gay City News* (🌐 www.gaycitynews.nyc), *Next Magazine* (🌐 www.nextmagazine.com), *GO* magazine (🌐 www.gomag.com) or the listings in the weekly *Time Out*.

Health

Drugstores can be found every few blocks – CVS and Duane Reade are the city's major chains, and many open 24hr (such as the Duane Reade at 1470 Broadway, near Times Square).

If you do get sick or have an accident, medical costs can be incredibly expensive; organize insurance before your trip, just in case. It costs upwards of $100 simply to see a doctor or dentist, and prescription drugs can be prohibitively expensive – if you don't have US medical insurance, you'll have to cough up the money and make a claim when you get home.

In the unlikely event that you are involved in a serious accident, a medical service (ambulance) will pick you up and charge later (typically $600–$1200 in Manhattan). Note that basic emergency care will cost at least $200, ranging to several thousand for serious trauma – that's in addition to fees for drugs, appliances, supplies and the attendant physician, who will charge separately.

Should you find yourself requiring a doctor or dentist, ask if your hotel has links to a local practice, or look in the *Yellow Pages* under "Clinics" or "Physicians and Surgeons".

Doctors in Manhattan often have long waiting lists, however, and will be reluctant to see a new patient at short notice – if you have an accident or need immediate attention, head to the 24hr emergency rooms at these and other Manhattan hospitals: New York Presbyterian (Cornell), E 70th St, at York Ave (☏ 212 746 5050); and Mount Sinai, Madison Ave, at 100th St (☏ 212 241 7171).

Internet

Wireless is king in New York. Most hotels offer it for free, and it's also available at wi-fi hotspots like Times Square and complimentary at cafés like Starbucks. Wi-fi is also free in many of New York's parks (select "attwifi"): Battery Park, Brooklyn Bridge Park, Central Park (southern section) and The High Line among them. Limited free wi-fi ("Guest-WiFi"), with a choice of a ten-minute free pass, or a day pass for $0.99, is available at Madison Square Park. Bryant Park offers its own free high-speed wi-fi network (ⓦ www .bryantpark.org), as does Union Square ("unionsquarewifi"). If you're travelling without your own computer, accessing your email is still possible at internet cafés, though their numbers are dwindling. Try Postal Connections at 200 W 39th St (Mon–Fri 8.30am–8pm, Sat & Sun 10.30am–6pm).

A great, free alternative is to stop by a branch of the New York City Public Library, where wi-fi and computer internet access and printing are available. You first need to get a guest pass at the Stephen A. Schwarzman Building (the main library building; Mon and Thurs–Sat 10am–6pm, Tues and Wed 10am–8pm, Sun 1–5pm), at 42nd St and Fifth Ave. With the pass, you can reserve time slots at computers in person or via ⓦ www.nypl.org.

Left luggage

The best place to leave luggage is your hotel, but you can also use Schwartz Travel Services (daily 8am–11pm; ☏ 212 290 2626, ⓦ www.schwartztravel.com; $2.50/hr to a maximum $10/day) at 357 W 37th St, near Penn Station.

Lost property

If you lose something on a bus or on the subway, contact NYC Transit Authority, at the W 34th St/Eighth Ave Station on the lower-level subway mezzanine

(Mon, Tues & Fri 8am–3.30pm, Wed & Thurs 11am–6.30pm; ⓦ lostfound .mtanyct.info). For items lost in a taxi call ☎ 311 or file a report online (ⓦ www.nyc.gov/taxi); try to get the taxi's medallion number (printed on your receipt).

Money

On a moderate budget, expect to spend at least $200–250 per night on accommodation in a low-to mid-range, centrally located hotel in high season, plus $30–40/person for a moderate sit-down dinner each night and about $25 more per person per day for takeout and grocery meals. Getting around will cost $31/person per week for unlimited public transportation, plus $10 for the occasional taxi ride. Sightseeing, drinking, clubbing, eating haute cuisine and going to the theatre will add exponentially to these costs.

With an ATM card you'll have access to cash from machines all over New York, though, as anywhere, you will usually be charged a fee for using a different bank's ATM network (usually $3). Most banks are open Monday–Friday 8.30am–5pm, and a few have limited Saturday hours (major Citibank branches tend to open Sat 9am–3pm). Major banks – such as Citibank and Chase – will exchange travellers' cheques and currency at a standard rate. For banking services – particularly currency exchange – outside normal business hours and at weekends, try major hotels, though the rate won't be as good.

Opening hours

The opening hours of specific attractions are given throughout the Guide. As a general rule, most museums are open Tuesday to Sunday, 10am–5 or 6pm, though most have one night per week where they stay open at least a few hours later. Government offices, including post offices, are open during regular business hours, usually 9am–5pm. Store hours vary widely, though you can generally count on them being open Monday–Saturday from around 10am–6pm, with limited Sunday hours. Many of the larger chain or department stores will stay open to 9pm or later, and you generally don't have to walk more than a few blocks anywhere to find a 24-hour deli. On national public holidays, banks and offices are likely to be closed all day, and some shops have reduced hours.

Phones

In the US, AT&T and T-Mobile use the GSM standard for mobile phones, and most foreign companies partner with them to provide service to travelling customers. Note that unless you have a tri-band phone, it is unlikely that a mobile bought for use outside the US or Canada will work inside the States. If you have a Blackberry or smartphone these should work in the US, but roaming charges, especially for data, can be extortionate; even checking voicemail can result in hefty charges. Check with your phone company before you travel.

The cost of a local call on a public payphone is 25¢ for three or four minutes, depending on the carrier (each phone company runs its own booths). Calls elsewhere within the US are usually 25–50¢ for one minute; overseas rates are much pricier, so buy a prepaid calling card ($5, $10 or $20), from a grocery store or newsstand.

To call home internationally: dial 011 + country code + number, minus the initial 0 (to call Canada, just start with the area code). Country codes are as follows: Australia (61), New Zealand (64), UK & Northern Ireland (44) and Ireland (353).

Post
International letters and postcards usually take about a week to reach their destination; rates are currently $1.15 for all international letters and postcards. To find a post office or check up-to-date rates, see ⓦ www .usps.com or call ☎ 1 800 275 8777.

Smoking
Smoking has been banned in virtually all indoor public areas (including malls, bars, restaurants and most work places) in New York – fines start at around $100 for breaking this law.

Time
New York City is on Eastern Standard Time (EST), which is five hours behind Greenwich Mean Time (GMT), three hours ahead of Pacific Standard Time, fourteen to sixteen hours behind East Coast Australia (variations for Daylight Savings) and sixteen to eighteen hours behind New Zealand (variations for Daylight Savings).

Tipping
Tipping in a restaurant, bar, taxi, or hotel lobby, on a guided tour, and even in some posh washrooms, is a part of life in New York. In restaurants in particular, it's unthinkable not to leave the minimum (fifteen percent of the bill or double the tax) – even if you disliked the service.

Tourist information
For general enquiries, call ☎ 311. The best place for information is the Official NYC Information Center, Broadway Plaza, between 43rd and 44th streets at Times Square (daily 9am–6pm; ☎ 212 484 1222, ⓦ www.nycgo.com). They have bus and subway maps, information on hotels and accommodations (including discounts), touch-screen databases and up-to-date leaflets on what's going on in the arts and elsewhere. You'll find other small tourist information centres and kiosks all over the city; inside Macy's, Herald Square (Mon–Fri 9am–7pm, Sat 10am–7pm, Sun 11am–7pm); inside Federal Hall, at 26 Wall St (Mon–Fri 9am–5pm); City Hall Park, on Broadway opposite the Woolworth Building (Mon–Fri 9am–6pm, Sat & Sun 10am–5pm); and Pier 15, South Street Seaport (daily: May–Aug 9am–7pm, Sept–April 9am–5pm).

For information about what's on, the *Village Voice* (free in Manhattan, ⓦ www.villagevoice.com) is a widely read free weekly, mainly for its comprehensive arts coverage and investigative features. Other leading weeklies include glossy *New York* magazine ($5.99; ⓦ mymag.com), which has reasonably comprehensive listings, the venerable *New Yorker* magazine (ⓦ www.newyorker .com; $7.99) and *Time Out New York* (ⓦ timeout.com/newyork; free every Wednesday) – a clone of its London original, combining the city's most comprehensive what's-on listings with New York-slanted news stories and entertainment features.

The *New York Times* ($2.50; ⓦ www .nytimes.com) is an American institution and prides itself on being the "paper of record". It has solid, sometimes stolid, international coverage, and places much emphasis on its news analysis.

Travelling with children
Perhaps contrary to belief, New York is a child-friendly city: there's tons

to keep their attention, including many sights specifically geared towards kids, and lots of public spaces in which to blow off steam.

Though some parents might have fears of taking small children on the subway, it's perfectly safe; indeed, the kids will probably get a kick out of it, crowds, noise and all. Your main problem will be getting your stroller (if you're using one) up and down the stairs – though you'll often find people willing to lend a hand. Most restaurants, save perhaps the fanciest and trendiest, easily accommodate children.

If you're in need of a babysitter, consider contacting the Babysitters' Guild (☎212 682 0227, ⓦwww .babysittersguild.com), a fully licensed organization with a carefully selected and experienced staff.

For listings of what's going on when you're in town, check out ⓦwww .nymetroparents.com or ⓦwww .newyorkfamily.com, or magazines like *Time Out* and its specialized edition for kids (ⓦtimeout.com/ new-york-kids), *TONY Kids*.

Travellers with disabilities

New York City has had disabled access regulations imposed on an aggressively disabled-unfriendly system. There are wide variations in accessibility, making navigation a tricky business.

At the same time, you'll find New Yorkers surprisingly willing to go out of their way to help you. For wheelchair users, getting around on the subway is next to impossible without someone to help you, and even then is extremely difficult at most stations. Several, but not all, lines are equipped with elevators, but this doesn't make much of a difference. The Transit Authority is working to make stations accessible, but at the rate they're going it won't happen soon.

Buses are another story, and are the first choice of many disabled New Yorkers. All MTA buses are equipped with wheelchair lifts and locks. To get on a bus, wait at the bus stop to signal the driver you need to board; when he or she has seen you, move to the back door, where he or she will assist you. For travellers with other mobility difficulties, the driver will "kneel" the bus to allow you easier access. For more travel information for people with disabilities call ☎718 596 8585 (daily 6am–10pm).

Taxis are a viable option for visitors with visual and hearing impairments and minor mobility difficulties. For wheelchair users, taxis are less of a possibility unless you have a collapsible chair, in which case drivers are required to store it and assist you; the unfortunate reality is that most drivers won't stop if they see you waiting. If you're refused, try to get the taxi's medallion number and report the driver at ☎311. Most of the major hotels in New York have wheelchair-accessible rooms, including roll-in showers.

Traveler's Aid (ⓦwww .travelersaid.org), a nonprofit organization, has professional and volunteer staff who provide emergency assistance to disabled or elderly travellers at JFK Airport: you can find volunteers at the Ground Transportation Counters in each terminal or via their main office in the arrivals area of Terminal 4 (daily 10am–6pm). They also operate at Newark Airport. The Mayor's Office for People with Disabilities, 100 Gold St, 2nd floor (☎212 788 2830, ⓦwww.nyc.gov /html/mopd), offers valuable general information and resources for travellers with disabilities.

Festivals and events

CHINESE NEW YEAR

The first full moon between Jan 21 and Feb 19

Chinatown bursts open to watch a giant red, green and gold dragon made of wood, cloth and papier-mâché run down Mott Street.

ST PATRICK'S DAY PARADE

March 17 Ⓦ www.nycstpatricksparade.org

Irish bands and organizations celebrate an impromptu 1762 march by Irish militiamen on St Patrick's Day. A parade heads up Fifth Avenue between 44th and 86th streets.

CELEBRATE BROOKLYN/ SUMMERSTAGE

June–Aug

These two summer-long music festivals, featuring many free events, take place in Prospect Park's Bandshell and Rumsey Playfield in Central Park.

GAY PRIDE

Third or fourth week of June

Ⓦ nycpride.org

The world's biggest Pride event kicks off with a rally and ends with a parade, street fair and dance. Activities centre on the West Village.

Public holidays

January 1: New Year's Day; **3rd Monday:** Dr Martin Luther King Jr's Birthday; **February 3rd Monday:** Presidents' Day; **May Last Monday:** Memorial Day; **July 4:** Independence Day; **September 1st Monday:** Labor Day; **October 2nd Monday:** Columbus Day; **November 11:** Veterans' Day; **4th Thursday:** Thanksgiving Day; **December 25:** Christmas Day

US OPEN

First two weeks of September

Ⓦ www.usopen.org

Try to catch a day session for this Grand Slam tennis tournament, held in Flushing, Queens.

WEST INDIAN AMERICAN DAY CARNIVAL

Labor Day Ⓦ wiadcacarnival.org

Held on Eastern Parkway, Brooklyn's largest parade is modelled after the carnivals of Trinidad and Tobago and features music, food, dance and colourful floats with sound systems.

VILLAGE HALLOWEEN PARADE

Oct 31 Ⓦ halloween-nyc.com

New Yorkers get their freak on at America's largest Halloween celebration. Spectacular puppets, sexy cross-dressers and scary monsters parade up Sixth Avenue from Spring to W 23rd sts.

NEW YORK CITY MARATHON

First Sunday in November

Ⓦ www.tcsnycmarathon.org

Some 50,000 international runners assemble for this 26.2-mile run through the five boroughs. One of the best places to watch is Central Park South, near the finish line.

MACY'S THANKSGIVING DAY PARADE

Thanksgiving Day

Ⓦ social.macys.com/parade

New York's most televised parade, with big corporate floats, marching bands from around the country and Santa Claus's first appearance of the season. It winds its way from W 77th Street down Central Park West to Columbus Circle, then down Broadway to Herald Square.

Chronology

Early days > New York and the surrounding area is occupied by Native Americans, most notably the Lenape tribe.

1609 > English explorer Henry Hudson, working for the Dutch, sails past Manhattan upriver as far as Albany.

1624 > Dutch colony established on Governors Island.

1626 > Peter Minuit arrives as governor. He moves the Dutch settlement to Manhattan, which is named New Amsterdam, and numbers some 300 inhabitants.

1647 > New Amsterdam's most famous governor, Peter Stuyvesant, is appointed.

1664 > Revolt against Stuyvesant's dictatorial rule coincides with surrender to British naval troops, who rename the colony New York.

1754 > Ivy League Columbia University founded as King's College.

1776 > British naval vessels arrive to capture New York after the Declaration of Independence; fire destroys much of the city, which is occupied by British troops until 1783.

1789 > George Washington takes the oath as America's first president on Wall Street. New York is capital of the new nation for one year.

1792 > Buttonwood Agreement, signed by 24 stockbrokers on Wall Street, signals beginning of New York Stock Exchange. It is formally organized in 1817.

1812 > British blockade of Manhattan during the War of 1812.

1825 > Opening of the Erie Canal makes New York a major shipping port. Fulton Street dock and market area built.

1830–50 > First wave of mass immigration, principally German and Irish. The Lower East Side developed.

1831 > Founding of New York University (NYU).

1835 > Great Fire of New York destroys most of the buildings on the southern tip of Manhattan around Wall Street.

1856–71 > The city is ruled by a corrupt group of politicians known as Tammany Hall. Their leader is deputy commissioner William "Boss" Tweed, who is finally indicted for corruption in 1873.

1858 > The first Chinese immigrants arrive in what would become Manhattan's Chinatown; 12,000 live here by 1890.

1861–65 > Though not a theatre of the Civil War, class and racial tensions lead to the Draft Riots of 1863, in which 1000 people are killed.

1876 > Central Park opens to a design by Fredrick Law Olmsted and Calvert Vaux.

1880s > More immigrants (southern Italians and eastern European Jews) settle in the Lower East Side.

1883 > The Brooklyn Bridge links Manhattan with Brooklyn.

1885 > Emergence of Tin Pan Alley on 28th St in Manhattan, where music publishers and popular songwriters like George Gershwin ply their trade.

1886 > The Statue of Liberty, a gift from the French people to America, is unveiled.

1891 > Carnegie Hall completed, funded by Scottish-born steel magnate and philanthropist Andrew Carnegie.

1898 > The outer boroughs of Brooklyn, Queens, the Bronx and Staten Island are formally incorporated into New York City. The population swells to three million.

Early 20th century > The first skyscrapers are built, most notably the Flatiron Building (1902) and the Woolworth Building (1913).

1902 > Macy's opens at Herald Square.

1913 > The New York Highlanders baseball team (established here in 1903) becomes known as the New York Yankees.

1915 > The Equitable Building fills every square inch of its site on Broadway, propelling zoning ordinances in 1916 that demand a degree of setback to allow light to reach the streets.

1920 > Prohibition forbids the sale of alcohol. Economic confidence of the 1920s brings the Jazz Age and Harlem Renaissance.

1925 > Jimmy Walker is elected mayor. New York Giants football team established.

1927 > Duke Ellington's band begins famous residency at the Cotton Club in Harlem.

1929 > Wall Street Crash. America enters the Great Depression. Many of the lavish buildings commissioned and begun in the 1920s reach completion. Skyscrapers combine the monumental with the decorative in a new and distinctive Art Deco style: Chrysler Building (1930) and Empire State Building (1931). Rockefeller Center, the first exponent of the idea of a city-within-a-city, is built throughout the decade.

1932 > Lucky Luciano takes control of the Five Families of the New York mafia; he is imprisoned in 1936.

1934 > Fiorello LaGuardia elected Mayor (which he would remain until 1945). To rebuild New York after the Depression, he increases taxation, curbs corruption and improves the city's infrastructure with new bridges, roads and parks (with much federal funding).

1939 > Blue Note Records founded. Jazz legend Charlie Parker moves to New York, where he helps create bebop; he dies in the city in 1955.

1949–50 > Miles Davis records his seminal album *Birth of the Cool* in New York for Capitol Records, heralding a new era in jazz.

Late 1940s to 1950s > The East Village becomes home to the Beat poets – Jack Kerouac, Allen Ginsberg and William Burroughs.

1950 > United Nations established in New York. The UN secretariat building introduces the glass curtain wall to Manhattan.

1958 > The plaza of the newly built Seagram Building causes zoning regulations to be changed again – this time to encourage similar public spaces.

1959 > Frank Lloyd Wright's Guggenheim Museum opens.

1961 > Bob Dylan moves to Greenwich Village and becomes a leading figure in the folk music movement.

1964 > Race riots in Harlem and Brooklyn. Jimmy Hendrix moves to Harlem and becomes a regular performer at *Cafe Wha?* in Greenwich Village. The minimalist Verrazano Narrows Bridge links Brooklyn to Staten Island.

1965 > Malcolm X is assassinated at Washington Height's Audubon Ballroom.

1968 > New Madison Square Garden is built on the site of the old Penn Station.

1969 > The Stonewall riots in Greenwich Village inaugurate the gay-rights movement.

Early 1970s > A low point for New York as the city struggles to attract investment; Harlem drug lords Frank Lucas and Nicky Barnes flood the city with heroin. However, The World Trade Center Towers are built in 1972, dramatically altering the New York skyline; hip-hop emerges on the streets of the South Bronx.

1973 > CBGB opens on the Lower East Side; becomes epicentre of punk music; Blondie and the Ramones perform in 1974.

1975 > Mayor Abraham Beame presides over New York's decline as city financing reaches crisis point and businesses leave Manhattan. New York comes close to financial collapse, as its lack of essential services and collapsing infrastructure drive people away.

1977 > New York City Blackout (25hr): city suffers looting and civil unrest. *Discothèque Studio 54* opens – remains home of cool until 1986.

Late 1970s > Vociferous Ed Koch elected mayor (1978). Virtually no new corporate development until the Citicorp Center (1977) adds a new profile to the city's skyline; its popular atrium is adopted by later buildings.

1979 > The first hip-hop record, *Rapper's Delight*, released by The Sugarhill Gang (actually from New Jersey).

1980 > John Lennon is murdered outside his apartment on the Upper West Side.

1980s > Corporate wealth returns to Manhattan. The mixed-use Battery Park City opens to wide acclaim. Donald Trump emerges as a major real-estate developer.

1984 > Rick Rubin and Russell Simmons create Def Jam Records. Beastie Boys become their first major success.

1987 > Black Monday: the stock exchange crashes and the Dow Jones index plunges 508 points in one day.

1988 > The Tompkins Square Park Police Riot, which inspires a scene in the musical *Rent*.

1989 > David Dinkins becomes first black mayor of New York City, defeating Ed Koch and Rudolph Giuliani.

Early 1990s > NYC's budget deficit again reaches record proportions. East Coast hip-hop renaissance led by Nas, Notorious B.I.G. and later Mos Def and Jay-Z.

1993 > Puerto Rican salsa superstar Héctor Lavoe, "El Cantante", dies in New York.

1994 > Rudolph Giuliani is elected mayor – the city's first Republican mayor in 28 years, signalling a desire for change.

1996 > Prosperity returns to New York. Times Square is redeveloped, and the city becomes one of the safest and statistically most crime-free cities in the country.

2001 > World Trade Center's Twin Towers destroyed on September 11 by two planes hijacked by terrorists; Downtown Manhattan essentially shut down for several weeks. Mayor Rudy Giuliani cuts a highly composed and reassuring figure as New Yorkers struggle to come to terms with the assault on their city. Michael Bloomberg succeeds Giuliani as mayor a few months later.

2002 > Tribeca Film Festival established with the backing of Robert De Niro.

2003 > Daniel Libeskind is selected to design the new World Trade Center. His initial design goes through many revisions under pressure from the city and victims' relatives.

2005 > Michael Bloomberg is re-elected mayor.

2006 > Legendary punk club CBGB closes.

2007 > New York Giants win Superbowl XLII.

2008 > US mortgage crisis finally hits Wall Street in a big way: the Dow Jones slumps 500 points and, after more than 150 years, Lehman Brothers goes bankrupt; several other merchant banks are sold.

2009 > Michael Bloomberg is re-elected mayor for a third time, after backing a controversial extension of term limits. Yankees win World Series for 27th time. Miracle on the Hudson: Captain "Sully" Sullenberger lands his Airbus on the Hudson River after a bird strike takes out the engines at LaGuardia Airport.

2012 > NY Giants and Eli Manning win Superbowl XLVI. The city is hammered by Hurricane Sandy, with several neighbourhoods in Downtown Manhattan and Brooklyn flooded: the damage takes many months to clear up.

2013 > Bill de Blasio becomes the first Democratic mayor since 1993, winning the election by a landslide.

2016 > New York tycoon Donald Trump runs for US president.

PUBLISHING INFORMATION

This fourth edition published February 2017 by **Rough Guides Ltd**.
80 Strand, London WC2R 0RL
11, Community Centre, Panchsheel Park, New Delhi 110017, India
Distributed by the Penguin Group
Penguin Books Ltd, 80 Strand, London WC2R 0RL
Penguin Group (USA) 375 Hudson Street, NY 10014, USA
Penguin Group (Australia) 250 Camberwell Road, Camberwell, Victoria 3124, Australia
Penguin Group (NZ) 67 Apollo Drive, Mairangi Bay, Auckland 1310, New Zealand
Rough Guides is represented in Canada by Tourmaline Editions Inc., 662 King Street West, Suite 304, Toronto, Ontario, M5V 1M7
Typeset in Minion and Din to an original design by Henry Iles and Dan May.
Printed and bound in China
© Stephen Keeling and Andrew Rosenberg 2017
Maps © Rough Guides
No part of this book may be reproduced in any form without permission from the publisher except for the quotation of brief passages in reviews.
208pp includes index
A catalogue record for this book is available from the British Library
ISBN 978-0-24125-617-6
The publishers and authors have done their best to ensure the accuracy and currency of all the information in the **Pocket Rough Guide New York City**, however, they can accept no responsibility for any loss, injury, or inconvenience sustained by any traveller as a result of information or advice contained in the guide.
1 3 5 7 9 8 6 4 2

ROUGH GUIDES CREDITS

Editor: Rachel Mills
Layout: Ankur Guha
Cartography: Ed Wright
Picture editor: Phoebe Lowndes
Proofreader: Jan McCann
Managing editor: Keith Drew
Production: Jimmy Lao
Cover photo research: Ankur Guha, Roger Mapp, Nicole Newman
Photographers: Greg Roden, Curtis Hamilton, Nelson Hancock, Angus Oborn, Susannah Sayler
Editorial assistant: Freya Godfrey
Senior DTP coordinator: Dan May
Programme manager: Gareth Lowe
Publishing director: Georgina Dee

THE AUTHORS

Stephen Keeling has been calling New York City home since 2006. He worked as a financial journalist for seven years before writing his first travel guide and has written several titles for Rough Guides, including books on Puerto Rico, New England, Florida and Canada.

Andrew Rosenberg is a copy editor and sometimes writer. He lives in Brooklyn with his wife, Melanie; son, Jules; and cats, Caesar and Louise. Feel free to send comments about the book to nycroughguide@gmail.com.

ACKNOWLEDGEMENTS

Stephen Keeling would like to thank Victor Ozols, Gordon Polatnick, fellow author Andrew Rosenberg for his hard work, advice and support, Rachel Mills for her enthusiasm and fine editing, and Tiffany Wu, for the love, support and inspiration.

Andrew Rosenberg would like to thank Rachel Mills for her diligence and patience; Keith Drew and Mani Ramaswamy for kicking things off; fellow author Stephen Keeling for chalking up another edition in the books; Sarah Hull for creating the bones of some of the new listings; and Melanie and Jules for their help, love and support.

HELP US UPDATE

We've gone to a lot of effort to ensure that the fourth edition of **The Pocket Rough Guide to New York City** is accurate and up-to-date. However, things change – places get "discovered", opening hours are notoriously fickle, restaurants and rooms raise prices or lower standards. If you feel we've got it wrong or left something out, we'd like to know, and if you can remember the address, the price, the hours, the phone number, so much the better.

Please send your comments with the subject line "**Pocket Rough Guide New York City Update**" to mail@roughguides.com. We'll credit all contributions and send a copy of the next edition (or any other Rough Guide if you prefer) for the very best emails.

Find travel information, read inspiring features and book your trip at roughguides.com.

PHOTO CREDITS

All images © Rough Guides except the following:
(Key: a-above; b-below/bottom; c-centre; f-far; l-left; r-right; t-top)

1 Alamy Stock Photo: RooM the Agency Mobile/alyfromuk2us
2 AWL Images: Michele Falzone
4 Dreamstime.com: Typhoonski
6 Dreamstime.com: F11photo
8 Getty Images: Atlantide Phototravel (b)
9 Dreamstime.com: Afagundes (t)
10 Alamy Stock Photo: Stockimo/ lauren_fisher
12-13 Alamy Stock Photo: Brian Jannsen
14 Dreamstime.com: Littleny
15 Dreamstime.com: Rabbit75 (cra). **Getty Images:** Christophe Launay (t)
16 Getty Images: Scott W Baker
17 4Corners: Richard Taylor (t); Richard Taylor (cra). **Smorgasburg:** (b)
19 Alamy Stock Photo: Christian Reister (b). **Whitney Museum of American Art:** Ed Lederman (cr)
21 Alamy Stock Photo: dbtravel (bl); Ted Pink (c). **Momofuku Noodle Bar:** Gabriele Stabile (crb)
23 Alamy Stock Photo: Andreas Argirakis (t); Patti McConville (ca). **The Delancey Nightclub:** (br)
24 Getty Images: Gaelle Beri
25 Esther Montoro: Esther Montoro (crb)
Gordon Polatnick: Gordon Polatnick (b)

26 Beacon's Closet
27 Brooklyn Flea: (tl)
28 Alamy Stock Photo: Stacy Walsh Rosenstock
29 Alamy Stock Photo: PCN Black (cla); PureStock (b). **Getty Images:** Gavin Hellier (l)
30-31 Getty Images: Atlantide Phototravel
37 Jewish Heritage Museum: David Paler (b)
39 AWL Images: Jon Arnold
41 Alamy Stock Photo: Randy Duchaine
44 Robert Harding Picture Library: Wendy Connet
46 Alamy Stock Photo: dbimages
47 Alamy Stock Photo: Ed Rooney
48 ApexArt
52 TriBeCa Grand Hotel: Poul Ober
65 Alamy Stock Photo: Ed Rooney
68 urban75.com
75 Alamy Stock Photo: Stefano Politi Markovina
78 Mermaid Inn: Melissa Hom
92 AWL Images: Gavin Hellier
112 New York Public Library
114 Robert Harding Picture Library: Gavin Hellier
116 4Corners: Massimo Borchi

Index

Maps are marked in **bold**.

SO NOW WE'VE TOLD YOU
ABOUT THE THINGS NOT TO
MISS, THE BEST PLACES TO
STAY, THE TOP RESTAURANTS,
THE LIVELIEST BARS AND THE
MOST SPECTACULAR SIGHTS,
IT ONLY SEEMS FAIR TO
TELL YOU ABOUT THE BEST
TRAVEL INSURANCE AROUND

 WorldNomads.com
keep travelling safely

RECOMMENDED BY ROUGH GUIDES